*MAMMALS OF THE INTERMOUNTAIN WEST*

# Mammals of the Intermountain West

by
Samuel I. Zeveloff

Original Paintings and Drawings
by
Farrell R. Collett

University of Utah Press
Salt Lake City
1988

**Library of Congress Cataloging-in-Publication Data**

Zeveloff, Samuel I., 1950–
  Mammals of the Intermountain West.

  Bibliography: p.
  Includes index.
  1. Mammals — West (U.S.) 2. Alpine fauna — West (U.S.)
I. Collett, Farrell R.   II. Title.
QL719.W47Z48   1988        599.0978        88-20462
ISBN 0-87480-296-2
ISBN 0-87480-327-6 (pbk.)

To my parents, Harold and Muriel,
with love and affection.
—Samuel I. Zeveloff

To my wife, Martie, who has shared my love of
nature and art for some forty-eight years.
—Farrell R. Collett

# Contents

# Checklist

Use this list to keep track of the mammals that you have seen in this region.

Marsupials
_____ Virginia opossum

Insectivores
_____ Masked shrew
_____ Mt. Lyell shrew
_____ Preble's shrew
_____ Vagrant shrew
_____ Dusky or montane shrew
_____ Inyo shrew
_____ Dwarf shrew
_____ Water shrew
_____ Trowbridge's shrew
_____ Merriam's shrew
_____ Pygmy shrew
_____ Desert shrew
_____ Broad-footed or California mole

Bats
_____ California or Waterhouse's leaf-nosed bat
_____ California myotis
_____ Western small-footed myotis
_____ Yuma myotis
_____ Little brown bat
_____ Long-legged myotis
_____ Fringed myotis
_____ Long-eared myotis

_____ Silver-haired bat
_____ Western pipistrelle
_____ Big brown bat
_____ Red bat
_____ Hoary bat
_____ Spotted bat
_____ Allen's big-eared bat
_____ Townsend's big-eared bat
_____ Pallid bat
_____ Brazilian free-tailed bat
_____ Big free-tailed bat

Pikas, Rabbits, and Hares
_____ Pika
_____ Pygmy rabbit
_____ Nuttall's or mountain cottontail
_____ Desert or Audubon's cottontail
_____ Snowshoe hare
_____ White-tailed jackrabbit
_____ Black-tailed jackrabbit

Rodents
_____ Least chipmunk
_____ Yellow-pine chipmunk
_____ Townsend's chipmunk
_____ Cliff chipmunk
_____ Hopi chipmunk
_____ Colorado chipmunk
_____ Panamint chipmunk
_____ Uinta chipmunk
_____ Palmer's chipmunk
_____ Yellow-bellied marmot or rockchuck
_____ White-tailed antelope squirrel
_____ Townsend's ground squirrel
_____ Wyoming ground squirrel
_____ Uinta ground squirrel
_____ Belding's ground squirrel
_____ Thirteen-lined ground squirrel
_____ Spotted ground squirrel
_____ Rock squirrel

_____ California ground squirrel
_____ Round-tailed ground squirrel
_____ Golden-mantled ground squirrel
_____ White-tailed prairie dog
_____ Utah prairie dog
_____ Gunnison's prairie dog
_____ Abert's squirrel
_____ Red squirrel or chickaree
_____ Douglas' squirrel
_____ Northern flying squirrel
_____ Northern pocket gopher
_____ Idaho pocket gopher
_____ Wyoming pocket gopher
_____ Mountain pocket gopher
_____ Botta's pocket gopher
_____ Townsend's pocket gopher
_____ Olive-backed pocket mouse
_____ Plains pocket mouse
_____ Great Basin pocket mouse
_____ Silky pocket mouse
_____ Little pocket mouse
_____ Long-tailed pocket mouse
_____ Desert pocket mouse
_____ Rock pocket mouse
_____ Dark kangaroo mouse
_____ Pale kangaroo mouse
_____ Ord's kangaroo rat
_____ Chisel-toothed kangaroo rat
_____ Panamint kangaroo rat
_____ Banner-tailed kangaroo rat
_____ Merriam's kangaroo rat
_____ Desert kangaroo rat
_____ Beaver
_____ Western harvest mouse
_____ Cactus mouse
_____ Deer mouse
_____ Canyon mouse
_____ Brush mouse
_____ Piñon mouse
_____ Rock mouse

_____ Northern grasshopper mouse
_____ Southern grasshopper mouse
_____ White-throated woodrat
_____ Desert woodrat
_____ Stephens' woodrat
_____ Mexican woodrat
_____ Dusky-footed woodrat
_____ Bushy-tailed woodrat
_____ Southern or boreal red-backed vole
_____ Heather vole
_____ Meadow vole
_____ Montane vole
_____ California vole
_____ Long-tailed vole
_____ Mexican vole
_____ Water vole
_____ Sagebrush vole
_____ Muskrat
_____ Western jumping mouse
_____ Porcupine

Carnivores
_____ Coyote
_____ Gray or timber wolf
_____ Red fox
_____ Kit fox
_____ Gray fox
_____ Black bear
_____ Grizzly bear
_____ Ringtail or cacomistle
_____ Raccoon
_____ Marten
_____ Fisher
_____ Ermine or short-tailed weasel
_____ Long-tailed weasel
_____ Black-footed ferret
_____ Mink
_____ Wolverine
_____ Badger
_____ Western spotted skunk

_____ Striped skunk
_____ River otter
_____ Mountain lion or cougar
_____ Lynx
_____ Bobcat

Odd-Toed Hooved Mammals
_____ Horse
_____ Burro

Even-Toed Hooved Mammals
_____ Elk or wapiti
_____ Mule deer
_____ White-tailed deer
_____ Moose
_____ Pronghorn
_____ Bison
_____ Mountain goat
_____ Mountain or bighorn sheep

# Preface

The Intermountain West of North America is surely one of the world's most picturesque places. A land with so many different environments, it is appealing to people with a wide diversity of nature interests. The two land types that first come to mind are the incomparable western flank of the Rocky Mountains and the austerely beautiful Great Basin. Yet, within the region are also fantastic canyons, rushing rivers, meandering streams, hot springs, and a multitude of small, virtually undiscovered mountain ranges, each beckoning their visitors in new ways at every turn.

A great assortment of animal life abounds in this highly differentiated region. Although this is readily apparent for the more visible fauna, such as birds and insects, the situation is not the same for mammals. As with the other groups, the variety of habitats has spawned a proliferation of species. But the large majority of mammals are small and secretive. Encountering one often requires luck, patience, cunning, and trapping skills. Perhaps because it is so difficult to observe mammals, the experience of doing so ultimately is a more exciting one.

This book is designed to assist learning about the region's mammals in several ways. It is written in a popular style to make the material understandable to those without formal biological training. At the same time, it is up-to-date and thorough so as to be useful to students, professionals in the field, and demanding naturalists. Presently, there is no other book which offers current information about the life histories and ranges of the region's mammals. Excellent texts with in-depth accounts of the mammals in the area's two major states do exist: S. D. Durrant's *Mammals of Utah* and E. R. Hall's *Mammals of*

*Nevada*. Yet, both are too technical for the average reader, emphasizing the taxonomy or classification and distribution of the states' mammals.

One of the primary aims of this book is for it to serve as a field guide. The account of each of the 151 mammal species begins with a section that describes the animal's appearance, how it may be distinguished from similar forms, and its occurrence in the region. Together with the succeeding information about its habitat, the range map, and illustration, the reader should be able to determine each mammal's identity. The maps reflect species' distributions based on data available when this book was completed in the fall of 1987. Some are more detailed than others, and many will change as the mammals expand their ranges or are discovered in new places. Users of the maps should keep these points in mind. The portion on habitat continues with a discussion of food habits, predators, and unique behaviors. Concluding each account is a section about the animal's reproduction, including information about its breeding period, pregnancy duration, litter size, and social behavior. Longer accounts are provided for species about which additional material offers a perspective on an animal's history or role in the region, such as that of the bison. This book is not designed to provide recognition of species based upon tracks or signs. For those wishing to pursue natural history in such a fashion, I recommend the field guides by W. H. Burt and R. P. Grossenheider, J. O. Whitaker, Jr., or O. J. Murie cited in the general references list.

Three of the accounts deal with species that have been introduced to the region: the opossum, the horse, and the burro. Each is significant in different ways, topics which are fully explored in the accounts. The opossum, the continent's only marsupial north of Mexico, is continually expanding its range and might eventually play an important role in the region's ecology. The horse and the burro each already have a great impact on the habitat and other species where they occur. Other introduced species have become established in the region, including the house mouse (*Mus musculus*), Norway rat (*Rattus norvegicus*). black rat (*Rattus rattus*), and fox squirrel (*Sciurus niger*). Accounts for these were not included due to their limited distributions, a lack of current information about them, and their low popular appeal relative to other nonnatives.

A substantive way in which this book differs from similar ones is in the attention it gives to the life history evolution and behavioral ecology of many species. The discipline of biology known as "life history evolution" attempts to discern how an organism's basic characteristics, such as litter size, age of maturity, and survival, are shaped by its environment and ancestry. In recent years, innovative studies have given us both tantalizing clues and exciting answers for understanding species within this framework. Where appropriate, I present such information to offer a more complete and modern understanding of mammalian biology. Behavioral ecology is a category of animal behavior which examines an organism's actions within the context of its habitat. Research in this field has given us insights into the ecological factors that influence phenomena as diverse as feeding strategies, territoriality, and parental care. Again, the incorporation of such material provides a more holistic perspective on the animal's life.

This book offers a dimension that will draw its possessors deeply into the world of mammals: the brilliant and sensitive artwork of Farrell Collett. By depicting the animals in poses reflecting specific behaviors and through accurate habitat depictions, he enhances the reader's understanding and appreciation of the Intermountain West and its mammals. As a result, the book is more than a treatise on the region's mammals; it is a portfolio of outstanding wildlife art. Mr. Collett brings to life the animals that he has spent a lifetime studying and illustrating, work for which he has earned international recognition. His work has opened my eyes to mammals in a new and vibrant way.

It was only through synthesizing material from other works that I was able to provide such thorough species accounts. Most body size measurements, as well as additional information, come from Whitaker's *The Audubon Society field guide to North American mammals*. The book *Mammals of the northern Great Plains*, by J. K. Jones, Jr., et al., and the Mammalian Species series of the American Society of Mammalogists were invaluable sources. Range maps are usually based on those in

Hall's *The Mammals of North America* unless more recent work revealed distributional changes. Virtually all of the mammal scientific names are from the *Revised checklist of North American mammals north of Mexico, 1986* by Jones et al. For convenience, the literature that was consulted is listed at the end of each section. References used throughout the text are compiled in a general list at the back of the book.

# Acknowledgments

I am indebted to many people for their assistance with this book. Financial support for the artwork and maps was generously donated by a group of Ogden, Utah, physicians and their families: Dr. and Mrs. Rex M. Alvord, Dr. and Mrs. Robert S. Brodstein, Dr. and Mrs. A. Steven Cain, Dr. and Mrs. Clayton R. Gabbert, Dr. and Mrs. O. Marvin Lewis, J. Ralph Macfarlane, M.D., Dr. and Mrs. Carl A. Mattsson, Dr. and Mrs. Dean W. Packard, Dr. and Mrs. Winn L. Richards, Dr. and Mrs. Harvey Ruskin, Dr. and Mrs. John D. Schirack, and Richard S. White, M.D. One of them, Robert Brodstein, devoted his energies to organizing this fund-raising effort. Without his involvement, the book's publication would have faced a long delay.

Harold Egoscue and Jerran Flinders provided thoughtful and constructive reviews of the manuscript. Through my discussions with them and Clyde Pritchett, I was alerted to recent changes in the distributions of several species. I learned much about the history of Utah's wildlife from Jack Renzel. The illustrations of the fisher and marten are based on the personal slides of Roger Powell and Bill Zielinski. My colleague at Weber State College, Carl Marti, told me about several key references on the region's mammals. Norma Mikkelsen, editor at the University of Utah Press, showed an early and sustaining faith in this work. Her many suggestions, always offered in a gracious style, improved my writing. I also appreciate the fine production work of Rodger Reynolds of the University of Utah Press. My wife Linda produced the maps with her usual keen sensibility for graphics. Her love and that of our daughters, Abby, Naomi, and Susannah, provided me with a positive working environment. Finally, there are four key individuals who have influenced my thinking about mammalian ecology: the late Fred Barkalow, Mark Boyce, John Christian, and Phil Doerr. In many ways, their teachings have contributed to this book. It is nice to have the opportunity to collectively thank them.

—S.I.Z.

When the University of Utah Press asked me if I would be interested in writing and illustrating a book on the mammals of the Intermountain West, I was delighted for two reasons. First, I had seen a need for such a book, and, second, I had a long-standing interest in illustrating this kind of work. After some consideration, I informed the Press that I would be privileged to do the illustrations but that I had neither the time nor the qualifications to do the writing.

At this time, Samuel Zeveloff, unaware of the project underway, called the Press and asked if it would be interested in a manuscript on mammals of the Intermountain West. His credentials and timing were perfect. It has been a pleasure to work with Samuel Zeveloff; he has given me invaluable help in many ways and has provided some of the references for the illustrations.

I hope that my work in this book would have pleased the late Ernest Thompson Seton, Charles Livingston Bull, and Paul Bransom. These men, through their writings and art work, were the first to kindle my interest in wildlife and the outdoors. They have inspired me and fired my enthusiasm for drawing and painting all of my life. I will be eternally grateful to them.

—F.R.C.

*MAMMALS OF THE INTERMOUNTAIN WEST*

# Introduction

## THE INTERMOUNTAIN WEST—
## THE REGION AND ITS BOUNDARIES

The Intermountain West is not an easy area to define. Although
most people have a general idea of what it refers to, they would
probably become flustered if asked to come up with precise
boundaries for the region. This is partially because the term is
more often used to describe a commercial or political region
rather than a geographical or ecological entity. Since the name
alludes to that space between the Sierra Nevada and the Rocky
Mountains, agreement on its eastern and western borders is
comparatively easy to come by. But even here difficulties creep
in. Should the eastern edge be along the Wasatch Range, the
westernmost chain of the Rocky Mountains? Or is it more
logical to place this border on the western edge of Colorado's
central Rockies? This appears justified because of the extensive
basins and plateaus lying to their west, which are thus part
of an intermountain zone. Establishing the region's northern
and southern boundaries is troublesome because there are several natural features in both directions where borders can be
justified.

   I wrestled with determining boundaries until I located a map
of the region in the volume *Intermountain Biogeography: A
Symposium* from the Great Basin Naturalist Memoirs series.
Kimball Harper, an organizer of this symposium, informed me
that the map's borders were agreed upon by a consensus of its
participants, which included many of the area's leading
biogeographers. After deciding that the boundaries were indeed

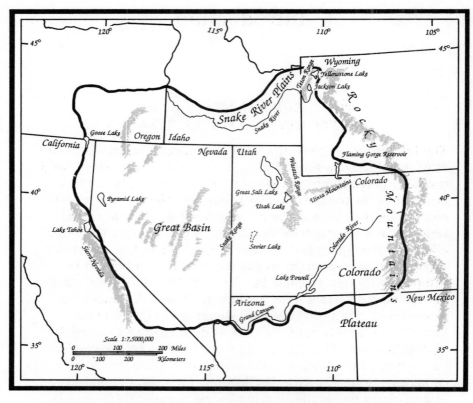

MAP OF THE INTERMOUNTAIN WEST DEPICTING THE REGION'S
BOUNDARIES AND MAJOR PHYSIOGRAPHIC FEATURES.

justified, I accepted them for this book. Most important, they circumscribe an area with integrity as a biogeographical unit, taking into account its fauna, vegetation, climate, and topography. It is also based on the historical use of the term "Intermountain West." The region includes all of Utah, virtually all of Nevada, a slice of eastern California, the southeastern quarter of Oregon, the southern two-fifths of Idaho, the southwestern quarter of Wyoming, western Colorado, a corner of northwestern New Mexico, and section of northern Arizona. It encompasses the eastern flank of the Sierra Nevada, the Great Basin, the Snake River Plains, the northern two-thirds of the Colorado Plateau, and several major Rocky Mountain ranges.

This area is similar to the one described in *Intermountain Flora* by A. Cronquist and his colleagues. The major difference between it and the area chosen is that it has Utah's eastern border as its eastern boundary. As the authors point out, this was an arbitrary decision guided by the then recent publication of a book on Colorado's flora. That aside, several of their notions are helpful in characterizing the region. First, they consider the area as the "dryland region" between the Sierra Nevada and the Rocky Mountains, bordered by the moist Pacific Northwest and the warmer drylands to the south. They further contend that the region's mountains are generally discontinuous and surrounded by desert. Hence, although they exclude western Colorado, it seems logical to include it — using their own criteria — since the arid canyon and plateau country between the Wasatch Range and central Colorado Rockies is similar to intermontane areas throughout the region.

I accept their claim that the Intermountain West is the "core of a region in which the foothills and lowlands are mostly dominated by sagebrush and shrubs such as shadscale" (quote modified from original). Indeed, just three plant communities thoroughly characterize the region's valleys and lower mountain slopes: shadscale, sagebrush, and pinyon-juniper. Evidence suggests that many of these places historically were grasslands. They were probably replaced by woody vegetation due to fire suppression and heavy cattle and sheep grazing. To the south of the region are markedly hotter summers, milder winters, and deserts dominated by creosote bush. Here, several mammals characteristic of the Great Basin steppe country are absent. The climate and vegetation to the northwest are heavily subject to maritime influences.

In the following, I review the boundaries of the region in detail. Beginning at the southern end of Nevada's straight eastern border, the line heads west into southern California, where it encompasses the Inyo Mountains. The line then runs north-northwest, along the Sierra Nevada, cutting through the corner of Nevada south of Reno. It continues along this course, but veers more directly north as it approaches the Oregon border, crossing it near Goose Lake. From here, the line continues basically northward, following the Cascade Range. Close to Horse Ridge, south of Bend, it turns east, following the low mountains of east-central Oregon and enters Idaho around where the Snake River turns north. Throughout Idaho, the boundary follows the northern border of the Snake River Plains. Where the Snake winds eastward north of Idaho Falls, the line heads northeast, crossing into Yellowstone National Park south of West Yellowstone, Montana. This is the only place where Montana joins the region. Going east, the line enters Wyoming and travels south around the eastern shore of Yellowstone Lake. Moving southeast, it leaves the park and continues to the west of the Wind River Range. West of South Pass City, Wyoming, the boundary then heads southwest. Near the Green River, it moves east-southeast above Flaming Gorge Reservoir, crossing into Colorado by the Sierra Madre. Here the line travels virtually south, crossing into New Mexico near Dulce, south of the San Juan River. It then heads west-southwest along the Navajo Reservoir. Continuing west, the line enters Arizona, veering north below Page. It then shifts south, staying east of the Colorado River, and goes around the Grand Canyon. Below the canyon it heads west again, returning to our starting point.

Naturally, criteria used in establishing such a precisely delineated area are subject to debate. Distinct lines are always difficult to justify since there rarely are sharp demarcations between natural areas. Even when boundaries exclude the plants that typify surrounding regions, many can still easily travel across regions. Many animals can cross these boundaries even more readily. Yet, for the reasons reviewed, I am confident that the area selected will at least stand the test of present geological time as the standard for the Intermountain West.

## THE PROVINCES OF THE INTERMOUNTAIN WEST

The Intermountain West is composed of several different geological provinces: the Colorado Plateau, the Rocky Mountains, the Great Basin, and the Snake River Plains, each distinguished by its own geology, climate, flora, and fauna. Yet, the provinces share such features to a degree greater than do comparable land units outside of the region, aspects of which are reviewed in the previous section. In this portion, we shall take a brief look at the environment of each province to get an in-depth perspective on the entire area. The Sierra Nevada, which form only the western edge of this region, are not included.

### Colorado Plateau

The Colorado Plateau is a large province of some 200,000 square miles; its northern half lies within the Intermountain West. Here, it covers the southeastern half of Utah, adjacent western Colorado, and northern New Mexico and Arizona. It actually is composed of many plateaus, often arrayed in terrace-like formations, and the valleys lying between them. To many, the majestic canyons that form at the plateau's junctures are the region's most impressive features. Both these canyon walls and those of the solitary plateaus seem to be routinely carved into beautifully colored, often bizarre formations. Within this province are such magnificent national treasures as Glen Canyon National Recreation Area and its Lake Powell, Capitol Reef National Park, Zion National Park, Bryce Canyon National Park, and the granddaddy of them all, Grand Canyon National Park. Except for the eroded valley floors of the Colorado and San Juan rivers, the entire plateau is above 5,000 feet, with portions rising up to 12,000 feet. An unusual landscape feature which results from such high plateaus is expansive flat surfaces rising above the neighboring mountains.

The rugged canyons are formed by a combination of several factors: (1) the high elevation of the plateau, (2) a dry climate which erodes the resistant rock cliffs slowly, and (3) the regular availability of water from nearby mountains, providing a steady stream which sculpts the rocks. The province's most important watercourse is the Colorado River. Water from almost the entire plateau drains into it. The Colorado, the Green River, and most of the plateau's streams have a southwesterly flow.

There is considerable variation in the climate and dominant vegetation of this province. In the north, it is desertlike with warm, dry, and windy weather. The habitats of its central portion include grasslands and open forests. Yet, its southern section, which lies outside the Intermountain West, is nourished by greater precipitation and contains large stands of dense forest.

The plateau is mostly covered by sagebrush, shadscale, and pinyon-juniper, the three most common plant communities in the region. Nevertheless, it has several unusual floristic features. First, the canyon area of southeastern Utah is richer in endemic plants than any other part of the region. These are plants that are confined to a certain place. More than 70 species are found here, many of which could have evolved in this locale since it is surrounded by mountain barriers. Another unusual area is extreme southwestern Utah, known as "Dixie," and bordering Arizona, some of which is in the Great Basin. This is the only place in the region where Mojave Desert plants, such as Mojavean creosote and mesquite, are abundant. Finally, there is the Kaibab Plateau, the highest one of all, in the province's far southeastern corner. This is where the largest ponderosa pine forest in the region occurs; it is also the location of the North Rim of the Grand Canyon.

## Rocky Mountains

It is entirely reasonable to assume that words like "serene," "majestic," and "grandeur" were invented to describe the Rocky Mountains, so commonly are they used in reference to these inspiring giants. They first arise, as if in a vision, from the plains of eastern Colorado, occupying much of it and the surrounding states. In the Intermountain West, the major ranges of the Rockies include the Wasatch Range, the Uinta Mountains, and the Teton Range. Along with the region's many other mountain formations, they dominate the landscapes where they occur.

Considered the westernmost chain of the Rockies' main spine, the Wasatch Range extends for some 220 miles from the big loop of the Bear River in southeastern Idaho to the pass south of central Utah's Mount Nebo. The range's highest peak, Mount Nebo, is close to 12,000 feet high. Whereas the eastern slope of the Wasatch Range rises gradually, the western slope is characterized by abrupt, almost horizontally rising faces. Here, these mountains present incomparable vistas to the inhabitants of Utah's major population centers: Salt Lake City, Ogden, and Provo. Because the snow that falls on the Wasatch is first "blow-dried" over the Great Basin, it offers some of the world's finest skiing. Equally impressive are the steep canyons and rivers which cut through the range. It is a must to travel through Ogden Canyon at the height of the fall foliage, a trip every bit as delightful as an autumn drive through the New England countryside. Another recommended stop is Timpanogos Cave National Monument between Salt Lake City and Provo. Common trees in the higher parts of the range are conifers, such as white fir, subalpine fir, blue spruce, Engelmann spruce, and Douglas fir. Lower slopes tend to be dominated by a community of Gambel oak and bigtooth maple.

In northeastern Utah is the only range in the Rockies that appears to have forgotten which way it was supposed to go: the Uinta Mountains. This is the largest range in the hemisphere situated on an east-west axis. Surely though, great expanses of pristine wilderness characterize this range as much as any geological anomaly. The Uintas are an essentially undeveloped, primitive area with terrific appeal to those wanting to get away from it all. The state's highest point, 13,528-foot Kings Peak, is found here. Cirques, rock-walled amphitheaters at the heads of glaciers, are abundant in the high country. Directly to the east of the range lies Dinosaur National Monument. Here, one can see remains of the animals which ruled the Intermountain West and much of the planet before the mammals acquired ascendancy. The monument has an active fossil quarry and excellent displays.

Few ranges anywhere compare to the awesome Tetons of northwestern Wyoming. Although the entire range is only about 40 miles long, its precipitous eastern front has a magical appeal. The mountains and the valley to the east, Jackson Hole (early trappers referred to a valley ringed by mountains as a "hole") is one of those special places which one is compelled to return to time after time. The word "teton" is derived from the name the early French explorers gave to the range's highest peaks: *les trois tétons*, the three breasts. The geological history of the mountains and valley floor have combined to produce a vertical rise that is approximately 7,000 feet at its highest point. About nine million years ago, the block of earth which became the mountains began to surge upward and the valley started to sink. The abrupt rise occurred along a fault, or fracture in the earth, resulting in the mountains' eastern front being much higher than the rest of the range. This is unusual since most ranges are highest in the center. In the last 15,000 years, the peaks have undergone additional remodeling. Accumulated snow formed large glaciers which lumbered across the mountains with tremendous force, creating the current masterpieces. Today, there are still several active glaciers in the range.

The many watercourses that lace the area make it attractive to humans and wildlife. Jackson Lake, the largest one, was originally smaller than it now is. Before the founding of Grand Teton National Park, it was enlarged to impound water for irrigation in Idaho. Flow from the lake is regulated at the Jackson Lake Dam before entering the Snake River. The Snake winds around dozens of islands, providing its travelers with changing views of the mountains at every turn. Ultimately, it gives rise to white-water rapids south of the park. Also impressive are the Gros Ventre and Buffalo rivers and the brilliant small jewels lying at the foot of the Tetons: Jenny, String, and Leigh lakes.

Great Basin

The Great Basin is not a large basin at all, but is composed of a multitude of "basins": areas of interior drainage without outlets from which water can escape, except by evaporation. Many of these are elongated valleys lying between the more than 150 north-south mountain ranges here. Most mountains form by compression of segments of the earth's crust against one another. Those of the Great Basin have formed in a different manner. Here, the crust is broken up into enormous blocks, each separated by faults that usually enter the surface at about 60-degree angles. This has caused the blocks to tilt toward the faults, resulting in their exposed ends becoming mountaintops.

Faulting responsible for this basin and range formation has been dated back to the late Miocene, about eight million years ago. Even now, the entire area is being stretched apart, an event which has played a key role in this geological turmoil.

The area was termed the Great Basin by the great explorer John C. Frémont. It is actually only the northern part of a much larger geological area, the Basin and Range Province. The Basin itself is bordered by the Sierra Nevada to the west, the Columbia Plateau and Snake River Plains on the north, and by the Wasatch Range to the east. Although it is difficult to establish a southern boundary, I have selected the one largely coinciding with that of the Mojave Desert for reasons cited earlier.

Approximately half of this country is a cold desert, the Great Basin Desert. Extremely dry to begin with, the area's aridity is exacerbated by the rapid evaporation of incoming water. Much of the dryness results from the Sierra Nevada and other ranges to the west capturing a large fraction of the air's moisture before it ever reaches the basin. As a result, Nevada and Utah are the two driest states in the nation. The cold and snowy winters here are a function of both the high latitude and high altitude; much of the area is above 4,000 feet. Summers can be uncomfortably hot, as in Death Valley, the lowest spot in the entire Western Hemisphere.

Mountain environments here are considerably moister than those in the desert. Some even harbor permanent streams which flow off the slopes, terminating in lakes and underground sinks. Here, flash floods can move water with a strength sufficient to sculpt these mountains. Larger ranges are about 50 miles long, yet few are more than 15 miles wide. Many of the mountains are from 7,000 to 8,000 feet, but a couple, such as Wheeler and Boundary peaks, soar to over 13,000 feet. Part of the Snake Range of eastern Nevada, Wheeler Peak is located in the country's newest national park, Great Basin National Park, established in the fall of 1986. Comprising some 76,800 acres, it includes many interesting features, such as Lehman Caves, Lexington Arch, stands of ancient bristlecone pine, and even a small glacier. The one national park in Nevada, this is also the only one that showcases the Great Basin. For far too long, the Great Basin has been viewed as a desolate place, worthy at best of the many bombing ranges which scar it. Those who take the time to explore it, though, will be taken by its stark, if not serene, beauty.

Finally, there is a diversity of wetlands in the Great Basin, a habitat type vital to many species. Pyramid Lake in western Nevada contains what has been the continent's largest breeding colony of white pelicans. Mono Lake in California, which unfortunately is drying up due to water demands, has served as the breeding area for more than 20 percent of the world's California gulls. In this book, we shall see how wetlands are vital to many mammals as well. Because virtually all of the province's lakes lack outlets, many are either alkaline or salty. As their water evaporates, their mineral levels become increasingly concentrated.

At the end of the Pleistocene, two enormous lakes covered much of the present-day Great Basin. The former Lake Bonneville is now divided into the Great Salt Lake, Utah Lake, and Sevier Lake. On the benches of the Wasatch Range and elsewhere, one can easily discern several former levels of this prehistoric lake, which was once about the size of Lake Michigan. Similarly, Lake Lahontan formerly occupied the western end of the Great Basin in northwestern Nevada. Its remnants include Honey Lake, Pyramid Lake, and Winnemuca Lake, some of which are essentially freshwater.

From its valley to the mountaintops, the plant life of the basin follows a typical sequence. Ascending from the valleys, we first find shrub or grass-shrub habitat dominated by shadscale on the saline desert floors; big sagebrush above, especially on well-drained soils; low, widely spaced trees occasionally followed by more grass-shrubs; taller, more closely spaced trees; and stunted and widely spaced trees at the higher altitudes. Plant cover is usually greatest in the higher, central part of the basin. The woodlands are dominated by pinyon pine and Utah juniper, composing the so-called pinyon-juniper forest. Red fir occurs on the higher slopes, with Douglas fir, white fir, and blue spruce at the highest elevations. Exceptions to this pattern exist, particularly in north-central and northeastern Nevada, where the pinyon-juniper is often replaced by shrublands. The exact combination of species is always the result of various site-specific factors.

Snake River Plains

Of the four provinces in the Intermountain West, the crescent-shaped Snake River Plains of southern Idaho is the smallest. The name "Snake" is not, as many assume, due to the tortuous route the river follows. Rather, the river became known as the Snake during the fur trapping era in reference to the region's Snake Indians, who were likened to snakes due to their skill at concealing themselves.

The province is characterized by relatively flat lava plains which slope toward the river. Some of the lava is less than a thousand years old. Occasionally, the plains are interrupted by volcanic cones, such as in Craters of the Moon National Monument in the northeastern part of the province. Some cones are impressive; south of Arco, Idaho, Big Butte ascends 2,350 feet above the plains. As the Snake River flows west across Idaho, it descends about 3,000 feet in only 350 miles. At its western end, where the entire province narrows, the Snake enters a majestic deep gorge: the Grand Canyon of the Snake River. Streams entering the Snake River can be permanent or intermittent. Not all in the area flow into the river since they may be intercepted by joints in the lava.

The predominant vegetation here is sagebrush. At the lower elevations closer to the river, shadscale is well represented. Limber pine and some Douglas fir often occupy the higher reaches of the volcanic cones. The pinyon-juniper forests, so typical of the region's higher altitudes, are not present here. Much of the area without lava is farmed; the Snake River Plains is one of the Intermountain West's richest agricultural zones. Major crops include potatoes and sugar beets.

Along the border of the Great Basin in the province's southwest, surrounded by a relatively flat desert, lie the Owyhee Mountains. Although similar in appearance to the mountains of the Great Basin, they differ in having granite and other older rocks in their core. The name "Owyhee" has an unusual history. A corruption of "Hawaii," it was first given to the area's Owyhee River by the trapper Peter Skene Ogden. He named it after two Hawaiian members of his expedition who were killed by the Snake Indians.

## THE CLASS MAMMALIA

### Beginnings

There are only some 4,060 species in the Class Mammalia, far fewer than the numbers of reptiles or birds. Yet, because of their great competitive abilities, intelligence, and predatory skills, mammals are regarded as the dominant group of vertebrates, animals with backbones. They exist in a terrific diversity of forms, including burrowers, runners, flyers, and swimmers, and occupy many niches. But it was not always this way. Today's mammals are the products of a long evolutionary history. As an environment changes, some individuals are better suited to survive and so leave more offspring than others; they are regarded as having greater "fitness" than their less successful counterparts. By such differential survival and reproduction of individuals, the composition of a population and thus a species can change over time. This process, natural selection, was proposed as the mechanism for the evolution of life by the great nineteenth-century British biologist, Charles Darwin. Although evolution is unacceptable to some fundamentalist religious groups, scientific evidence for it and for natural selection as its chief mechanism is conclusive.

Mammalian origins can be traced back to the Synapsida, one of the earliest groups of reptiles. Synapsids were present on Earth some 300 million years ago in the Paleozoic Era, long before the appearance of the dinosaurs. These "mammal-like reptiles" were especially abundant about 280 to 230 million years ago and persisted into the Triassic Period, the first part of the Mesozoic Era. Although it is not clear why, synapsids were virtually extinct by the end of the Triassic, some 180 million years ago. Mammals arose from a synapsid order, the Therapsida, about 200 million years ago. It is curious that a group which became so successful had its origins in one which was rapidly declining. Some therapsids possessed several mammalian features, including one of great significance for mammals: the secondary palate. This palate, which lies beneath the roof of the mouth, creates a chamber permitting air inhaled through the nostrils to be sent to the back of the mouth. As a result, therapsids probably could breathe while eating and thus should have been able to sustain a high metabolic rate. This was crucial in the development of homeothermy or "warm-bloodedness," the maintenance of a constant body temperature.

Remains of the earliest mammals have been found on several continents. Certain aspects of their existence are reasonably clear despite a spotty record. They were small, with a head and body length of about two feet. The majority resembled shrews, likely ate insects, and probably had some climbing skills. Most had a characteristic articulation between a knob of the jawbone and the skull's squamosal bone. The three bones which play a role in jaw articulation in lower vertebrates ultimately migrated to the middle ear in mammals, becoming the hammer, anvil, and stirrup. These have a vital role in the transmission and amplification of sound. Indeed, mammals are characterized by superb hearing. Finally, many early mammals had powerful and complex cheek teeth compared to those of their reptilian predecessors.

Until the end of the Mesozoic, some 70 million years ago, the major categories of mammals were largely different from the modern ones. One, the multituberculates, is notable. They were the first herbivorous mammals and had unusually large bladelike lower premolars, apparently for cutting plants. They were successful for an extensive period, about 100 million years. Competition from the rodents, today's most successful mammals, appears to have been the final straw in their extinction. The Mesozoic, however, was the "Golden Age of Reptiles," a time when the dinosaurs and their allies ruled the roost. It was not until after their demise, at the juncture of the Mesozoic and Cenozoic Eras, that mammals evolved into a considerably greater diversity of forms. Most modern mammalian orders, including those occurring here, burst upon the scene early in the Cenozoic, the current geological era. Present-day mammals are divided into three major categories: the Monotremata, three species that have retained the egg-laying habit; the Marsupialia, a group that produces extremely immature young which are almost always reared in pouches; and the Eutheria or placentals, in which development is characterized by attachment of the fetus to the uterus across a rich, nurturing tissue called the placenta.

Characteristics

As is true of any group, the successes of mammals can be traced to particular characteristics. Certainly, several of these are unique to them and thus are useful in defining the word "mammal." But it must be recognized that many seemingly distinctive traits are just mammalian versions of features found in other groups. An example is homeothermy, for birds can also maintain a constant body temperature. Moreover, as we proceed from less to more complex animals, there is a trend toward increasing constancy in physiological processes, a balance called "homeostasis." In attaining a constant temperature, mammals have ascended to the pinnacle of homeostasis. It is a vital trait, one which has enabled them to live in many otherwise inhospitable environments.

Another example of a trait that reaches its highest level in mammals is intelligence. Mammals have the largest brains relative to body size of any vertebrate group. What is more, their relative brain size has increased over evolutionary time; in reptiles it has remained about the same. Relative brain size, computed by dividing brain size by body size, is a crude but useful measure of comparative intelligence. Of critical consideration is that the large size is due to great development of the neopallium, or gray matter, of the cerebrum, whose surface area and nervous connections are commonly increased by complex folds. The neopallium acts as a command center, processing information based upon memory and learning before coordinating appropriate motor responses. The advanced behaviors that typify mammals largely result from its presence.

Hair is the first feature to be mentioned which is uniquely mammalian. Although some mammals, particularly whales and other aquatic species are essentially hairless as adults, even they possess hair as embryos. It is common knowledge that hair is composed of dead cells, but few people realize that it consists of several layers of such cells. On the outside is the usually transparent cuticle. It covers a layer of highly packed cells, the cortex, which may surround a core region termed the "medulla." Either cortex or medulla contains the pigment which gives the coat its color. The arrangement of the hair cells is unique to each species, and mammalogists often use hair samples for identification. Hair's primary function is to provide insulation. But the coat or portions of it commonly play an instrumental role in other aspects of the animal's life, especially protective coloration and sexual advertisement.

Several aspects of mammalian reproduction merit discussion, not only because they characterize the group but also because of the role they play in the mammals' overall success. The word "mammal" is derived from one of their most distinctive features, the mammary gland; the Latin "mamma" means breast. It even has been suggested that the word evolved from the sound that infants make while nursing. Mammary glands are just one of several unique mammalian skin glands, which include sweat and scent glands. All female mammals lactate, or produce milk, for their young. However, there is considerable variability in the period of dependency on the mother for sustenance. In addition, the composition of milk varies between species. In rapidly growing mammals, such as in some seals, it often has a high fat content. There also are differences in how the young obtain the milk. In monotremes, they lick it from hairs over the skin patches that exude it. Most marsupials and placentals have some type of nipple from which the milk is sucked. Whales use muscles to force the gland into the mouth of the young since they lack lips and thus cannot suck.

Lactation has great consequences for mammals. The close association that develops between the mother and her young has been implicated in their high learning levels. Furthermore, the availability of milk generally should reduce dependency on the father for food. Paternal care is linked with monogamy, the system in which one male mates only with one female. Thus, the fact of lactation could help explain the relatively low incidence of this mating system in mammals.

As in reptiles and birds, the mammalian fetus develops in a fluid-filled sac, the amnion. A major difference, though, between mammals and other vertebrates is that virtually all mammals are viviparous; they bear live young. A few other vertebrates do have live offspring. But among the mammals, only the monotremes — two spiny anteaters and the duck-billed platypus — lay eggs. Marsupial young are so immature that they resemble embryos. In placental mammals, which includes all in this region except the opossum, the newborn are well developed.

This is due in large part to their namesake, the placenta, a richly vascularized tissue between the fetus and the uterus. It aids in the transfer of nutrients and gases between the fetal and maternal bloodstreams, facilitating growth. Some marsupials and even several lower vertebrates have a placenta. But it is only the eutherian mammals with their highly developed placentas that consistently produce live young.

Within placental mammals there is, of course, variation in the degree of maturity of the newborn. A distinction commonly made is that between species producing altricial or relatively immature young, such as the wolf, and those giving birth to precocial or more mature offspring, such as the mule deer. An "either/or" approach is not realistic because there actually is a range of newborn maturity levels. With Mark Boyce, an ecologist at the University of Wyoming, I determined that mammal species with relatively immature newborn typically have litters with at least three young. In such species, females usually also have comparatively short pregnancies. Investing relatively little time in pregnancy apparently enables them to produce more young. Such mammals also tend to be monogamous, likely because producing immature offspring increases the opportunities for a father to assist in raising them. Alternately, species bearing precocial young usually have litters of one or two offspring, longer pregnancies, and tend to be polygynous (i.e., a harem-style mating system). Such associations show that close links occur between such life history traits as newborn developmental status or litter size and a behavioral characteristic like the mating system.

Recent studies have revealed that many mammalian life history traits are "scaled" to body size. This means that as we go from smaller to larger species, the magnitude of certain traits changes accordingly. Larger mammals usually have longer gestations, smaller litters, older age of sexual maturity, and longer life-spans. Body size is a key life history character which apparently drives the direction of many other such traits. There still is variation in the magnitude of these traits; litter size and the time to weaning are the most flexible and hence adaptive among closely related, similarly sized species.

Many factors are involved in the determination of mammalian body size, such as climatic conditions, food availability, and diet. In recent years, it has become clear that both within and among mammalian species, larger forms occur in the more seasonal areas. As Boyce points out, this is likely a result of larger mammals having proportionately greater fat reserves and thus being better able to withstand the food shortages of severe seasons.

There are several other features specific to the mammals. These include having three bones or "ossicles" in the middle ear, red blood cells which lack nuclei, and a muscular diaphragm separating the pulmonary or lung cavity from the abdominal cavity. The last is said to be the only one that can always distinguish a mammal, regardless of sex or age. Surely, any of the unique traits as well as the numerous specializations of mammals could be and often are the subjects of voluminous texts. In this brief introduction, I have presented an overview of which features I consider to be most crucial to mammalian success, flavored by the incorporation of items of personal interest.

## MAMMAL DISTRIBUTIONS IN THE INTERMOUNTAIN WEST

It is difficult to assess any overall influence of the Intermountain West's environment on the distributions of its mammals. Because the region is so large and physiographically diverse, it contains an exceptional number of different habitats. There are many climatic regimes here as well, considering its pervasive dryness. As a result of this environmental diversity, the region includes mammals common to many areas; the great majority of Intermountain mammalian species are not unique to the region. Mammalian distributions here closely follow the boundaries of the main topographic types: mountain ranges, plateaus, and rivers. As will become evident, the region's geologic history and resultant topography have strongly influenced the biogeography of its mammals, especially in the Great Basin.

Dominant Patterns: Climatic and Vegetation Influences ´

Except for the mountains and a few rivers and lakes, the Intermountain West is exceptionally arid. Nevada and Utah, the two driest states, account for most of its land. Many members of the mammalian fauna are desert-adapted, with such traits as light coloration and an ability to live without free-standing water. There are some species, mammalian and otherwise, which have found a niche only within the confines of the region. Most are adapted to the conditions of one of its two predominant zones: deserts and shrublands. Mammals for which the Intermountain West contains virtually their entire range are the pygmy rabbit, the Uinta chipmunk, Palmer's chipmunk, Townsend's ground squirrel, Belding's ground squirrel, the Utah prairie dog, the dark kangaroo mouse, the pale kangaroo mouse, and the chisel-toothed kangaroo rat. In addition, there are several species which, although largely unique to the region, have substantive range extensions beyond its borders. In this category are the Colorado chipmunk, the white-tailed antelope squirrel, the Uinta ground squirrel, the white-tailed prairie dog, Gunnison's prairie dog, the Great Basin pocket mouse, the little pocket mouse, the long-tailed pocket mouse, the canyon mouse, and the desert woodrat. Several from either group, such as long-tailed pocket mice and desert woodrats, inhabit rocky locales. Others, such as the pale kangaroo mouse, have a predilection for sand.

Conversely, there are several mammals which barely occur here, despite a strong presence over much of the continent. Their absence could be attributed to their reliance on free-standing water or on the organisms which depend on it. Moles, for example, essentially do not occur here because of their reliance on moist soils for burrowing. Distributions of the Yuma myotis and red bat appear limited to moist areas. A lack of water in much of the Great Basin is also a likely factor in the relative absence of two otherwise ubiquitous carnivores: black bears and raccoons. The Intermountain West is but one of a few regions in North America where aquatic mammals, such as beavers, muskrats, and river otters, do not occur over large areas. Finally, white-tailed deer are absent from the Great Basin. However, this may not only be due just to the dearth of water but may also be because of competitive exclusion by mule deer. Others do not occur here because of historical factors not solely accounted for by climate. For example, opossums are virtually absent from the region but can survive here as evidenced by their introduction in western Colorado.

Several of the region's mammals which normally occupy the northern part of the continent are referred to as boreal species. Here, most of these are restricted to moist and cool mountain areas. Their occurrence results from a southern extension of their ranges along the region's mountains. Within this category are masked shrews, pygmy shrews, northern flying squirrels, southern red-backed voles, heather voles, water voles, marten, fishers, wolverines, lynx, moose, and mountain goats. Mountains are also the only Intermountain zone where tree-dwelling species occur with any regularity. Mountains serve as dispersal routes for many such species as well. For example, the Uinta Mountains appear to have facilitated contact between the boreal mammals of northwestern Wyoming and central Colorado. These mountains are also a transition zone between the mammals of the Great Plains and those of the Southwest.

Even within the Great Basin, a seemingly homogeneous region, differences occur in mammalian faunas. In northeastern Nevada, for example, the small mammalian assemblages vary with vegetation type. Great Basin pocket mice and chisel-toothed kangaroo rats are the primary species in big sagebrush-shadscale communities; deer mice and least chipmunks prevail in greasewood stands; and montane voles, western harvest mice, northern pocket gophers, and vagrant shrews are the typical small mammals in marsh-meadow environments.

The Landscape

The region's varied topography and its great altitudinal relief assure the existence of many habitats, each with a distinct mammalian community. Sharp separation between land formations creates barriers, preventing the movements of animals from one area to another. As a result, there is a high degree of subspeciation here, the differentiation of species into types or races. In fact, the southwestern quarter of the United States, which includes most of the Intermountain West, has a larger number of mammalian subspecies than any other equally sized continental area in the world. Subspeciation is a key process in the formation of new species. Its high level of occurrence here provides us with another clue to understanding the region's rich variety of mammals.

*Insular Biogeography.* In 1967, Robert MacArthur and Edward Wilson, two influential ecologists, proposed a theory to explain the regulation of the number of species on islands. They predicted that two processes, immigration of species from the mainland and extinction of species on an island together determine the species number. Rates of immigration should be greater on islands closer to the mainland, those of extinctions are expected to be lower on larger islands. Therefore, large islands close to the mainland would have the most species. This association between island size and species number is strengthened by the fact that larger islands usually have a greater diversity of habitats. The composition of species would change over time, but the number would remain relatively constant, producing a "dynamic equilibrium." Many tests have shown the theory to be basically valid, particularly if modifications are made for the characteristics of individual islands. Interestingly, it is also useful in explaining the number of species on isolated patches of continental habitats, a finding which has been applied to the design of nature reserves.

Upon examination, the mountain ranges of the Great Basin appear as isolated, elongated islands emerging from the surrounding desert. Indeed, they are even separated from the "mainland" habitats of the major mountain chains, the Rockies and the Sierras. This analogy prompted one ecologist, James Brown, to investigate whether island biogeographic principles apply to the number of small- and medium-sized mammalian species on Great Basin mountaintops. He suggested that the distribution of mammalian species on the mountaintops could be explained by (1) colonization of these areas during the Pleistocene, followed by extinction of populations in the lowlands between the mountains and (2) extinctions on the mountaintops themselves. To begin, he examined the number of species of marmots, pikas, chipmunks, ground squirrels, jumping mice, woodrats, shrews, and weasels occurring at altitudes over 10,000 feet on mountains in the Great Basin. He found that the numbers of these species were greater than what would be expected simply based upon the sizes of the mountaintop zones and their distances from the major ranges.

These "islands" have only been separated from one another and the larger ranges for a relatively short time: since the end of the last Pleistocene ice advance, approximately 10,000 years ago. Brown surmised that the numbers of such species had not yet reached the equilibrium predicted by the theory. If environmental conditions remain relatively similar, one would ultimately expect the numbers of such mammalian species in these zones to eventually decline. His hypothesis that mammals reached Great Basin mountaintops in the Pleistocene and then became isolated and extinct to varying degrees on them has been greatly supported by recent paleontological evidence.

This theory has also been examined in one of the region's more striking landscapes: Craters of the Moon National Monument in southeastern Idaho. Here are hundreds of "kipukas," sagebrush covered islands which have not been buried by recent lava flows. They are isolated from the "mainland" vegetative habitat by their lava surroundings. Although the degree of a kipuka's isolation is unrelated to its number of small mammalian species, larger kipukas do indeed support more species. It may be that some species have their habitat requirements met only on these larger ones. Interestingly, the most distant kipukas also contain the highest densities of mammals, perhaps because they encounter less predation there.

Effects of Rivers and Lakes

Just as mountains and canyons prevent populations from mixing, leading to subspeciation and speciation, so do the region's waterways. The predominant river involved in such processes is the Colorado. Rising in the high country of Wyoming and Colorado, it crosses the Uinta Mountains and then cuts through the Colorado Plateau in Utah's southeastern corner. Continuing southwest, it crashes through its most well-known corridor, the Grand Canyon. Particularly where confined within such deep canyons, the Colorado prevents many mammals from crossing it. It is a greater barrier to movements downstream than it is upstream. But because the river has a southwesterly flow, it stops many northern mammals from extending their range to the south and vice versa. In comparison, the Green River continues upstream in a northerly direction above its confluence with the Colorado. Terrestrial mammals attempting to extend their range north or south would not have their movements so hampered.

In Idaho, the Snake River also is a factor in mammal distributions. Davis found that the mammals likeliest to occur in different forms on either side of the Snake, or not cross it at all, were either hibernating and/or burrowing species with restricted territories. Mammals not hampered by these criteria were apt to exist as the same subspecies on both sides of the river. Such relationships are dependent on the ease of crossing the river at any given point.

Two enormous prehistoric lakes that apparently played a role in mammal distributions were Lake Lahontan in western Nevada and Lake Bonneville of western Utah. At its highest level, Lahontan covered almost 8,500 square miles and surrounded an area in its center of about half that size. In comparison, its present-day remnants, Pyramid and Walker lakes, occupy some 250 square miles. The drying of Lahontan may have resulted in a sharp increase in the number of mammals. After lake bed sediments became exposed, large areas of wind-drifted sand and other fine soils were created. These ultimately provided superb habitat for many rodent species. By functioning as a barrier between populations, Lahontan has also been implicated in the subspeciation of several small mammals, including the long-tailed pocket mouse, the dark kangaroo mouse, and Ord's kangaroo rat.

Lake Bonneville, like its Nevada counterpart, was formed by the joining of many smaller lakes. At its highest level some 70,000 years ago, Bonneville covered about 19,750 square miles. Since then it has fluctuated dramatically, beginning to recede to the Great Salt Lake approximately 12,000 years ago. Estimated age of the current lake is about 2,000 years. Such a huge body of water undoubtedly has had a great impact on mammal distributions. It has been implicated in restricting the southern extension of northern pocket gophers and the northward expansion of Botta's pocket gophers. Over time, lake fluctuations appear to have isolated many pocket gopher populations, contributing to the considerable subspeciation which characterizes this group. As with Lahontan, the drying of Bonneville probably increased the habitat for the heteromyids (kangaroo rats and mice and pocket mice) and other sand-dwelling rodents.

## *HOW TO USE THIS BOOK*

This book is written in a manner that should make it easy to distinguish the mammals of the region. Readers should first gain familiarity with the appearance of the species in each of the major groups: the insectivores, bats, rabbits and hares, rodents, carnivores, and hooved mammals by reviewing the illustrations located throughout the text. For the comparatively diverse groups, there are illustrations of representatives of the major types of species within each group. For example, those of the rodents include mice, ground squirrels, and voles; illustrations of carnivores cover canids, weasels, and cats. By learning about the general appearance of the mammals, the reader will know where in the book to look for the detailed descriptions.

An example of how to proceed with an identification is as follows. Assume you spot a small- to medium-sized mammal. After having used the illustrations in the above-stated manner, you should be able to place the animal into a broad category, such as ground squirrels. It is a good idea to double-check a first impression by considering all illustrations of similar animals. Once an initial confirmation is made, the next step in narrowing down possibilities is to examine the range maps. This will enable you to determine which from the group of similar species occurs in the area under consideration. After reviewing the species accounts of the potential choices, you should be able to make a positive identification. This is accomplished by comparing the possible species' size, coloration, and other external traits, summarized in the account's first paragraph, and the likely habitat, in the following paragraph, of the alternates.

It is rarely a simple or straightforward task to know exactly what you have just seen. More often than not, you catch but a fleeting glimpse of a wild mammal. You should use the utmost care to remain unnoticed by the animal. Facial markings, stripe patterns, and any other distinctive marks should be quickly noted. Do not wait until a later time to figure out what animal you have just seen. Chances are that the important details will become blurred by the time you try to sort out all of the information. The most successful natural history observers I know use field guides *in the field* to identify the item at hand. Further, it is only through repeated observations and familiarity with a guide that you become confident in this activity. But for those willing to invest the time and effort, natural history becomes more of a passion than a hobby. For many, it is intrinsically rewarding to learn about an environment by being able to recognize its inhabitants.

Much of the information in the accounts is not useful in making identifications. Rather, discussions of food habits, reproductive biology, and behavior are offered to provide a deeper understanding of the mammals and the region. By spending the time to read an entire account, you will obtain a better understanding of what the animal's life is all about. For the large majority of this region's mammals, we are still learning just the basic details. Novices and experts alike often can take satisfaction in knowing that they are observing an unknown facet of a mammal's existence. I hope that this book stimulates this learning process and encourages its users to share their observations with others.

## REFERENCES

Bowers, M. A. 1982. Insular biogeography of mammals in the Great Salt Lake. *Great Basin Naturalist* 42: 589–596.

Boyce, M. S. 1979. Seasonality and patterns of natural selection for life histories. *American Naturalist* 114: 569–583.

Brown, J. H. 1971. Mammals on mountaintops: Nonequilibrium insular biogeography. *American Naturalist* 105: 467–478.

————. 1978. *The theory of insular biogeography and the distribution of boreal birds and mammals*. Great Basin Naturalist Memoirs no. 2: 209–227. Provo: Brigham Young University.

Carter-Lovejoy, S. H. 1982. The relationship between species numbers and island characteristics for habitat islands in a volcanic landscape. *Great Basin Naturalist* 42: 113–119.

Cronquist, A., A. H. Holmgren, N. H. Holmgren, and J. L. Reveal. 1972. *Intermountain Flora, vascular plants of the Intermountain West, U.S.A.* Vol. 1. New York: Hafner Publishing Co.

Eisenberg, J. F. 1981. *The mammalian radiations, an analysis of trends in evolution, adaptation, and behavior.* Chicago: University of Chicago Press.

Fiero, B. 1986. *Geology of the Great Basin.* Reno: University of Nevada Press.

Grayson, D. K. 1987. The biogeographic history of small mammals in the Great Basin: Observations on the last 20,000 years. *Journal of Mammalogy* 68: 359–375.

Harper, K. T., and J. L. Reveal, symposium organizers. 1978. *Intermountain biogeography: A symposium.* Great Basin Naturalist Memoirs no. 2. Provo: Brigham Young University.

Honeycutt, R. L., M. P. Moulton, J. R. Roppe, and L. Fifield. 1981. The influence of topography and vegetation on the distribution of small mammals in southwestern Utah. *Southwestern Naturalist* 26: 295–300.

Jones, J. K., Jr., ed. 1969. *Contributions in mammalogy: A volume honoring Professor E. Raymond Hall.* University of Kansas Museum of Natural History Miscellaneous Publication no. 51. Lawrence.

Jones, J. K., Jr., D. C. Carter, H. H. Genoways, R. S. Hoffmann, D. W. Rice, and C. W. Jones. 1986. *Revised checklist of North American mammals north of Mexico, 1986.* Texas Tech University Museum Occasional Papers no. 107. Lubbock.

Kirkland, G. L., Jr. 1981. The zoogeography of the mammals of the Uinta Mountains region. *Southwestern Naturalist* 26: 325–339.

Lanner, R. M. 1984. *Trees of the Great Basin, a natural history.* Reno: University of Nevada Press.

McPhee, J. 1981. *Basin and Range.* New York: Farrar, Straus, Giroux.

Millar, J. S. 1977. Adaptive features of mammalian reproduction. *Evolution* 31: 370–386.

O'Farrell, M. J., and W. A. Clark. 1986. Small mammal community structure in northeastern Nevada. *Southwestern Naturalist* 312: 23–32.

Ryser, F. A., Jr. 1985. *Birds of the Great Basin, a natural history.* Reno: University of Nevada Press.

Tueller, P. T., C. D. Beeson, R. J. Tausch, N. E. West, and K. H. Rea. 1979. *Pinyon-juniper woodlands of the Great Basin*. U.S. Department of Agriculture Forest Service, Intermountain Forest and Range Experiment Station Research Paper INT-229. Washington, D.C.: U.S. Government Printing Office.

Vaughan, T. A. 1978. *Mammalogy*. 2d ed. Philadelphia: W. B. Saunders.

Western, D. 1979. Size, life history and ecology in mammals. *African Journal of Ecology* 17: 185–204.

Zeveloff, S. I., and M. S. Boyce. 1980. Parental investment and mating systems in mammals. *Evolution* 34: 973–982.

# The Marsupials — Order Marsupialia

Marsupials are characterized best by their mode of reproduction. Almost every species produces extremely immature, virtually embryonic young which are nurtured in a pouch, or marsupium. The most well-known forms, kangaroos, wombats, and koala bears, reside in Australia. Less appreciated is the fact that South America, too, has several marsupial species. The earliest marsupial records, however, are from North America. From here they apparently traveled to South America. Before the continents moved to their present positions, Australia was connected to the southern part of South America by Antarctica, which then was far to the north of its present position. Recent finds of marsupial fossils on Antarctica support the notion that they crossed it en route to Australia. After the continents separated, marsupials flourished in Australia, undergoing an "adaptive radiation" into the many available niches there. There they were free from competition with placental mammals.

Placentals and marsupials have had separate lineages for over 100 million years. Marsupials are regarded as the more primitive group, both in their method of reproduction and in their less complex, relatively smaller brains. Yet, this does not imply any lack of adaptation. Producing such immature young could even be an advantage in the unpredictable climates many of them face. The loss of an offspring in which little energy has been invested is considerably less costly to the mother than losing a mature one.

## NEW WORLD OPOSSUMS — FAMILY DIDELPHIDAE

Didelphids are the most primitive and oldest known family of marsupials. The 66 species in this group are primarily subtropi-

29

cal and tropical. Throughout South America, other opossum species abound. In Mexico, small mouse opossums (*Marmosa* spp.) are abundant in many locales.

## VIRGINIA OPOSSUM
### (*Didelphis virginiana*)

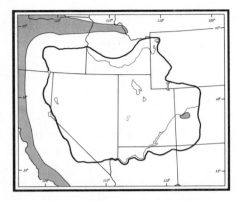

DISTRIBUTION OF VIRGINIA OPOSSUM; INTRODUCED IN BOTH AREAS SHOWN.

Total length: 25 3/8 to 40 inches; tail length: 10 to 21 inches.

The only marsupial in North America north of Mexico is the opossum. It would be difficult indeed to mistake any other animal for an opossum. It has a distinctive, grizzled appearance due to a thick, occasionally black-tipped white underfur which is overlaid by pale guard hairs. Other distinguishing features include a somewhat bulbous pink fleshy nose at the end of a pointed snout, paper-thin ears, and a long scaly tail. Opossums resemble large unkempt rats; males weigh about six pounds and females average about four pounds. Although abundant in much of the United States, particularly the Southeast, opossums are essentially nonexistent in the Intermountain West. They occur in the region due to an introduction near Grand Junction, Colorado. But opossums are unique, and since they are presently expanding their range on the continent and can survive in a variety of habitats, they could conceivably become more abundant in the area. Thus, they do merit discussion.

Opossums occur in various habitats but prefer wet ones. They eat what is readily available, concentrating on an animal diet. They are one of a few mammals that regularly prey upon shrews and moles. Many feed on carrion or animal remains. Fruits and vegetables are also important. Daytime dens include holes in the ground, cracks in trees, hollow logs, and stumps. A most interesting behavior is their ability to enter a state resembling death when faced with a highly threatening situation. This condition is often accompanied by the discharge of a greenish, foul-smelling substance from their anal glands. Apparently, they can "play possum" for several hours if the situation warrants it.

Breeding occurs throughout most of the year but within two distinct periods. Thus, there are usually two litters per year. After just 12 to 13 days in the womb, about eight young are born in an extremely immature or altricial state. As with other marsupials, the young pull themselves into the pouch using their well-developed forelimbs. The actual number of offspring is quite variable and may be as high as 16. However, there are only 13 teats in the pouch, so additional newborn perish. Each young remains attached to a nipple, which becomes swollen in its mouth, for approximately two months. Once this attachment stops, the young continue to nurse periodically for a short while longer. Both social and parental behaviors are very weakly developed in the opossum. Since opossums are nocturnal, the best opportunities for viewing them is at night along streams and rivers.

## *REFERENCES*

Low, B. S. Environmental uncertainty and the parental strategies of marsupials and placentals. *American Naturalist* 112: 197–213.

# The Insectivores — Order Insectivora

Insectivores are the most primitive placental mammals. Their ancestors are considered to be the group from which the placentals arose. Most, such as shrews, are small. There are, however, exceptions; the tenrec (*Tenrec ecaudatus*) of Madagascar may weigh over three pounds. In general, insectivores have poor vision and rely on hearing, touch, and odors to orient themselves. They usually possess five clawed toes on each foot. As the name implies, most feed on insects. There are about 400 species in this order, including well-known ones, such as hedgehogs and moles, as well as the lesser known solenodons (*Solenodon* spp.) and the moon rat (*Echinosorex gymnura*), which looks remarkably like an opossum. In the Intermountain West, there are 13 species: 12 shrews and 1 mole.

## SHREWS — FAMILY SORICIDAE

The soricids include the world's smallest mammals. In addition to their tiny size, they are characterized by elongated pointy snouts, small eyes, and reduced ears which are usually hidden under the fur. A unique feature of shrews is the presence of tiny peglike teeth, or unicuspids, the arrangement of which are often used to distinguish the species. All North American soricids have teeth that are pigmented on the tips with a brownish color. Due to the tiny size of a shrew's body, there is a large amount of exposed surface area relative to its volume. As a result, shrews lose a great amount of heat, necessitating a voracious appetite to replenish the lost energy. On the average, they must feed once every three hours throughout the day. Their typically high metabolic rates are also reflected in their heart rates; the heart of an excited shrew can beat over 1,000 times per minute.

## MASKED SHREW
(*Sorex cinereus*)

Total length: 2 3/4 to 4 3/8 inches; tail length: 1 to 2 inches.

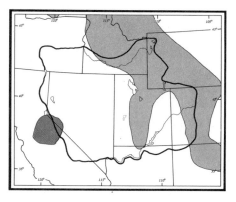

DISTRIBUTIONS OF MASKED SHREW (LIGHT) AND MT. LYELL SHREW (DARK).

The masked shrew is a medium-sized, light grayish brown shrew with a fairly long bicolored tail. It is generally dark tan to ash brown on its upper body, with a light brownish color below. In some regions, it has a tricolored pattern, with an intermediate brown on the sides. It is very difficult to tell this shrew apart from the vagrant shrew. Although a trained mammalogist could distinguish them by their tooth characteristics, the casual observer might only be able to tell them apart by the masked shrew's narrower snout. As with most other shrews, the masked shrew is extremely light, weighing between a tenth to a fifth of an ounce. It has the greatest distribution of any North American shrew. In the Intermountain West, it is found throughout southeastern Idaho, western Wyoming, and in two wide north-south belts extending through central Utah and Colorado.

Although the major habitat of masked shrews is the coniferous forests of the mountains and foothills, these tiny mammals also occur in a variety of other habitats, such as along river bottomlands or marshes. They thrive in moist environments, being common in some spots. Masked shrews eat a wide variety of invertebrate animals, as might be expected of an insectivore which exists in so many habitats. Most of their diet consists of insects, such as beetles, flies, and ants. But they also consume small vertebrates, such as salamanders, and some vegetation. Due to their largely invertebrate diet, they can be rather beneficial to humans by reducing populations of such harmful forest insects as the larch sawfly.

Masked shrews begin breeding in the spring, producing a litter of from 4 to 10 highly immature young after a pregnancy of 19 to 22 days. The young weigh approximately 0.28 grams (several thousandths of an ounce) at birth. Adult females generally have two or three litters a year. They usually construct individual nests in the cavities of old stumps or logs.

## MT. LYELL SHREW (*Sorex lyelli*)

Total length: 4 inches; tail length: 1 1/2 inches.

The Mt. Lyell or simply Lyell shrew is a close relative of the masked shrew. It is brownish above, olive gray or smoke-gray below, and has a bicolored tail. Compared to the masked shrew, its skull is slightly wider between the eyes and flatter on top. Although only about a dozen have been found, Lyells are known to occupy several different habitats: grassy spots or those among willows and alders in moist areas, sagebrush steppe communities, and clumps of wild rye. They appear to be restricted to elevations of over 6,000 feet in the central Sierra Nevadas of California. Since they occur close to the border, they are also likely to inhabit adjacent areas of Nevada. Almost nothing is known about their life history.

## PREBLE'S SHREW (*Sorex preblei*)

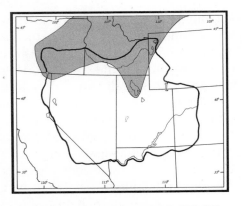

DISTRIBUTION OF PREBLE'S SHREW.

Total length: 2 to 2 1/4 inches; tail length: 1 1/2 inches.

Little is known about Preble's shrew, also referred to as the Malheur shrew. It is one of the smallest western shrews, yet no reliable records of its weight are available. Undoubtedly, though, based on its length, it is lighter than the masked shrew. Most specimens have light brownish gray upperparts, with slightly paler underparts. The coloration pattern of the tail closely matches that of the body. A trained observer can distinguish Preble's shrew from the masked shrew by the former's smaller size, flatter skull, and broader rostrum, or nose, area. Positive identification relies on examination of tooth characteristics.

Preble's shrew probably occurs throughout much of Montana, central Idaho, eastern Oregon, and surrounding areas in semiarid to arid habitats. The word "probably" is used since records of it are only from that area's borders. Until recently, it's occurrence in southeastern Oregon placed it just within the Intermountain region. But there are now records of it in Timpie Springs, along the southern border of the Great Salt Lake, so there is no question that it inhabits our region. This tiny beast occupies marshy areas, such as creeks and bogs bordered by willows and other brushy plants. They are occasionally found in the wetter areas of open conifer tree stands. Recently, it was caught in a montane-sagebrush community in northeastern California.

### VAGRANT SHREW
(*Sorex vagrans*)

Total length: 3 3/4 to 4 3/4 inches; tail length: 1 1/4 to 2 inches.

The vagrant or wandering shrew is a medium-sized shrew with a considerably different appearance from those already reviewed. Individuals found in most of the region, the

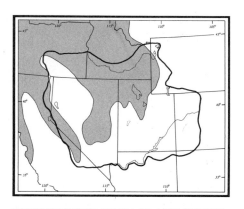

DISTRIBUTION OF VAGRANT SHREW.

northern Great Basin and adjoining Columbia Plateau and the Snake River Plains, are reddish in summer and become blackish in winter. The feet are rather dark, and the tail is slightly bicolored. In the Rocky Mountains, vagrant shrews tend to be larger, more grayish brown in summer, and not as black in winter. In parts of Nevada, they are relatively pale. Clearly, they display considerable variation, and many subspecies are recognized. The terms "vagrant" or "wandering" have nothing to do with how far they travel. They go by this name due to a large distribution which covers most of the western part of the continent. They occur throughout much of the northern part of this region.

Vagrant shrews largely occur in wetter areas within conifer forests but are also found in more arid locales, such as sagebrush prairies. Wet places that they inhabit include cattail and tule marshes, sphagnum bogs, and areas with lush fern growth. Compared to dusky shrews, they seem less capable of surviving at high altitudes, in boreal forests, or on dry soils. Within the Uinta Mountains proper, dusky shrews appear to occur alone, but both vagrant and dusky shrews occupy the lower slopes of the western Uintas. The vagrant shrew probably moves about underground in vole runways or tunnels, since it has been successfully trapped in them. Just as it is found in many different habitats, it also eats a variety of items: insects and their larvae, centipedes, spiders, earthworms, slugs and snails, vegetation, and a subterranean fungus, *Endogone*. The shrews are believed to be active both day and night at certain times. Evidence exists of their being preyed upon by snakes, such as the Mormon racer, and barn owls.

As is the case for most other shrews, only the bare facts about reproduction are known. Apparently, vagrant shrews can breed from late January through May. They may breed again in the fall, but most produce one litter a year. After about 20 days, from two to nine immature young are born. Six is the average number of young in Washington. Nests consist of grass or leaves in stumps and logs. After about a week, the young open their eyes. They are weaned after approximately 20 days. When they disperse from their birth area, they weigh about five or six grams (less than a fifth of an ounce). At maturity, a year after birth, they will weigh only about two grams more. Their life-span rarely exceeds 16 months.

## DUSKY OR MONTANE SHREW (*Sorex monticolus*)

Total length: 4 1/8 to 4 7/8 inches; tail length: 1 3/4 to 2 1/4 inches.

Until recently, the dusky or montane shrew was considered to be a subspecies of the vagrant shrew. Now it is clear that they are unique species, each usually occupying a distinct "microhabitat" where they occur together. What had appeared to be rare cases of interbreeding between them might be better explained by "character convergence." This is a resemblance between species which can occur as a result of their facing similar environmental pressures. In the summer, dusky shrews have a short,

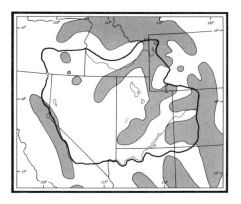

DISTRIBUTION OF DUSKY OR MONTANE SHREW.

rust-brown fur above but are lighter and less reddish below. Their fur is darker and longer in the winter. Although the tail is bicolored, the color separation is not clear. Vagrant shrews are generally smaller than dusky shrews where they occur together. Further, the tail of the former is shorter. The pigmentation patterns on their incisors differ, a distinction that is apparent only to a trained zoologist. The paper by Junge and Hoffmann listed at the end of this section provides illustrations of these traits, which are helpful in distinguishing their skulls. Dusky shrews occur throughout northwestern North America and into much of the Rocky Mountains and other ranges of the western United States and Mexico.

As one of the common names indicates, dusky shrews are ordinarily found in the mountains. Common habitats include forested areas near streams and wet meadows, but they appear less dependent on wet areas than do vagrant shrews. At high altitudes in the northern Rockies, they occur in spruce-fir forests and alpine tundra. At lower altitudes of about 3,000 feet, they occupy conifer forests composed of such species as Douglas fir, lodgepole pine, and western larch. They may also be present in pinyon-juniper and sagebrush communities in the northern Great Basin. Foods include insects, spiders, and snails.

Reproductive data for this species are scanty. In high altitude populations in Montana, births have been observed to occur in March and April.

## INYO SHREW (*Sorex tenellus*)

Total length: 3 3/8 to 4 inches; tail length: 1 3/8 to 1 5/8 inches.

The Inyo shrew is a small, rare species found only in some of the Great Basin mountains along the southern Nevada-California border. Individuals weigh between 3.4 to 4.1

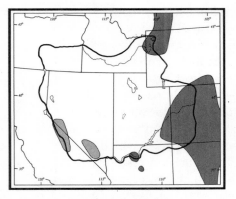

DISTRIBUTIONS OF INYO SHREW (LIGHT) AND DWARF SHREW (DARK).

grams, roughly about a tenth of an ounce. In the summer, Inyo shrews are drab gray above and a lighter smoky gray tinged with buffy white below, with a similarly bicolored tail. By winter, they become considerably lighter all over. Although they will occur in the foothills down to about 4,500 feet, they seem to be more common above 8,000 feet, primarily around streams flowing by rock ledges and canyon bottoms. A preferred habitat is the shaded rocky areas in subalpine conifer forests. They have also been found in swampy areas and atop a 14,000-foot mountain. Surely this is one animal about which much remains to be learned.

## DWARF SHREW (*Sorex nanus*)

Total length: 3 1/4 to 4 1/8 inches; tail length: 1 1/2 to 1 3/4 inches.

The dwarf or Rocky Mountain dwarf shrew is a close relative of the Inyo shrew. They live in similar habitats and resemble each other anatomically. But the dwarf shrew is even smaller than its cousin. With weights ranging from 1.8 to 3.2 grams (for a midvalue of less than a tenth of an ounce) and a slightly shorter length, it is one of the smallest North American shrews. In summer, its upper hair, which extends far down the sides, is usually brown to olive brown. Its undersurface is smoky gray to whitish. In winter, its hair is both lighter and grayer, particularly on the back. The tail is indistinctly bicolored. Dwarf shrews occur in the Intermountain West in eastern Utah, north-western Wyoming, and western Colorado. At one time, they were believed to be extremely rare, but their high rates of capture in some areas reveal that this is not always the case.

As with the Inyo shrew, this species is primarily found in montane areas. In a study in the Medicine Bow Mountains of southeastern Wyoming, most dwarf shrews were collected from rockslides in subalpine and alpine zones. They also occur in areas ranging from sedge marshes to dry, shortgrass prairies. Little information exists about their food habits. In a study of captive individuals, however, some interesting behaviors were observed. Individuals selected soft-bodied spiders and insects but refused to eat slugs. They also piled up unused food in the corners of their cages, presumably for later use. Evidence exists that they are preyed upon by barn owls.

There is some information about dwarf shrew reproduction from trapped individuals. In alpine areas, breeding begins after snowmelt in the beginning of summer. First litters are born between late July and early August, second litters occurring about a month later. Females probably go into heat after giving birth (postpartum estrus); several that were producing milk were also pregnant. This is common in many small mammals. The average number of young produced in second litters is about six and a half. No information on the size of first litters is available. There is no evidence that females reproduce in their first year. It appears that males reach maturity late in their first summer.

## WATER SHREW (*Sorex palustris*)

Total length: 5 1/8 to 6 5/8 inches; tail length: 2 1/4 to 3 1/2 inches.

Almost the size of a house mouse, the water shrew is easily the largest long-tailed shrew in the Intermountain West. Its weight of a third to a half an ounce may not seem like much, but it is quite a bit for a shrew. In winter, it ranges from velvety brown to a black-gray which appears frosted in some individuals. It is browner in the warmer months. The fur has a shiny, almost iridescent look. The undersurface is silvery, and its tail is distinctly bicolored. Its hair is dense and very soft, permitting water bubbles to be trapped above the skin surface. This makes the hair relatively impervious to water.

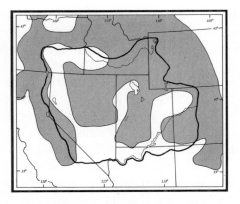

DISTRIBUTION OF WATER SHREW.

One characteristic which distinguishes the water shrew from all other shrews in the region is the stiff whitish hairs that stick out along the sides of its hind feet. In addition, there is a thin webbing joining the third and fourth toes of the hind feet for about half their length. Clearly, these are adaptations to an aquatic existence. Water shrews are excellent swimmers and the stiff hairs and webbing give them extra propulsion as they move through the water. The fringes can trap bubbles, enabling the shrew to briefly run across the water's surface. But its talents do not stop with an ability to "walk on water." If it becomes too wet, it shakes itself dry and combs out its fur with the fringe hairs. It is also fully capable of moving about on land. Because of its unique aquatic adaptations, it has also been called the marsh shrew (the name *palustris* is from the Latin for marshy), beaver mouse, and muskrat shrew. Indeed, it has been discovered to inhabit both beaver and muskrat lodges. Water shrews are widely distributed throughout most of the region.

Water shrews are most often found in and near fast-running, cold mountain streams at high altitudes. Investigators in both Nevada and Idaho reported that they were not found below about 5,000 feet. They may also occur around ponds or lakes. Grass-sedge marshes and willow-alder shrub zones are typical of water shrew habitat. Regardless of the watercourse, good cover, such as rocks and large roots, appears to be attractive to them. This could be because, as an aquatic shrew, they are probably more susceptible to predation than the others. They are preyed upon by various weasels, birds of prey, snakes, and fish. Of course, their excellent swimming abilities enable them to use the water for escape. They appear to be most active shortly before

WATER SHREW

dusk and dawn, perhaps either to avoid predators or to take advantage of an abundant food source. Aquatic insects and their larvae commonly compose over half of their diet. Other morsels tasty to this creature include small fish, snails, flatworms or planaria, earthworms, leeches, slugs, snails, and even other shrews and mice. Green plants and fungi are important to some populations.

Water shrews have their first litters between February and June; the length of pregnancy is unknown. The average litter size is six, but litters may range from four to eight young. Some females may give birth to three litters per year. Although they are exceptions, females have occasionally been found to reproduce in their first year. Alternately, males have not been found to breed at this age. Maximum life-span for these mammals is about one and a half years.

## TROWBRIDGE'S SHREW (*Sorex trowbridgii*)

Total length: 4 3/8 to 5 1/4 inches; tail length: 1 7/8 to 2 3/8 inches.

Trowbridge's shrew occurs only in a small part of our area, in far northeastern California and directly above it in Oregon. It

42

has a large distribution in the Pacific states, where it is found along the coast in conifer forests. Apparently, it is restricted to environments that are more humid than those in this region. This rather large shrew is dark gray-brown and has a sharply bicolored tail. It has the unusual habit, for a shrew, of including seeds of the Douglas fir tree in its diet.

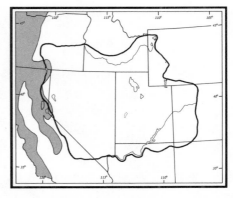

DISTRIBUTION OF TROWBRIDGE'S SHREW.

## MERRIAM'S SHREW
(*Sorex merriami*)

Total length: 3 1/2 to 4 1/4 inches; tail length: 1 3/8 to 1 3/4 inches.

It is odd that so little is known about Merriam's shrew since it is one of the most widely distributed shrews in the Intermountain West. Indeed, it is also one of the region's most ubiquitous shrews, largely occurring in the dry habitats which characterize it. Because it exists in relatively sparse populations, it may seem rare at times. This small shrew is light gray on top, has a whitish underbelly and feet, and a sharply bicolored tail. Its sides are a bit paler than the upper surface. In the winter, its pelage is brighter. Compared to those of other shrews, the skull is short and broad. This species was named after the great mammalogist, C. Hart Merriam (1855–1942), the first chief of the U.S. Biolog-

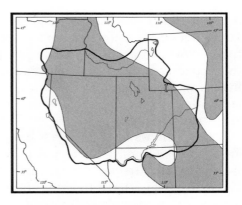

DISTRIBUTION OF MERRIAM'S SHREW.

ical Survey. As we shall see, there are several other mammals that bear his name.

The occurrence of a shrew in dry areas is unusual. But Merriam's shrew is commonly found in sagebrush, mountain mahogany, and arid grassland communities. It manages to prosper in these areas by utilizing the burrows and runways of voles to search for food. A particularly close association has been discovered between Merriam's shrew and the sagebrush vole. In Washington, foods include beetles, cave crickets, wasps, and caterpillars, which are the most common food in the summer. In turn, it suffers from predation by owls although there is slim evidence of its being preyed upon. It should enjoy some protection from predators in the vole runways.

The timing of its reproductive events are probably similar to that of other members of the genus. Limited samples indicate that it has litters of about six young. An unusual aspect of its reproduction is that the males develop large flank glands, approximately a quarter of an inch long, on their sides throughout the spring. They are larger than those of any shrew, with the exception of the desert shrew, which barely appears here. These glands have a strong odor that may attract mates, repel predators, or even both. To accomplish both at once undoubtedly would be convenient.

## PYGMY SHREW
*(Sorex (Microsorex) hoyi)*

Total length: 3 1/8 to 3 7/8 inches; tail length: 1 1/8 to 1 7/8 inches.

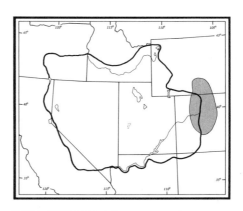

DISTRIBUTION OF PYGMY SHREW.

The pygmy shrew has the dubious yet distinctive honor of being the smallest mammal in North America. Here we have a shrew among shrews. Although some individuals of other species might be smaller than any given pygmy shrew, it is still recognized as the continent's littlest mammal. Its weight of approximately an eighth of an ounce is equal to about that of a dime; you would barely feel its presence in your hand. Varying from reddish brown to gray on top, it has a lighter, silvery coloration below. Red predominates on the upper body in the summer, although some females remain gray at this time. Around the venter, or hind region, it is light gray. Compared to the similar masked shrew, the pygmy shrew is slightly smaller and has a shorter, more distinctly bicolored tail. This miniscule mammal has a limited distribution in our region, occurring only along the center of the Wyoming-Colorado border and to the south of it. Some texts show it in southeastern Idaho and throughout central Colorado. Elusive and often rare, it could occur in these places, but the finds have not been documented.

The most typical habitat of pygmy shrews is the deep woods of the boreal forest. They are also found in fields, sphagnum bogs, and other wet areas. They feed on a variety of larval and mature insects and other small invertebrates. They have been found living beneath logs and in the roots of tree stumps. As with other shrews, they have been caught in vole runways. They are preyed upon by snakes and likely have to deal with many of the same predators as their relatives.

Their breeding habits have not been studied much, although scanty evidence indicates that their litter size is similar to that of other long-tailed shrews. It is believed that they do not produce more than one litter per year, which could account for their suspected low population sizes. In Colorado, they were observed to reach their maximum population density several weeks before similar species did. As with Merriam's shrew, male pygmy shrews have sizable and smelly flank glands.

DESERT SHREW (*Notiosorex crawfordi*)

Total length: 3 to 3 3/4 inches; tail length: 7/8 to 1 1/4 inches.

The fact that such an animal as the desert shrew occurs in the Intermountain West is a strong reminder of just how arid parts of this region are. Primarily a denizen of the southwestern and south-central United States and northern Mexico, this species appears as far north as the southern portions of Nevada,

Utah, and Colorado. It may be distinguished from the other shrews here by its more visible ears. It is gray on top with a paler gray bottom.

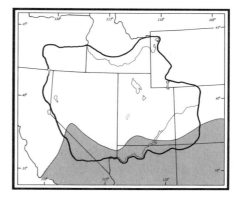

DISTRIBUTION OF DESERT SHREW.

Desert shrews are found in many habitats, as is expected of a species with such a broad distribution. Typically, they are found in semidesert scrub communities with such plants as mesquite or agave. Like many desert dwellers, they do not require a permanent source of water. Instead, they can obtain water from their food, mostly the soft body parts of their prey. They will drink water when it is available. Various plants are used for cover, and they often rely on woodrat dens for their homes. Although they use pathways created by other animals, they are not fossorial; that is, they do not dig or create burrows. They probably eat many of the small invertebrates that occur in their areas, but there is little documentation of their food habits. Studies of captive animals suggest that crickets are an appealing item. Great horned owls and barn owls are their only known predators. But rather than worry about being devoured, they enjoy a particularly deep sleep. This behavior might be the result of periodic decreases in metabolic rate to slow up respiratory water loss.

Nests are built from various materials, such as moth web-silk, cornsilk, grass, and feathers. Litters are notably smaller than those of other shrews, about three to five young. Length of the gestation period is not known. Newborn are extremely altricial, being both naked and blind. At about 40 days, they leave the nest. Interestingly, desert shrews appear more even tempered than most shrews. When placed together in cages with a food surplus, they express little antagonism toward each other. In many ways, the desert shrew stands apart from its relatives here.

## MOLES—FAMILY TALPIDAE

This family includes the moles, shrew-moles, and an aquatic group, the desmans. With the exception of the shrew-mole, *Neurotrichus gibbsii*, of the Northwest, all North American talpids are moles. They are rat-sized animals whose head and forelimbs are highly modified for burrowing. As with the shrews, their velvety fur can lie either backward or forward. This assists in moving through the underground tunnels they inhabit. Such adaptations have enabled moles to become one of the most subterranean groups of mammals, a life-style which has resulted in their suffering little predation for a mammal their size. The association that most people have with moles is a negative one. After all, they cause extensive damage in two of our favorite places: gardens and golf courses. To their credit, it should be mentioned that their digging aerates the soil. And, plumbers have found their short, thick-napped fur to be excellent for cleaning pipe threads.

**BROAD-FOOTED or CALIFORNIA MOLE**
(*Scapanus latimanus*)

Total length: 5 1/4 to 7 1/2 inches; tail length: 3/4 to 1 3/4 inches.

The broad-footed mole is the sole mole in the region and even it has only barely found a home here. Most of its distribution is throughout California. But

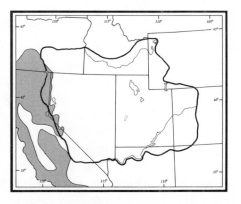

DISTRIBUTION OF BROAD-FOOTED OR CALIFORNIA MOLE.

because it crosses the border into northwestern Nevada, it is included as one of our more unique citizens. As is true for other moles, the broad-footed mole lives almost its entire life underground. Here, it relies on its excellent tactile senses to find its way around. The naked nose and other body parts have many nerves directly under their surfaces. Its eyes are tiny and virtually sightless, and it lacks external ear pinnae, or flaps. It digs underground tunnels with its huge spade-shaped hands; its shoulder girdle is also enlarged and structured in a way that provides much power to the forelimbs. Although its hands are broad, they actually are not broader than those of most other moles. Moles are larger than shrews and this one is no exception. These chunky fellows weigh approximately two ounces. Their color varies from brownish to grayish.

Their preferred habitats are within the porous soils of mountains and meadows. Earthworms are their major food item. Other small animals, such as slugs and insects, are not ignored when encountered. The production of one litter a year is the norm; between two to five young are born in March or April.

## REFERENCES

Armstrong, D. M., and J. K. Jones, Jr. 1971. *Sorex merriami*. Mammalian Species no. 2. American Society of Mammalogists.

Armstrong, D. M., and J. K. Jones, Jr. 1972. *Notiosorex crawfordi*. Mammalian Species no. 17. American Society of Mammalogists.

Beneski, J. T., Jr., and D. W. Stinson. 1987. *Sorex palustris*. Mammalian Species no. 296. American Society of Mammalogists.

Findley, J. S. 1955. *Speciation of the wandering shrew*. University of Kansas Museum of Natural History Publications, vol. 9: 1–68. Lawrence.

Hennings, D., and R. S. Hoffmann. 1977. *A review of the taxonomy of the* Sorex vagrans *species complex from western North America*. University of Kansas Museum of Natural History Occasional Papers no. 68: 1–35. Lawrence.

Hoffmann, R. S., and J. G. Owen. 1980. Sorex tenellus *and* Sorex nanus. Mammalian Species no. 131. American Society of Mammalogists.

Hoffmann, R. S., and R. D. Fisher. 1978. Additional distributional records of Preble's shrew (*Sorex preblei*). *Journal of Mammalogy* 59: 883–884.

Junge, J. A., and R. S. Hoffmann. 1981. *An annotated key to the long-tailed shrews (genus* Sorex*) of the United States and*

48

*Canada, with notes on Middle American* Sorex. University of Kansas Museum of Natural History Occasional Papers no. 94: 1–48. Lawrence.

Kottler, B. P. 1985. A record of *Notiosorex crawfordi* (Insectivora: Soricidae) from the Great Basin Desert, Nevada. *Southwestern Naturalist* 30: 448–449.

Long, C. A. 1974. Microsorex hoyi *and* Microsorex thompsoni. Mammalian Species no. 33. American Society of Mammalogists.

Mullican, T. R. 1986. Additional records of *Sorex merriami* from Idaho. *Murrelet* 67: 19–20.

Ports, M. A., and J. K. McAdoo. 1986. *Sorex merriami* (Insectivora: Soricidae) in eastern Nevada. *Southwestern Naturalist* 31: 415–416.

Tomasi, T. E., and R. S. Hoffmann. 1984. *Sorex preblei* in Utah and Wyoming. *Journal of Mammalogy* 65: 708.

Williams, D. F. 1984. Habitat associations of some rare shrews (*Sorex*) from California. *Journal of Mammalogy* 65: 325–328.

# The Bats — Order Chiroptera

Bats are the only mammals capable of true flight. Several other orders include efficient gliders, but only bats fly. Furthermore, they have great maneuverability and can fly over long distances. Their wings are formed by a membrane of skin stretched across the fingers. An additional flight surface is the interfemoral membrane, or uropatagium, a thin tissue which extends between the hind limbs. In most bats, this membrane has two cartilaginous supports for its exposed edge, the calcars, one of which is anchored to each foot.

With over 850 species, bats are the second largest group of mammals. They are divided into two suborders, the Megachiroptera and the Microchiroptera. Megachiropterans, which include the flying foxes, subsist largely on fruit, nectar, and pollen. Most reside in the Old World tropics. The other suborder, Microchiroptera, is much more diverse. The majority orient themselves in space by echolocation. During this process, bats emit ultrasonic waves through the mouth or nose, and then determine the position of an object by the manner in which the wave is reflected. Most "microbats" are insectivorous and can use echolocation to locate prey on even the darkest of nights. Another noteworthy feature of bats is their remarkable ability to conserve energy. In addition to lowering metabolism during the day, many microchiropterans hibernate in the winter. Such energy savings have resulted in long life-spans for several species. There are records of little brown bats living for over 20 years.

Although bats have long been the victims of fear and superstition, they can be highly beneficial to our interests. They can devour large numbers of harmful insects, pollinate flowers, and aid in seed dispersal. One of the few dangers they do present is

49

transmission of rabies by biting. Unprovoked attacks are rare, but bats should be handled only by trained persons. Today, they face a much greater threat than an occasional killing by a frightened person. The indiscriminate use of chlorinated hydrocarbon pesticides and habitat destruction has placed several species in threatened statuses.

## LEAF-NOSED BATS—FAMILY PHYLLOSTOMATIDAE

The leaf-nosed bats compose one of the most diverse bat families, containing some 140 species. In addition, they demonstrate a great variety of body structures and food habits. Some are insectivorous, whereas others feast upon fruit. Of special interest is the vampire bat, *Desmodus rotundus*, which feeds on the blood of living mammals. In parts of Central America, it is a significant pest to domestic cattle. Most phyllostomatids are distributed in southerly climes: Mexico, Central America, and the Carribean. Only five species enter the southwestern United States, with just one barely crossing into this region.

CALIFORNIA or
WATERHOUSE'S
LEAF-NOSED BAT
(*Macrotus californicus*)

Total length: 3 3/8 to 3 5/8 inches; forearm length: 1 7/8 to 2 1/4 inches.

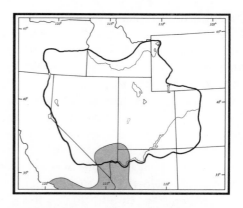

DISTRIBUTION OF CALIFORNIA OR WATERHOUSE'S LEAF-NOSED BAT.

The California leaf-nosed bat is the only phyllostomatid in the region. It thus can be readily distinguished from any other bat in the area by the erect, lancelike, approximately quarter-inch flap on its nose. This "leaf" has a role in directing the emissions of the high frequency sounds which are used in echolocation. The bat's odd appearance is accentuated by the large ears, which measure about one inch in height and are joined at their bottoms by a ridge of skin. The forearms, which reside within the relatively broad wings, are fairly long. The fur is gray to dark brown on the upper body, becoming almost white at its base, with a paler undersurface. The tail either extends to or goes slightly beyond the interfemoral membrane. This bizarre-looking mammal has a wide distribution in much of western and southern Mexico, throughout Cuba, and some nearby islands. It reaches its northernmost distribution in the southwestern corner of our region, principally around the bottom of Nevada.

These bats usually roost in relatively small groups of up to 100 individuals. Most often, they roost around the entrances of abandoned mine tunnels and caves. In winter, however, they have been located deep within caves, perhaps because of the more constant temperature there. Most of their diet, predominantly grasshoppers, beetles, and moths, is taken on or near the ground. They have been observed hunting for insects flying within a few feet of the ground, close to short vegetation. As with the other bats in this family, they do not hibernate. Undoubtedly, this is responsible for their southern distribution since they cannot adjust to the cold by slowing up their metabolism as do hibernating bats.

Little is known about their reproduction, but much of what has been discovered is fascinating. Their early development is "delayed": ovulation, the shedding of the egg within the female, and the subsequent fertilization occur in autumn, but embryo development is very slow until March. Then, after approximately an eight-month actual pregnancy, quite long for a small animal, usually one young is born in early summer. Males appear to leave the females and young alone in the maternity colony. Whereas females may breed in their first year, males do not.

## EVENING BATS—FAMILY VESPERTILIONIDAE

The vespertilionids, a family of some 280 species, are the most numerous and widely distributed bats in the region and the world. In the Intermountain West, there are 16 species from this family. There is a report of an additional one, the cave myotis (*Myotis velifer*), from near Idaho Falls, but it has not been substantiated. Most of these bats are plain-looking, usually lacking the bizarre facial structures evident in other groups. The majority are small and insectivorous. In capturing insects "on the wing," they commonly demonstrate remarkable agility.

## CALIFORNIA MYOTIS
### (*Myotis californicus*)

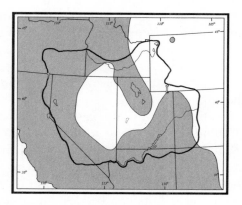

DISTRIBUTION OF CALIFORNIA MYOTIS.

Total length: 2 7/8 to 3 3/8 inches; forearm length: 2 7/8 to 3 3/8 inches.

One of the smaller of the "myotis," or mouse-eared bats, the California myotis is distinguished by its diminutive quarter-inch-long foot. Its upper body ranges from brown to yellowish, tending toward a buffy color where it occurs in the drier areas so typical of our region. The upper fur has alternately been described as possessing a yellowish to orangish cast. In some areas, such as the Southwest, the relatively light fur contrasts sharply with its black ears. In this bat, the calcar is keeled, meaning that it has a flat portion which projects into the membrane, increasing its stiffness. Several other bats in the region are difficult to distinguish from the California myotis. The Yuma myotis is usually larger with a larger foot; the western small-footed myotis has a black mask across its face; and the others are generally larger. All of the above have smaller ears. Obviously, such characteristics are useful only if comparing the bats up close. The California myotis is prevalent throughout the western and southwestern United States, including the Intermountain West except for areas of eastern Nevada and central Utah.

These bats occur primarily in rocky canyon habitats in desert and semidesert regions. They are also found in grasslands and around ponderosa pine stands. They usually live in crevices in mine tunnels, hollow trees, and loose rocks. Yet, they may select human-made structures, such as bridges and buildings, moreso than other bats. They live in small colonies or alone. When foraging, which is usually among trees, they rarely fly higher than 15 feet. Oddly, when going after insects, they have the uncanny ability to suddenly veer sideways, up or down, and even zigzag, making for rather erratic flight patterns. In the winter months, some hibernate but others remain active.

For most of the year, the sexes are separate. After the usually one young is born, in either May or June, mothers remain with their offspring in nursery colonies. The newborn is naked and helpless and begins to feed on its own within a few weeks.

## WESTERN SMALL-FOOTED MYOTIS
(*Myotis ciliolabrum*)

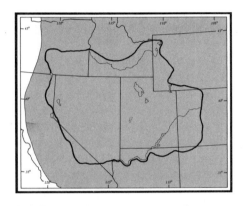

DISTRIBUTION OF WESTERN SMALL-FOOTED MYOTIS.

Total length: 1 1/3 to 1 7/8 inches; forearm length: 1 1/6 to 1 4/10 inches.

The western small-footed myotis is slightly smaller than the California myotis. Its fur is typically a long, silky yellow which varies from tan to golden brown, with hair tips that occasionally are glossy. The characteristic black facial mask is hard to recognize from afar because the rest of the face is blackish as well. And as is true for the California myotis, the ears are black. The top of the head, the area around the base of the ears, and the underparts are all buffy white. Its name reveals that the feet are tiny, yet they are not necessarily any smaller than the quarter-inch-long foot of the California myotis. The calcar is keeled. Distributed throughout the western United States except for northern Pacific coastal areas, western small-footed bats occur in all of the Intermountain West.

By most accounts, they prefer the same types of roosting sites as those of the California myotis and tend to occur around rocky environments. They may also be found in a variety of other habitats, such as forests, near watercourses, and even in desertlike areas in central Idaho. They search for insects while flying low among the trees or brush. These small creatures may occur either in groups or alone and typically hibernate. Usually, a single young is born between May and July. Mothers remain with the newborn in small nursing colonies; groups of up to 20 individuals have been reported.

## YUMA MYOTIS
(*Myotis yumanensis*)

Total length: 3 3/8 to 3 7/8 inches; forearm length: 1 3/8 to 1 1/2 inches.

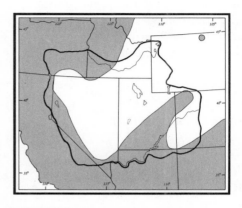

DISTRIBUTION OF YUMA MYOTIS.

Perhaps it is unfortunate to be distinguished by dullness, but the Yuma myotis is described as having a short, dull brownish upper body fur. The lower body is lighter and the throat region occasionally is whitish. Yuma bats are larger than the California myotis or the western small-footed myotis. They appear similar to little brown bats but tend to have darker ears and a more sloping forehead. One of their distinctive features is the hairiness of the interfemoral membrane; it is furred nearly to the knees. The edge of this membrane is almost white and there is no keel on the calcar. Not as widely distributed in the region as some other myotis bats, the Yuma myotis is still common in portions of southern Idaho and Oregon, western Nevada, and throughout much of southern Utah.

These bats may look dull, but they do not necessarily act that way. Nearly always by waterways, such as lakes and streams, they dart about the water in a low flight pattern searching for small insects. Moths and midges account for a large part of their diet in some places. In turn, they are known to be preyed upon by bobcats. Despite their penchant for wet spots, they most often are found in arid environments, including deserts and grasslands.

Female Yumas roost together with their young in large, clumped colonies in caves and tunnels. Some of these nursery colonies contain thousands of individuals. Usually one young is born between May and June.

## LITTLE BROWN BAT
### (*Myotis lucifugus*)

Total length: 3 1/8 to 3 3/4 inches; forearm length: 1 3/8 to 1 3/4 inches.

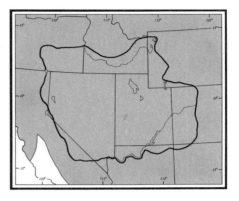

DISTRIBUTION OF LITTLE BROWN BAT.

The little brown bat or little brown myotis is perhaps the most common bat in North America. Its upper body fur is glossy, varying from yellowish to very dark brown; it is buffy below. The tragus, a small projection in the earflap, is short and rounded. Although the calcar usually lacks a keel, it may be slightly developed in some individuals. Males are typically bigger than females. If you can get a close look at one, it is relatively easy to tell it apart from other bats in the region. As mentioned, the calcar normally is not keeled. Alternately, that of the long-legged myotis is distinctly keeled. Little brown bats also have a shorter tibia and less fur on the wing undersurface than does the long-legged myotis. The long-eared myotis, as expected, has longer ears and a longer, thinner tragus. The Yuma myotis is typically smaller and a duller brown. Also smaller are the western small-footed myotis and the California myotis. The distribution of little brown bats encompasses all of the Intermountain West. This is but a small part of a range which includes almost the entire continent.

Perhaps more is known about this bat's habits than those of any other bat on the continent. Three types of roosting sites have been identified: day, night, and hibernation roosts. "Ordinary" day roosts occur in buildings or hollow trees, but small groups of nonnursing individuals may be found in wood piles and under rocks. Nursery roosts are usually in places with warm temperatures since these favor survival and rapid growth of the young. Adult males and nonpregnant females occupy sites apart from the nurseries. Bats in these cooler roosts often go into a daily torpor or lethargy. Openings to such roosts frequently have southwestern exposures, which warms them up in the morning, arousing the inhabitants. After the first evening feeding, little brown bats often congregate in smaller night roosts. This clustering results in these roosts being warmer than their daytime counterparts. Greater warmth might enable them to digest food more rapidly, an important process for species with high metabolic rates; their heart rates have been clocked at over 1,000 beats per minute. Females may travel over a hundred miles between summer and winter roosts; male migration patterns are less well understood. Hibernacula, or hibernation roosts, are usually in caves or mines because they tend to be warmer and more humid than abandoned buildings, which is important to overwintering individuals. They hibernate for up to eight months in northern areas beginning in September or for five months farther south starting in November.

Feeding habits of these bats vary with local food availability. In northeastern North America, they concentrate on aquatic insects, particularly chironomids, a group of mosquitolike flies and midges. Many different predators, such as snakes and small mammalian carnivores, eat little brown bats, especially where they are in thick concentrations.

Females become pregnant in the spring after emerging from hibernation. Because mating takes place in summer, a female must store the sperm of her partner for quite some time. Following a gestation period of 50 to 60 days, the young are born in nursery colonies. During birth, the single young is deposited in the mother's interfemoral membrane. At this time, the mother hangs right side up, the opposite of her usual posture. Eyes of the young open shortly after birth. The baby bats grow rapidly, ready to fly and feed on their own after about three weeks. Apparently, the mating system is unstructured; males try to mate with many females, each of which may have already mated with a different male. Much of their day is spent in self-grooming behavior.

## LONG-LEGGED MYOTIS (*Myotis volans*)

Total length: 3 3/8 to 4 1/8 inches; forearm length: 1 3/8 to 1 3/4 inches.

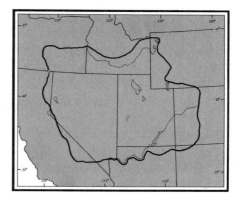

DISTRIBUTION OF LONG-LEGGED MYOTIS.

The long-legged or hairy-winged myotis has an upper surface which varies from tawny or reddish to almost black depending upon loca-tion. In this region, lighter, cinnamon individuals are common. Undersurface color, while lighter, also varies considerably. Other identifying features are a relatively large size, short rounded ears, a distinctly keeled calcar, and long, dense fur which covers much of the undersurface of the wings and interfemoral membrane. This last trait is one of the bats' most distinguishing characteristics; no other species in our region has this luxuriant growth. The nose area, or rostrum, is short, with the forehead rising from it at a steep angle. Whereas the western small-footed myotis and the California myotis also have keeled calcars, they are much smaller than their long-legged colleague. The little brown bat and the Yuma myotis also lack this keel. Long-legged bats occur throughout western North America, including the entire Intermountain West.

These bats primarily inhabit conifer forests but may also be found along watercourses and in deserts. Their roosts are usu-ally in places similar to those of other myotis species. Yet, they have even been found roosting in cracks in the ground, which is difficult to imagine since roosting implies an aboveground activ-ity. Long-legged bats are active throughout the night, when they fly in fast, directed patterns for long distances after their prey, in and over the forest. Moths are their most common food, but other soft-bodied insects, including flies and termites, are also taken.

Their reproductive habits are similar to those of related bats, as evidenced by the female's overwinter storage of sperm and the production of a single young. An unusual aspect of their breeding biology is that pregnant females are found throughout all of the summer. In other myotis species, pregnancy tends to be more synchronized. Birth occurs in nursery colonies composed of hundreds of individuals.

## FRINGED MYOTIS
(*Myotis thysanodes*)

Total length: 3 1/8 to 3 3/4 inches; forearm length: 1 1/2 to 1 3/4 inches.

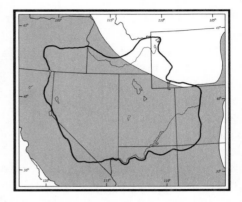

DISTRIBUTION OF FRINGED MYOTIS.

The fringe that gives this medium-sized bat its name is a distinctive set of stiff hairs which extend from the hind edge of the interfemoral membrane. The fringed myotis is also unusual in that the upper and lower body surfaces do not differ much in color: both range from yellowish to a deep reddish brown. Darker specimens occur in the northern parts of its range. Its ears are noticeably large. The fringed myotis occurs throughout most of the Intermountain region except for an area encompassing western Wyoming, southeastern Idaho, and northern Utah.

These bats inhabit a wide variety of environments, from desert scrub communities to fir tree stands in the mountains. Oak and pinyon woodlands are their most common habitats. They roost in the typical places mentioned for the other myotis species. Although they feed on insects, they occasionally concentrate on an unusual type: beetles. They begin to search for their prey shortly after sunset, flying in a slow, highly maneuverable manner, typically over watercourses. The fringed myotis is a hibernator.

Its reproductive cycle has been thoroughly studied only in northeastern New Mexico, an investigation which revealed that its habits are similar to those of many other myotis bats. In late spring, ovulation, fertilization by the stored sperm, and implantation of the egg in the uterine wall take place. The birth of the single young occurs in a nursery colony in early summer. Within the first hours of birth, the young's eyes open. The baby bats are capable of limited flight in just over two weeks.

## LONG-EARED MYOTIS (*Myotis evotis*)

Total length: 3 to 3 3/4 inches; forearm length: 1 3/8 to 1 5/8 inches.

This medium-sized bat resembles several of the myotis species. It, too, has glossy light brown to brown upper hair and a light undersurface. However, its long, dark ears make

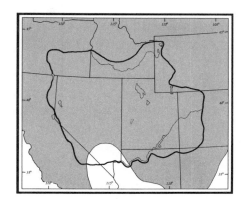

DISTRIBUTION OF LONG-EARED MYOTIS.

a big difference in its appearance. They are about one inch long and extend a quarter of an inch beyond the nose when laid forward. Often, the tail membrane has a sparse fringe of hairs, but this is hard to confuse with the conspicuously thick growth of the fringed myotis. Long-eared bats are a western species whose range occupies the entire Intermountain region, with the possible exception of some areas in far southeastern Nevada.

Their main habitat is the conifer forests of the mountains; they are most often found in pinyon-juniper communities. With all of the other species that roost in caves, buildings, and mine tunnels, one might anticipate a bat housing shortage. Yet, long-eared bats also frequent such dwellings. Their predatory habits are similar to those of the fringed myotis, particularly in regards to their reliance on beetles. Moths are another preferred food.

The single young are born in nursery colonies which are thought to be small, each of them numbering from 10 to 30 individuals. Several accounts indicate that birth occurs in early summer. Long-eared bats are a unique-looking species about which much remains to be learned.

## SILVER-HAIRED BAT
(*Lasionycteris noctivagans*)

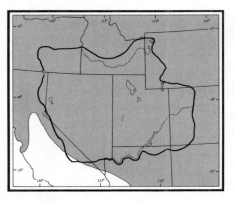

DISTRIBUTION OF SILVER-HAIRED BAT.

Total length: 3 5/8 to 4 1/4 inches; forearm length: 1 1/2 to 1 3/4 inches.

It would be difficult, indeed, to confuse any other species with the silver-haired bat. This is because of its exquisite frosted appearance, produced by the silvery white tips on its chocolate brown to black body hairs. Such coloration is particularly noticeable on the darker young; adults may lack the white tips or appear yellowish. Even though other bats in the region, the red bat and the hoary bat, are frosted, they are more lightly colored overall. The interfemoral membrane of the silver-haired bat is slightly furred above and its frosting may not be as apparent. Both its wings and short, rounded ears are black. It has a flattened skull with a broad, concave rostrum. This bat is found throughout the entire Intermountain West, although some populations are probably only migrating through. Our region encompasses but a small part of a distribution which includes most of the United States and southern Canada. In some areas, silver-haired bats are quite abundant.

These bats are often reported to be solitary, roosting under the bark and in the hollows of trees. But this tree-roosting tendency is not well documented. They also inhabit caves and mines, places typical of their cousins. As is true of many other bats, they usually feed near water, in their case within conifer or mixed deciduous forests. Silver-haired bats begin to feed both early and late in the evening and have two feeding periods in some locales. Such behavior could be a response to activity periods of prey or a function of attempts to avoid competition with other bats. They forage by flying slowly and erratically. They are opportunistic, feeding upon available insects and spiders. In some areas, they concentrate on moths and caddis flies. Predators include skunks and great horned owls. There is a documented case of an aerial attack by a rabid hoary bat; it's even hard to trust one's fellow bats. Interestingly, silver-haired bats have highly developed homing abilities. In one case, an individual returned over a hundred miles to its roost.

The timing of reproductive events is similar to that of related bats. Mating is in August or September, followed by the female's overwinter storage of sperm. Births occur between May and early July after a "real" pregnancy of 50 to 60 days. Either one or two young are born, with twins being more common. The tiny newborn only weigh about seven-hundredths of an ounce (two grams). They are highly altricial, with pink, hairless bodies, closed eyes, and folded ears, as if to emphasize their helplessness. Consistent with their solitary habits, silver-haired bats do not form the large maternity colonies typical of other evening bats. Small colonies consisting of about a dozen adults and their young have been found in hollow trees. The young nurse for slightly over a month and can become sexually mature in their first summer.

## WESTERN PIPISTRELLE
(*Pipistrellus hesperus*)

Total length: 2 3/8 to 3 3/8 inches; forearm length: 1 1/8 to 1 3/8 inches.

A bit of fanfare is in order as we consider the western pipistrelle, for it is the smallest bat in the United States. Adult weights of this wee beast

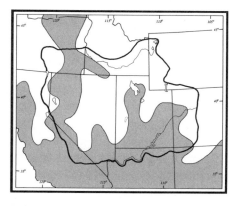

DISTRIBUTION OF WESTERN PIPISTRELLE.

range from but one-tenth to one-twentieth of an ounce. Gray to reddish brown above, it may also be yellowish gray in some locales; the belly is whitish gray. In Utah, grayer individuals are more prevalent toward the northwest, whereas southeastern natives are browner. Heightening their appearance, the nose, ears, feet, and flight membranes are almost black. The calcar is keeled. Although the western pipistrelle occurs throughout the Southwest, its Intermountain distribution is spotty. It inhabits much of Utah, extends into Arizona, and, from a stronghold in western Nevada, ranges up into the southern border area of Oregon and Idaho.

Its habitats include arid areas, such as greasewood flats, grasslands, deserts, and rocky cliff and canyon areas. But it is most often associated with canyons and is thus also referred to as the canyon bat. It is, in fact, the most common bat in the Grand Canyon. Since it is a weak flyer, its roosting sites are often located near its prey, close to water sources even in dry regions. Such sites include canyon or cliff walls, bushes, and trees. Often, it is the first bat species to begin feeding in the evening. It may even be seen in broad daylight, flying in a slow, jerky manner. Due to their size, western pipistrelles depend upon small insects, such as leafhoppers, small moths, and flying ants. In Idaho, they have been observed feeding around cliff swallow colonies. The pipistrelles and swallows foraged at separate times, thus avoiding competition for food. The extent to which they hibernate here is unknown, although there is some evidence of this behavior.

Usually two young are born in either June or July after a 40-to-50-day gestation. Females also exhibit overwinter sperm storage following an autumn mating. In warmer areas, where pipistrelles are more active, insemination occurs during the winter as well.

## BIG BROWN BAT (*Eptesicus fuscus*)

Total length: 4 1/8 to 5 inches; forearm length: 1 3/4 to 2 inches.

All descriptions of the big brown bat surely begin with its name. In this region only the hoary bat is larger, but the two are easily distinguished. The hoary bat is a frosted, whitish color; the slightly smaller big brown bat has a larger skull. Female big browns are about 5 percent larger than the males. To illustrate the size of this animal, it is useful to point out that western pipistrelles are about an inch smaller in length, quite a bit for a species which is so tiny to begin with. Color varies from light brown in those inhabiting deserts to a darker shade in forest dwellers. On the upper surface, the brown is glossy, whereas the belly hairs are paler. The wings and interfemoral membrane are black, with the body hair only slightly extended onto them. The calcar is keeled. Both the face and ears are darker than the body. Although big brown bats normally fly

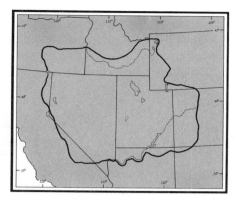

DISTRIBUTION OF BIG BROWN BAT.

in a slow, steady fashion, they can cruise at up to 40 miles per hour, the fastest reported for any bat. Some chatter loudly while in flight. Their homing ability is also well developed, with accounts of individuals returning to roosts from distances of 450 miles. It is easy to distinguish them from similarly colored species, such as many of the myotis bats, since these are considerably smaller. They are found throughout the lower 48 states, including the entire Intermountain area, as well as Mexico and most of southern Canada.

Clearly, a bat, or any species for that matter, with such a tremendous distribution occurs in a great variety of habitats. In New Mexico, big brown bats are most common in spruce-fir and other conifer stands. An interesting fact is that they often roost in buildings and other human-made structures. There is even a report of roosting in a storm sewer. They also roost in more typical spots, such as caves or mines. Hibernation begins in the fall in small groups of up to about 20 individuals. Usually in April, males and nonpregnant females leave the hibernacula but may stay nearby in small groups throughout the summer. Pregnant females band together in maternity colonies, which also often occur in human-made structures.

Big browns commonly begin their early evening feeding bouts, as do other bats, by drinking water. Food habit studies reveal a reliance upon beetles, but many other types of insects are also eaten. Moths, however, are taken infrequently. In winter, they may not eat at all, using fat reserves for energy

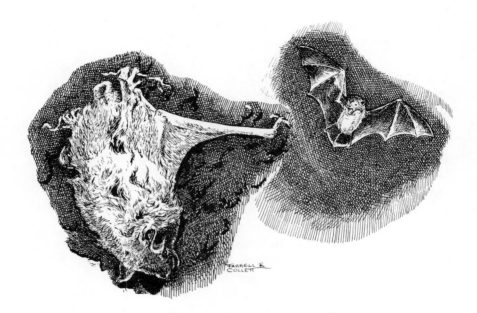

BIG BROWN BAT AND LITTLE BROWN BAT

instead. This might be possible only in such a large bat, since the bigger the mammal the proportionately greater is the fat reserve to be used in such situations. In this species, fat tissue can account for up to one-third of the body weight.

One young is born between May and July in the maternity colony. Twins are more common in eastern North America. This difference is fascinating because there are hardly any reported cases of longitudinal variation in mammal litter sizes. Mating occurs in the fall or winter; the two-month pregnancy begins in the spring following the storage of sperm. Juveniles are capable of flight after 3 weeks, reaching adult size at 10 weeks.

## RED BAT (*Lasiurus borealis*)

Total length: 3 3/4 to 5 inches; forearm length: 1 1/2 to 1 3/4 inches.

The red bat, with its striking upper body coloration, is one of the most easily recognized bats in the Intermountain West. It

is not always red; indi-
viduals vary from a
vibrant reddish orange
to a deep chestnut
brown. Males tend to be
redder and brighter, a
difference heightened by
the female's more
frosted look, which is
created by a preponder-
ance of white tips on the
upper body hairs. This
is one of a few mam-
mals in which the sexes

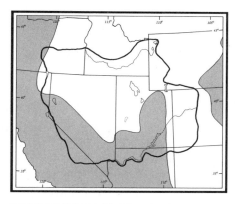

DISTRIBUTION OF RED BAT.

differ noticeably in color, a phenomenon called "sexual
dichromatism." In both sexes, there is a white patch of hair on
the shoulders. Both sides of the wings are furred up to the
elbow and the interfemoral membrane is completely covered
with fur. Indeed, the name *Lasiurus* is a combined form of two
Greek words meaning "shaggy tail." Under all of this fur and
where they are exposed, the wing membranes are brownish
black. And as if this beast were not hirsute enough, the hind
feet and most of the short, rounded ears are also well haired. At
least the undersurface is a bit lighter in color, if not any less
hairy. Hoary bats are similar in form but are substantially larger
and browner. In this region, red bats occur along the southwestern edge of Nevada into California and throughout eastern and
southern Utah into Arizona. Yet, they are not restricted to
southern locales, contrary to what one might surmise from their
Intermountain distribution. They have one of the largest ranges
of any North American bat, inhabiting most of the continent
and Central America and entering South America as well.

A likely reason for their absence from much of our region is
their preference for woods, which are relatively uncommon here.
Their occurrence in several Utah caves, however, reveals that
they may not be as restricted to forests as is generally believed.
Nevertheless, these bats typically roost in trees and occasionally
other vegetation, individually or in family groups of females
with their young. Although elms are favored for roosting, they
also dangle from box elder, assorted fruit, and various other

trees. Due to a tendency to hang by a foot with their wings wrapped around themselves, they resemble dead leaves from a distance. Red bats are one of the earliest species to feed in the evening, usually along forest borders. Although moths constitute the majority of their diet, many other insects are eaten. During feeding, they may land on vegetation to pick off their prey. Little is known about their winter ecology. Apparently, some groups migrate to warmer latitudes in colder months, whereas others hibernate. The factors that determine which population chooses either strategy are not understood. But an ability to increase metabolism to raise body temperature in winter and the ubiquitous dense fur are both adaptations which help them to survive the colder months.

Mating occurs either during the fall migration or in the wintering areas. The term "during migration" is accurate: red bats have been observed copulating in flight. As usual, females store sperm until early spring, when they begin a "real" pregnancy of 80 to 90 days. The most striking aspect of their reproduction is the litter size: between one to five young are born around June, with an average litter being three to four. This is regarded as the largest litter size of any bat. In fact, *Lasiurus* is the only bat genus in which females have four nipples. I suggest that this high production of young is a mechanism to compensate for the great mortality that juveniles must suffer by being so easily dislodged from trees during severe weather. Once displaced from their roost, they are highly susceptible to predation. Blue jays are significant predators on the juveniles.

## HOARY BAT (*Lasiurus cinereus*)

Total length: 4 to 6 inches; forearm length: 1 3/4 to 2 1/4 inches.

Hoary bats have the distinction of being the largest bat in North America and thus, of course, the Intermountain West. Their coloration and markings are also unique. The hoary appearance is due to the extensive silvery tips on the upper body hair, which ranges from yellowish brown to rich mahogany. On the neck, hairs are longer than average, forming a collar of sorts. The shoulders bear yellow-white patches which may join across the chest. Cream-colored spots are present near the wrists. Females are slightly larger, but the sexes are similar in overall appearance. The furring over much of the wings and ears, the interfemoral membrane, and upper feet is similar to that described for their close cousin, the red bat. The hoary bat's ears are short and rounded but are highlighted by a dark, naked rim.

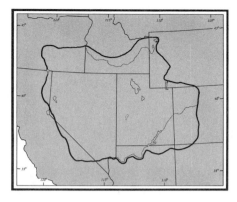

DISTRIBUTION OF HOARY BAT.

Belly hair is whitish to yellowish brown. This giant among bats has long, narrow wings. Hoary bats are found across the entire region, all of the United States, and much of Canada and Mexico. Incidentally, they are the only bats found on the Hawaiian islands, perhaps because of their strong flying capabilities.

This bat primarily inhabits the forested areas of the West, often spending its days hidden within dense foliage. Both deciduous and coniferous trees are used as roosts. It concentrates its feeding on moths and butterflies, although many types of insects are preyed upon. In an Iowa study, hoary bats were even found to eat pipistrelles. Feeding commences several hours later in the evening than for most bats, with a second bout afterwards. While aloft, they make a chattering sound which is audible to humans. They are a strongly migratory species, and some spend winters as far south as Central America. Migration may be undertaken by hundreds of individuals together. During the remainder of the year, they are relatively solitary. They leave their northern homes in the late summer, returning by April or May, with males arriving first. Hibernation is also an overwintering strategy they pursue. As with the red bat, it is not known what induces some groups to migrate and others to remain in an area in a state of torpor. In the summer, the sexes stay separate, with males at higher elevations and latitudes. Due to its solitary habits and late feeding schedule, the hoary bat is seldom observed. Both red and hoary bats appear to become impaled on barbed-wire fences more than do other bats. For now, the answer to this odd behavior will remain as mysterious as the red bat's large litters and the function of the longer collar hair of the hoary bat.

Between late May and early July, females give birth to usually two young. It is believed that this follows a late fall or winter mating and an overwinter sperm storage. The young are highly altricial at birth, being blind and only lightly haired. Their eyes do not open until their second week. Young hoary bats also fall out of tree roosts to the ground, where they undoubtedly are as helpless as their red cousins. Nevertheless, such a vulnerability has not favored as high a litter size in this species. After four or five weeks, the young are volant or capable of flight.

## SPOTTED BAT
### (*Euderma maculatum*)

Total length: 4 1/4 to 4 1/2 inches; forearm length: 1 7/8 to 2 inches.

The spotted bat is one of the most strikingly bizarre-looking mammals in the world. The clearly contrasting black and white pattern on its back, which has

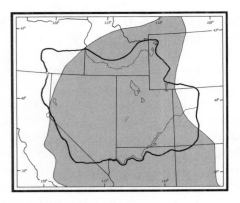

DISTRIBUTION OF SPOTTED BAT.

been likened to a "death's head" image, has few counterparts in the animal world. Only an Old World bat in the genus *Glauconycteris* has even a roughly comparable appearance. It has been suggested that this coloration is adaptive by making the bat inconspicuous while hanging on similarly patterned rocks. Yet, daytime roosts are also within horizontal rock crevices, so the pattern's significance, if any, remains a mystery. The three white spots are each slightly over a half-inch wide and are located over each shoulder and on the rump. The remainder of the upper body is grayish black to black. Although the undersurface appears white, parting the hairs reveals their black base. From this description, it would seem that the spotted bat is weird enough looking. But topping it off are its huge, naked, pinkish red ears. They are approximately two inches in length, the longest of any North American bat, yet are sturdy for their size. When at rest or when the animal is cooled, the ears roll back, resembling a ram's horns. On the throat of this alien-looking being is a small, circular, hairless spot which is hidden unless the head is tipped back. It is nonglandular and its purpose is unknown, although a temperature regulation function is suspected. Wing and tail membranes look similar to the ears. This is a Southwestern species which occurs throughout the entire Intermountain region except for small areas around northwestern Nevada and western Colorado. It is conceivable that the species inhabits these areas as well.

These bats occur in a variety of habitats, including forests and caves. Most often, though, they inhabit rough, desertlike terrain characterized by suitable roosting cliffs, areas similar to those frequented by other big-eared bats. They are a relatively solitary species but may hibernate in small groups. Moths are their food of choice; the bats have the unappetizing habit of pulling off and discarding their victims' heads and wings before devouring the abdomens. In turn, spotted bats are victimized by birds, such as kestrels. They cross flat surfaces with ease, and will pursue their prey on the ground. The ears are pointed for-ward in flight; they are believed to be fast flyers. Activity often takes place late at night. Spotted bats may be uncommon, but they have not been studied enough to know if their populations are healthy. Until recently they were listed as "rare" on the United States' Rare and Endangered Species List. Observations or finds of individuals should be reported to state or federal wildlife agencies.

Little is known about the reproductive habits of spotted bats. One researcher suggested that they do not exhibit the overwinter sperm storage typical of so many other bats, but this needs to be investigated further. Evidence points to birth occur-ring in early or mid-June, producing a single, highly immature young. The neonates, or newborn, have floppy ears and lack the distinctive coloration of their parents. But given time, they, too, will be fortunate enough to have those long pink ears and a death's head on the back.

## ALLEN'S BIG-EARED BAT (*Idionycteris phyllotis*)

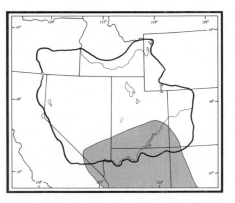

DISTRIBUTION OF ALLEN'S BIG-EARED BAT.

Total length: 4 1/8 to 4 5/8 inches; forearm length: 1 3/4 inches.

Allen's or the Mexican big-eared bat is another creature with unusual, oversized ears. In this case, though, the one-and-a-half-inch ears possess a feature that makes them unique. Projecting over the forehead from the front base of each ear is a "lappet," a slight enlargement of the lower ear lobe which resembles a rounded overhanging shelf. Furthermore, the ears are connected across the forehead by a membrane. Hair on the back is up to half an inch long, dark brown to blackish close to the body and tawny on the tips. On each shoulder there is a blackish patch. Not all individuals appear this way. When the hair is worn, the paler tips are lost, making them appear much darker. At the rear of each ear's base is a tuft of white hairs. Undersurface hairs are slightly lighter but resemble those of the upper body. Interestingly, the interfemoral membrane is braced with 12 or 13 transverse ribs, although the reason for these supports is not known. Sexual dimorphism occurs in this species: females are about 5 percent larger than males in head and body length but, oddly, their wings are about the same size. This bat is found in much of central Mexico and a substantial portion of the southwestern United States. In the Intermountain West, it occurs in the areas surrounding southern Nevada and Utah.

These bats are rare creatures of mountainous, forested habitats. But they are not restricted to any one forest type and occur in both conifer and deciduous forests as well as within cottonwood and willow stands along rivers and streams. Captures almost always occur in proximity to rocky areas, such as cliffs, boulders, or lava beds. It is widely believed that they roost in such sites although there are few actual observations. They prefer small moths and also eat a wide variety of beetles, including soldier, dung, and leaf beetles. Insects are taken either "on the wing" or picked off of leaves. While flying, they often emit a very rapid cheeping noise that sounds like clicking. They are capable of many flight styles, including slow, highly maneuverable flight; fast, directed flight; hovering; and even vertical flight. Such a repertoire coupled with echolocation enables them to exploit insects that are between, within, and below the tree tops.

From the little information available on reproduction, it appears that one young is born from mid-June to late July. During the summer, the sexes separate, with females staying in maternity colonies which have been located in mine tunnels and boulder piles. It is not known whether males remain together at this time. Similarly, the bats' winter habits and seasonal movements are not documented.

## TOWNSEND'S BIG-EARED BAT (*Plecotus townsendii*)

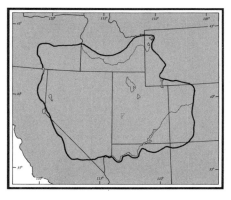

DISTRIBUTION OF TOWNSEND'S BIG-EARED BAT.

Total length: 3 1/2 to 4 3/8 inches; forearm length: 1 1/2 to 1 7/8 inches.

This species, also known as the lump-nosed bat, is perhaps the most common big-eared bat in most of the western United States. Its hair color is one of its most distinguishing features. On its back, the bases of the hairs are slate gray with the tips ranging from pale cinnamon to blackish brown. The color pattern is similar on the belly but with lighter tips. In total body length, females average slightly larger than males. Both the wings and tail membrane are hairless. The ears, as expected, are an obvious feature, ranging from one and a quarter to one and a half inches in length. As noted for several other big-eared bats, a Townsend's bat directs its ears forward in flight, suggesting that this provides lift. There is a profuse network of blood vessels in the earflaps. Thus, it is likely that they also have a temperature regulatory function since the proximity of blood to the air permits cooling. Most often, though, it is thought that these large flaps simply play a role in sound funneling. Ear positions can be slightly changed to pick up incoming sounds. Actually, these unusual structures could serve several functions, although the original one is difficult to discern. On the nose is another interesting trait: two large glandular lumps situated between the nostrils and the eyes. Their function is not known. Echolocation pulses can be emitted through the nose almost as effectively as from the mouth. Townsend's big-eared bat is distributed throughout western North America, including the entire Intermountain West.

This is a common bat in the highlands of the West, often found in scrub plant communities as well as pine, pinyon-juniper, and deciduous forests. Although these bats occur in deserts, they are generally uncommon in dry regions. They usually begin their feeding flights late in the evening, concentrating on small moths. Insects are caught off of leaves and other surfaces, but they chiefly feed in the air along the forest edge. They exhibit highly maneuverable flight and are capable of hovering.

In the spring and summer, females remain with the young in maternity colonies located in the warmer parts of caves, mines, and buildings. These are usually small groupings of 25 to 50 adults, rarely exceeding 100. Such colonies in the eastern United States are often substantially larger. At this time, males are solitary. In the winter, most bats roost alone but may also gather in small clusters. In Utah, they frequently hibernate in mines and caves, preferring the cooler parts, such as well-ventilated entrance areas. This could be the result of their tendency to slow down metabolism in these cool spots, thus decreasing the loss of fat reserves. Yet, they still may lose as much as half of their body weight while hibernating, perhaps because of frequent arousals and movements, even to other hibernacula, during this period. Townsend's big-eared bat seems to be a sedentary species, with some females returning to the same maternity roost year after year.

Much of what is known about their reproduction stems from a California study; it is likely that these findings apply to populations in our region. Females come into heat in the early fall, and copulation occurs throughout the winter. A precopulatory ritual is performed, characterized by males head-nuzzling with either hibernating or active females. After an overwinter storage of sperm in the uterus, births occur in the spring, following a pregnancy that is unusual in its highly variable length. It may last from 56 to 100 days depending upon spring temperatures and the amount of time a female spends hibernating. Warmer springs should accelerate the birth date. Litter size data are scarce, but normally one naked, helpless young is born; the large ears are draped over its closed eyes for several days. A baby Townsend has been described as grotesque due to its floppy ears and oversized feet and thumbs. It flies after two and a half to three weeks and is on its own at six weeks. Females are reproductively active in their first year, but males may not be. Birthrates are high, commonly ranging from 90 to 100 percent of the females in a population. Population densities may be rather high as well. Estimates of 100 individuals per square mile have been made, but this is probably at the high end of the scale. Although the importance of human-made structures as roosting sites has been questioned, the recent surge of construction in the western states may have led to an increase in the number of these bats.

## PALLID BAT
*(Antrozous pallidus)*

Total length: 4 1/4 to 5 3/8 inches; forearm length: 1 7/8 to 2 3/8 inches.

The large pallid bat is true to its name; its most distinguishing feature is probably the pale, light yellowish brown color. Even its belly tends to be white.

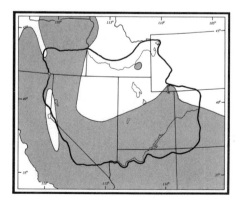

DISTRIBUTION OF PALLID BAT.

Such coloration may be an adaptation for camouflage on the desert floor, where it spends a fair amount of time feeding. An unusual aspect of the pelage is that tips of the hair are darker than the bases, the opposite of what typically occurs in bats. This ghostly creature is yet another large-eared bat; its ears measure from one to one and three-eighths inches long. Yet, the ears are separate at the bases, which is not the case for Allen's or Townsend's big-eared bats. It has rather large eyes and several wartlike bumps across the face. The latter are modified sebaceous glands which secrete an oily product. Its skunklike odor probably has a defensive function since it is most obvious when they are disturbed. Its charming appearance is enhanced by a squared-off muzzle that has a horseshoe-shaped ridge over the nostrils. The wings and interfemoral membrane are both hairless. Pallid bats are usually referred to as a Southwestern species although they do range up the Pacific coast states into British Columbia. They occur throughout most of the Intermountain area.

Their most common environment is the desert. Although they occur at altitudes of up to 8,000 feet, they are considerably more prevalent in low-elevation desert areas with rocky outcroppings. Most often, they prefer spots with available water, although this is not a necessity. The overwhelming majority of day roosts are in the crevices of rock outcroppings and cliffs; some roosts are in caves. Daytime roosts are often shared with other species, particularly the Brazilian free-tailed bat. At night, pallid bats roost in nearby spots, including shallow caves, cliff overhangs, and human-made structures, which may be selected because of their insulative properties. Most of their time is spent roosting, typically in groups of at least 20 individuals. Over 100 have been found living together. In winter they are inactive, likely hibernating at this time.

As indicated, these bats do most of their feeding on the ground. In fact, they are relatively good walkers. Usually, they emerge from the roost late in the day, slowly flapping their wings. They specialize in large insects, either on the ground or a few feet above it. Their favorite morsels include scorpions, ground crickets, and beetles. Insects nabbed off of plants include cicadas, katydids, and praying mantids. Because of the strength of their robust skull, pallid bats are particularly adept at devouring large, hard-bodied beetles. This is likely a factor in their ability to take vertebrates, such as silky pocket mice. They also eat the fruits and seeds of cacti and agave flowers. Clearly, pallid bats have quite a versatile diet. But along with their style of ground feeding come the penalties of injury and predation. In some locales, many suffer from ripped membranes (which may regenerate) and thorns or spines in the skin. Snakes and owls prey on them. To find their way about, they rely on echolocation, sight, and a well-developed sense of smell.

Following the pattern of most Intermountain bats, pallid bats copulate in the fall and winter, with sperm stored in the female until spring. Then, ovulation and fertilization occur, with embryonic development lasting for approximately nine weeks. Litter size varies from one to three, with an average of two altricial young. After four to five weeks they are capable of taking short flights and are weaned at six to eight weeks. The young may remain in association with the adults at their nursery roosts even beyond their first birthday. In fact, bats in the same family may stay at a site for several generations. Other aspects of their social behavior include vocal advertising of roost locations, positioning young at roost spots with advantageous temperatures, use of distress signals, and adult guarding of young.

## FREE-TAILED BATS — FAMILY MOLOSSIDAE

The free-tailed bats are a family of some 90 highly insectivorous species. Found throughout the world, they are especially evident in the subtropics and tropics. As their name indicates, they have a tail which extends beyond the border of the interfemoral membrane. They also have long, narrow wings which permit them to attain a sustained and rapid flight of up to 60 miles per hour. Oddly, another trait aiding them in this capacity is the shape of their ears. A side view reveals that the ear has the elliptical shape of an airfoil, that of an airplane wing in cross section. This shape assists in rapid flight by reducing turbulence and enhancing lift. Even the ears of these creatures are flightworthy! With their snub noses, the faces of free-tailed bats resemble those of mastiff dogs. Hence, they are also referred to as mastiff bats.

## BRAZILIAN FREE-TAILED BAT (*Tadarida brasiliensis*)

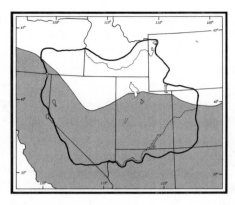

DISTRIBUTION OF BRAZILIAN FREE-TAILED BAT.

Total length: 3 1/2 to 4 3/8 inches; forearm length: 1 3/8 to 1 3/4 inches.

The small Brazilian free-tailed bat is one of two species in this family in the region; the other is the big free-tailed bat. In Brazilian free-tailed bats, the ears are separated at the base and have little bumps along their front edges. Their muzzles and wing membranes are nearly black. Most have a velvety, dark brown fur, but some may be dark gray. It has been said that it is the most common bat in the entire Southwest and one of the most numerous mammals in the United States. It inhabits the entire southern portion of the Intermountain West.

These bats are strongly migratory, only venturing into the colder reaches of their distribution when traveling north in spring. They will remain in some northern locales over the winter by hibernating, but migration is probably the more common method of avoiding cold in our region. Although they occupy various habitats, they are primarily a lowland species. Roosting takes place in the usual spots: caves, rock fissures, and mine tunnels. When they emerge from the roost at sundown, the appearance of large numbers of individuals at some sites can be spectacular. The bats seem to be part of an advancing, spiraling tube that stretches for miles. The famous Carlsbad Caverns of New Mexico were discovered due to the explosive nature of their emerging Brazilian free-tailed bats. As many as 5,000 to 10,000 bats a minute leave the caves at sunset. Yet, in this instance and similar ones, they hunt in small groups which break away from the larger one. Moths are one of their most common foods, but a variety of other insects, including ants, beetles, and leafhoppers, are taken. Colony size also is impressive in some Texas caves, where as many as 250 per square foot are crowded together in nursery populations of several million individuals. In these cases, the consumption of insects, including many pest species, may total 40 million pounds per year. Their only known predators are hawks and owls.

In the southern parts of their range, breeding occurs in late winter or early spring. This is later than the mating period of many North American bats. Ovulation takes place shortly thereafter, followed by an 80-to-100-day pregnancy. Thus, the young, which usually number one per litter, are born in early summer. Although females have two teats, twins are uncommon. Births are synchronized, resulting in all of the young arriving within a short time. In the cave, the newborn are deposited together in clusters or crèches away from the adults. When nursery colonies are vast, it would seem virtually impossible for a mother to be able to recognize her young. Previously, it was believed that mothers simply nursed the first one or two young that they came into contact with. This assumption is troubling since such females would be devoting substantial energy to unrelated individuals, an investment which would not enhance a mother's fitness. Recent studies by Gary McCracken have demonstrated that mothers usually do find and nurse their own offspring out of over the 1,000 young in a crèche. Experimental evidence suggests that after the mother returns to the crèche, she recognizes her offspring through a combination of auditory and olfactory cues. Interestingly, mothers make no attempt to save baby bats which fall to the ground. Successful little free-tails develop rapidly and are capable of flight after about five weeks. Males reside apart from the nursery colonies in much smaller groups.

The Brazilian free-tailed bat bears the indignity of being called the "guano bat." This is because its fecal matter, or guano, is so rich in nitrogen that it has been harvested as a commercial fertilizer. Considering the tremendous numbers that roost in some areas, it is easy to see how this industry could be profitable.

My first encounter with these bats was in central North Carolina, where I asked to investigate the bat infestation of a local Masonic temple. It was fascinating to watch several dozen fly about in the attic and then collect a few to verify the species. One of the Masons told a bizarre story of how he had also become a bat collector. One evening, he was standing at guard in one of the temple's doorways with an erect sabre in his hand. When an unlucky free-tail flew by, he attempted to swat it with the sabre and ended up neatly dividing the poor bat in two.

## BIG FREE-TAILED BAT (*Tadarida macrotis*)

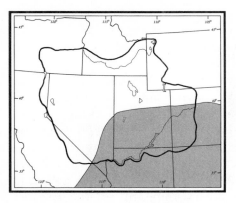

DISTRIBUTION OF BIG FREE-TAILED BAT.

Total length: 5 1/8 to 5 3/8 inches; forearm length: 2 1/4 to 2 3/8 inches.

From a distance, it would be difficult to distinguish the big free-tailed bat from the Brazilian free-tail. Of course, if one were close enough it would be useful to consider the size difference between the two. The largest Brazilian free-tails are about as large as the smallest big free-tails. Furthermore, the big free-tail has a much greater wing-span. Another telling feature is the length of the exposed tail. On big free-tails, the tail extends for at least an inch beyond the interfemoral membrane, about a quarter inch more than that of the Brazilian free-tail. Up close, some other differences are useful in telling the two mastiff bats apart. In the larger species, the ears are joined at the base, whereas they are separated in the Brazilian. In profile, the ears of the big free-tail are larger and possess more of the airfoil shape referred to in the previous account. Big free-tails vary from reddish brown to black, but many are dark brown. Thus, based upon color, it is hard to distinguish the two free-tails. The distribution of big free-tails is largely restricted to the southwestern United States and Mexico, although some have been discovered in the Midwest. In the Intermountain West, they occur along the southeastern edge of Nevada, throughout southern Utah and Colorado, and bordering areas.

However, they are very rare, and one should not expect to see them. Brazilian free-tails are much more common in the

Southwest and are more likely to be the free-tailed species sighted there.

Big free-tailed bats typically inhabit rugged, rocky environments with steep canyon walls. They also occupy arid sagebrush flats as well as riparian areas, those bordering rivers and streams. Roosting spots include caves, cliff crevices, and buildings. Although they may get into high altitude terrain, they are primarily a lowland species. Evidence suggests that they are not present in the northern areas of their distribution in the winter. Since the Intermountain region is within these northern boundaries, they probably emigrate from the area as the colder months approach. They begin to feed after dark, emitting a loud, piercing, chattering noise. Moths are taken most often, but ground insects, such as crickets and ants, are not overlooked.

A single young is born in June or July in nursery colonies that may include over 100 adult females. In Utah, the young emerge from these roosts in August. By then, they are close to full size. Big free-tailed bats remain a mystery in many respects. Despite their large size and unique appearance, they are too rare in this region for us to have learned much about their habits.

## REFERENCES

Anderson, S. 1969. *Macrotus waterhousii*. Mammalian Species no. 1. American Society of Mammalogists.

Czaplewski, N. J. 1983. *Idionycteris phyllotis*. Mammalian Species no. 208. American Society of Mammalogists.

Davis, R. B., C. F. Herreid, and H. L. Short. 1962. Mexican free-tailed bats in Texas. *Ecological Monographs* 32: 11–46.

Fenton, M. B., and R. M. R. Barclay. 1980. *Myotis lucifugus*. Mammalian Species no. 142. American Society of Mammalogists.

Finley, R. B., Jr., W. Caire, and D. E. Wilhelm. 1983. Bats of the Colorado oil shale region. *Great Basin Naturalist* 43: 554–560.

Haysenyager, R. N. 1980. *Bats of Utah*. Utah Division of Wildlife Resources, Publication no. 80–15. Salt Lake City.

Hermanson, J. W., and T. J. O'Shea. 1983. *Antrozous pallidus*. Mammalian Species no. 213. American Society of Mammalogists.

Kunz, T. H. 1982. *Lasionycteris noctivagans*. Mammalian Species no. 172. American Society of Mammalogists.

Kunz, T. H., and R. A. Martin. 1982. *Plecotus townsendii*. Mammalian Species no. 175. American Society of Mammalogists.

McCracken, G. F., and M. K. Gustin. 1987. Batmom's daily nightmare. *Natural History* 96(10): 66–73.

McMahon, E. E., C. C. Oakley, and S. P. Cross. 1981. First record of the spotted bat (*Euderma maculatum*) from Oregon. *Great Basin Naturalist* 41: 270.

O'Farrell, M. J., and E. H. Studier. 1980. *Myotis thysanodes*. Mammalian Species no. 137. American Society of Mammalogists.

Parsons, H. J., D. A. Smith, and R. F. Whittam. 1986. Maternity colonies of silver-haired bats, *Lasionycteris noctivagans*, in Ontario and Saskatchewan. *Journal of Mammalogy* 67: 598–600.

Warner, R. M., and N. J. Czaplewski. 1984. *Myotis volans*. Mammalian Species no. 224. American Society of Mammalogists.

Watkins, L. C. 1977. *Euderma maculatum*. Mammalian Species no. 77. American Society of Mammalogists.

# The Pikas, Rabbits, and Hares — Order Lagomorpha

The lagomorphs are a comparatively small order with only two families of some 63 species. One family, the Ochotonidae, consists of the pikas; the other, the Leporidae, includes the rabbits and hares. Lagomorphs occur on all continents except Antarctica, although they were absent from Australia before being introduced there by humans. Despite their low diversity, they are often important components of the environment. Many species, particularly among the rabbits and hares, exhibit dramatic population cycles which influence the status of the predators that depend on them. And when populations of leporids are high, they can have a great impact on the vegetation.

Like rodents, the lagomorphs have long, evergrowing incisors used to nip plant parts. A feature unique to the lagomorphs, though, is the presence of a tiny peglike incisor behind each of the upper two front ones. Differences such as this and those in the fossil record reveal that they are not closely related to the rodents, as was once assumed. Another interesting lagomorph feature is the presence of fenestrations, a latticework of openings on the sides of the skull. The term "fenestration" is from the Latin *fenestra* for window. During the stock-market crash of 1929, many brokers committed suicide by defenestration; they jumped out of the windows of their Wall Street offices.

## PIKAS—FAMILY OCHOTONIDAE

There are about 14 species of pikas worldwide. On this continent they occur only in the rocky areas of high mountains. But not all are restricted to alpine environments. In Europe and Asia, they are found in a diversity of habitats, including forests, open plains, and the desert-steppe. Pikas thrive on the high plains of China and Siberia. It was the Mongolians of northeastern Siberia that first gave this mammal its name, originally pronounced "peeka." Pikas are small, with adults usually weighing less than half a pound. Lacking the running ability of rabbits and hares, they ordinarily remain close to protective cover. Unlike those of leporids, the pika's ears are small and rounded, the opening of which is protected by a large skin flap.

### PIKA (*Ochotona princeps*)

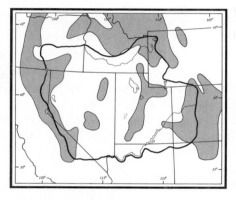

DISTRIBUTION OF PIKA.

Total length: 6 3/8 to 8 1/2 inches; no visible tail.

The curious little pika is a compelling creature. Perhaps our interest in it is first aroused when we learn that this animal, which resembles the guinea pig, a rodent, is actually a relative of the rabbit. Then there is its habit of storing hay for the winter, a behavior evocative of our own activities of farming and planning ahead for rough times. Whatever the reason, whoever has encountered this small mammal knows it as an intriguing representative of the high mountain country. Pikas are called "whistling hares" or "conies," although the latter name is more correct for the hyrax of the Middle East and Africa.

They have a dense grayish brown fur, small white-edged rounded ears, and virtually no tail. Other neighboring small mammals that they might be confused with, such as yellow-bellied marmots and golden-mantled ground squirrels, have bushy tails. A peculiar race of pikas has been found in Craters of the Moon National Monument in Idaho. Here, a melanistic or black race has evolved on the dark lava cinder cones. Unlike those of rabbits and hares, the hind limbs are not modified for jumping; the hind feet are only slightly larger than the forefeet. The soles of the feet are furred, which makes walking on snow easier. In the Intermountain West, as in much of western North America, pikas are found in mountainous areas. This includes the Wasatch and Uinta mountains of Utah, the Sierras of Nevada, and the San Juan range in southwestern Colorado.

In the mountains, pikas live in rocky areas, such as talus (rock debris) slides and boulder-strewn hillsides above timberline, typically at elevations of 8,000 to 13,000 feet. They have been found as low as 5,400 feet in southeastern Oregon. In this rarefied environment, they feed on a variety of green plants, mostly grasses and herbs. By late summer they begin to interrupt their meals with frequent bouts of clipping vegetation and hurriedly transporting it, in their mouths, to the rocks near their homes. The clippings are then spread out to dry before being piled into haystacks. These stacks are usually small, but some may weigh over 50 pounds. Farmers of our own species cure their hay in a similar manner. The pikas often move their piles of hay about to protect them from storms and to expose them to better drying sites before finally moving them to their homes in between the rocks. In this extreme environment, which so few other animals can tolerate, pikas stay active throughout the winter by eating this fastidiously prepared and maintained cache of food. A bit of lichen may spice up their winter diet. Predators include long-tailed weasels, pine martens, and various hawks.

Pikas are highly social and live in large colonies. Their sociality is revealed by a high level of chatter and other types of continuous vocal communication. In the fall, at least, they are territorial. Between two to six altricial young are born in May or June; the average litter size is about three. Occasionally, a second litter arrives by summer's end.

One sign of this animal is its black and sticky scat, which has been likened to pellets of tapioca. Its call is another feature by which it may be recognized. Seeming to come from afar, it resembles the bleating of a young goat. It is unmistakable, even to one who has never heard it before. One August day, I was hiking in the Snowy Range near Laramie, Wyoming, with a friend, John Connors, who was visiting from North Carolina.

As soon as he heard the cry, he turned to me and assuredly stated, "That's a pika!"

## RABBITS AND HARES — FAMILY LEPORIDAE

Leporids, the rabbits and hares, are a conspicuous group of animals. They are easily recognized by two features that permit them to detect predators: long ears and bulging eyes. Although both types of leporids have long hind limbs, those of the hares or jackrabbits are considerably longer, enabling them to make fantastic leaps. Of the 43 leporids in the world, six species are found in this region.

The members of this family provide the textbook example of the terms "altricial" and "precocial." Rabbits or cottontails produce altricial or immature young, ones that are naked with eyes closed at birth. Hares or jackrabbits give birth to more independent, precocial young which are able to move about within a few hours. I suspect that the explanation for this striking dichotomy lies both in the different habitats they generally occupy and in their burrowing tendencies. Hares, which do not construct burrows, are usually found in more open, exposed areas. There, the production of relatively mature, mobile young would be favored because they should be less susceptible to predation. Alternately, cottontails are typically found in brushy areas that provide concealment from predators, and may construct burrows. Given these conditions, the young should have a comparatively high survival, even in an immature state.

## PYGMY RABBIT (Sylvilagus (Brachylagus) idahoensis)

Total length: 9 3/4 to 11 3/8 inches; tail length: 3/4 to 1 1/4 inches.

Of all the North American leporids, the pygmy rabbit is the smallest. At its largest, this miniature rabbit is barely a foot long. It varies in weight from eight and a half ounces to a pound. Its upper body is buffy gray to blackish tinged with pink. The nape of the neck and front of the legs are an attractive cinnamon color. Both the upper and lower parts of its small

tail are buffy or gray; all
of the other rabbits in
the region have white
tail undersurfaces. This
is why they are called
cottontails and the
pygmy rabbit is not.
Another of its distin-
guishing features is the
whitish spots at the sides
of the nostrils. When the
new coat of hair arrives
in the fall, it is long and
silky. But by midwinter,

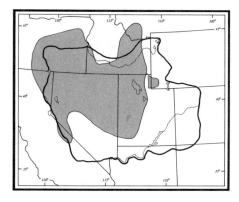

DISTRIBUTION OF PYGMY RABBIT.

it looks worn and silvery. The ears are not especially long, varying from one and three-eighths to one and seven-eighths inches.
Compared to other rabbits, its hind legs are also short and have
broad, heavily furred feet. Almost the entire distribution of
pygmy rabbits falls within the Intermountain West, primarily
the Great Basin and surounding areas. In the following discussion of their ecology we shall see why.

Pygmy rabbits most frequently occur in an environment
highly typical of this region: plains ranging from 4,500 to 7,000
feet dominated by sagebrush. They also are common where
dense stands of this and other brushy plants grow on alluvial
soils, those formed by deposition from streams and rivers.
Where they live, one typically finds a network of runways created by their movements within the brush. The pygmy rabbit
apparently is the only North American leporid which regularly
digs and uses an extensive burrow system. Tunnels often have
many entrances, from about three to five inches in diameter,
each located at the base of a sage plant. When frightened, the
rabbits retreat into shallow trenches that extend out from these
openings. There, only their ears and eyes stick out above the
ground. Below the surface, the tunnels widen to form chambers
where the rabbits rest during the day. They also "homestead" by
moving into burrows excavated by yellow-bellied marmots and
badgers. After all the energy that adults use to excavate and
maintain the burrows, juveniles may use them more. This is not

odd, considering the high rates of predation that the juveniles undoubtedly face. It should increase an adult's fitness to provide a haven which is safe not just for itself, but especially for its young. Nevertheless, rabbit populations are susceptible to decreases and even local extirpations, although the cause of this is not understood.

Based on the significance of big sagebrush as a haven for pygmy rabbits, it is not surprising that it is one of their most important foods. In fact, in the winter they rarely eat anything else. Fortunately for them, their strong sage flavor makes them less than desirable as a game species for many hunters. When summer rolls around, grasses may constitute about a third of their diet. Feeding usually occurs at dawn and dusk; that is, they are crepuscular. They also feed at midday and have been observed doing so right on top of the sagebrush. Mostly though, they rest in their burrows during the day and do not travel far from them when feeding. Principal predators of this bunny among rabbits are various weasel species; those occurring within their range include ermine and long-tailed weasels. These are natural predators on pygmy rabbits due to their great hunting efficiency in tunnels. Several other predators attack them on the ground, including coyotes, red foxes, owls, and marsh hawks. Fleas are yet another problem and can occur in such abundance that they create a waving motion in the rabbit's fur. Pygmy rabbits also have some nonthreatening companions in their relatives: black-tailed and white-tailed jackrabbits and mountain cottontails. The latter species has even been found to share a pygmy's burrow, though this might have been a chance occurrence.

At breeding time in the early spring, males and females may be found together in a burrow. Both are usually ready to mate by March although pregnancies occur from late February to late May. Females give birth to as many as three litters per year with an average of six young per litter. The newborn are highly altricial, as is typical of cottontails. The gestation period is probably similar to that of cottontails, ranging from 27 to 30 days. Much to the chagrin of those who have excavated the burrows of nursing females, neither nests nor nesting materials have been found. It is unknown where the nests of this little rabbit are sequestered.

NUTTALL'S or
MOUNTAIN
COTTONTAIL
(*Sylvilagus nuttallii*)

Total length: 13 3/4 to
15 3/8 inches; tail
length: 1 3/4 to 2
inches.

Nuttall's cottontail is
a medium-sized rabbit
named after the great
American naturalist
Thomas Nuttall

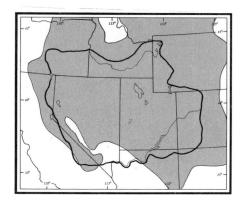

DISTRIBUTION OF NUTTALL'S OR
MOUNTAIN COTTONTAIL.

(1768–1859). Although similar in appearance to both the familiar eastern cottontail and the desert cottontail, it is paler than
the former and darker than the latter on its upper surface. It is
grayish brown with a yellowish cast above and is whitish below.
One distinguishing mark is the thin black line along the ear's
margins. The ears are relatively short, measuring two and one-
eighth to two and five-eighths inches, and are densely furred
inside. In contrast, the desert cottontail's ears are usually longer
and but slightly furred inside. The hind legs of Nuttall's cottontail are long and densely haired; again, those of the desert cottontail are not as hairy. Its large tail is dark and grizzled above
and white underneath, hence the name cottontail. For a rabbit,
the rostrum or nose area is long. As with the pygmy rabbit,
Nuttall's cottontail is truly a mammal of the Intermountain
West; it is found almost everywhere in the region. Its distribution extends south into Arizona and New Mexico and northward
into the southern portions of some Canadian provinces.

In most of their range, Nuttall's cottontails occur in thick
sagebrush stands, but in southern areas they also frequent conifer forests. Within the sage, they are prevalent in rocky hill and
canyon country and may be found in dry washes below the sage-
covered slopes. Narrow trails, barely penetrable by humans, are
made through the dense sage stands. They also inhabit cultivated fields. Much of the day is spent in rocky crevices or
"forms," resting places they create by depressing the vegetation
or soil. Burrows may be used more for concealment from preda-

NUTTALL'S or MOUNTAIN COTTONTAIL

tors where vegetation is sparse. At any rate, burrow occupation
is probably uncommon, and it is doubtful that they do their
own excavating. The most important food in all seasons is
sagebrush. Other items such as juniper berries are eaten, and
they prefer grasses in the spring and summer. Most feeding
takes place at either dawn or dusk in the shelter of brush or
close to it. They may wind up on the dinner plates of several
predators, including bobcats, coyotes, great horned owls, various
hawks, rattlesnakes, and humans, for whom they are quite palatable.

Compared to most other rabbits on the continent, a
Nuttall's has a solitary life-style. Yet, if the habitat will support
several individuals, as in grassy areas, feeding groups may
occur. This cottontail has an interesting behavior when
disturbed. When first aware of danger, it runs off for about 15
to 20 feet and then freezes, facing away from the intrusion. At
this point, it is keenly aware of the problem; and should it per-
sist, the rabbit hops off again in a semicircular path, presumably
to fool the intruder. Recently, another unusual behavior has
been documented: tree-climbing. During the summer in central
Oregon, Nuttall's cottontails have been observed in junipers up

to nine feet off the ground. They may be either licking water off of leaves or eating waterlogged leaves during what is an exceptionally dry time there.

The breeding season may begin as early as February but usually lasts from midspring until June. During this time, a female can exhibit a terrific fecundity, producing up to five litters, with about five young per litter. Litter sizes range from one to eight. The cuplike nest, lined with grass and fur is under a brush pile or rocks or in a burrow. Nuttall's bunnies are altricial at birth, weaned after about a month, and reach maturity in their first year. Breeding by juveniles is presumed to be rare.

## DESERT or AUDUBON'S COTTONTAIL
(*Sylvilagus audubonii*)

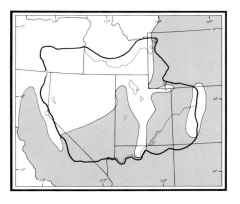

DISTRIBUTION OF DESERT OR AUDUBON'S COTTONTAIL.

Total length: 13 3/4 to 16 1/2 inches; tail length: 1 3/4 to 2 7/8 inches.

The "other" cottontail in the Intermountain West is the desert cottontail. In size, it is similar to Nuttall's cottontail. They are readily distinguished from each other in several ways, some of which are mentioned in the description of Nuttall's cottontail. Desert cottontails are colored the lightest of the rabbits in this region, nicely blending in with their arid habitats. Their upper body is pale gray with a yellowish tinge and a scattering of black hairs, the sides are paler yet, the lower body is whitish, and they have an orange-brown throat patch. They have the "required" cottontail: it is dark above and white below. Their ears, measuring two and one-quarter to two and three-quarter inches, are slightly longer than those of Nuttall's cottontail and lack the thick black tips and densely haired insides. As discussed, the hind feet are not heavily furred. The hind limbs are rather long. These rabbits are not as restricted to our region

PIKA

WHITE-TAILED JACKRABBIT

as the others found here; they also range throughout central Mexico and into a considerable portion of the Plains states. In the Intermountain West, they occur in southern Nevada, through western and eastern Utah (but not in the state's central section), across western Colorado and Wyoming, and adjacent areas.

It is difficult to pick out a characteristic habitat of this mammal because it occurs in so many different ones. These include dry desertlike areas, grasslands, shrublands, and riparian zones, those around watercourses. In the Southwest and Intermountain regions, these cottontails mainly inhabit deserts and lower elevations. Pinyon-juniper forests are also an important habitat. In California, they have been observed in the heavy brush and willows surrounding rivers, around brush piles, and in weed thickets. They are associated with such plants as arrowweed and screwbean mesquite in southern Nevada. In the canyons, valleys, and mesas of western Colorado, they prefer brushlands and woodland-edge habitats. Large differences can exist in the size of male and female home ranges. Whereas a male's may be as much as 15 acres, a female's in the same area can be less than 1 acre. Desert cottontails eat a wide variety of foods, concentrating on grasses in the open country. In colder months, they supplement their diet with sagebrush. They are not dependent on open water and can get most, if not all, of what they need from succulent vegetation and dew. Their predators are varied as well and include coyotes, gray foxes, badgers, red-tailed hawks and other raptors, and rattlesnakes. They are a common game species.

Desert cottontails are most active at dawn and dusk; during most of the day they remain inactive in burrows or forms. Although they may construct their own burrows, those abandoned by badgers, prairie dogs, and other mammals are also used. Activity periods may proceed longer into the day in areas with good cover. But when temperatures rise above 80° F, the rabbits are largely inactive. They can swim and climb trees and brush piles. It is clear that they use their tails as alarm signals. When one raises its tail exposing a large patch of white, the surrounding animals run for cover. Undoubtedly, this is also the function of such a tail in the other species. In the evenings, logs and tree stumps are used as lookout posts.

The breeding period for this species is relatively long. In Arizona, desert cottontails breed for eight to nine months, and in California, they may do so year-round. The young are born in ground cavities lined with grass and layered on the inside with rabbit fur. The typical litter size is small, varying from 2.5 to 3.6 young. But this is compensated for by the large number of litters; an average of five per year has been reported in Arizona. The young are highly immature at birth, finally opening their eyes at about 10 days. They remain near the nest for approximately three weeks after birth. Sexual maturity is reached after just over three months.

## SNOWSHOE HARE
(*Lepus americanus*)

Total length: 15 to 20 1/2 inches; tail length: 1 to 2 1/4 inches.

Snowshoe hares are midway in size between cottontails and jackrabbits. Yet they are more closely related to jackrabbits and are in the same genus, *Lepus*. In summer, they are dark

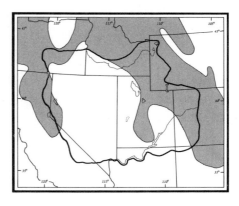

DISTRIBUTION OF SNOWSHOE HARE.

rusty brown above and grayish white below. Similarly colored, the tail can be even darker above. They have a white chin. In winter, they go through a molt which produces a white coat. This change is regulated by photoperiod or day-length, as is the case in other mammals which have a winter coloration. Clearly, it is a means by which they are camouflaged against the snow. Their summer coloration provides concealment among shrubs. In the late fall, the hair's patchy appearance also makes them difficult to see against a background of spotty snow. When both are in their winter coats, a snowshoe is easily distinguished from the white-tailed jackrabbit by its smaller size and shorter tail and ears. The soles of its feet are well furred, especially in winter. Many assume this to be the reason for its name. A likelier explanation is that the widely spread toes of its hind feet leave a

SNOWSHOE HARE

snowshoelike print in the snow. In the Intermountain West, snowshoe hares are most abundant in the northeastern part of the region: through southeastern Idaho, the mountains of Utah and Wyoming, and parts of Colorado.

These hares inhabit conifer and hardwood forests, especially in mountain country, and rarely venture from them. Here, they depend on the shrub understory. Burned areas with new woody growth are especially attractive. They also occur along water-courses in thick stands of alder and willow. Like other leporids, they spend their days resting in forms under shrubbery or in hollow logs and the burrows of other animals. They feed in the late evening. In the summer, food items include herbaceous vegetation, grasses, willows, and berries. In the winter, they browse on the buds, twigs, and bark of aspen, alder, and willow as well as conifer tree shoots. They frequently kill saplings by eating the bark in a circular fashion, a process known as "girdling." Although they rarely kill many trees in a concentrated area, they are still a source of concern for foresters. Compared with other hares, they have little impact on crops because they prefer woodlands. Unusual for their group, they eat carrion or animal remains.

The snowshoe hare is an important prey species for many northern forest animals. These include red foxes, coyotes, bobcats, lynx, various hawks, eagles, and owls. This dependency is evidenced by the fact that several of the predators, particularly the lynx, exhibit population cycles that follow those of the hare. Fluctuations are pronounced, with the length of a complete cycle being about 9 to 10 years. At their highest level, populations have 100 times the number of individuals that they have during their low point. Changes of ten- to thirtyfold are common. When snowshoes are extremely numerous, it is believed that a low availability of winter food precipitates a population decline. Another explanation is that at high densities, individuals suffer from a crowding-related stress which inhibits reproduction.

The breeding period lasts from early March through late August. After a pregnancy of some 36 days, about three young are born. Nests are not constructed; instead, the young are simply placed in a concealed depression. Litter sizes of up to seven have been reported, and there are usually two to four litters per year. That newborn hares are precocial or mature is curious. In the introduction to the Leporidae, it was suggested that hares and jackrabbits bear precocial young because this could increase their survival in exposed, open habitats. Yet, the snowshow hare is essentially a woodland creature. Its production of precocial young could be an "evolutionary holdover" from its shared ancestry with jackrabbits, one which has not been under pressure to change. Conceivably, the production of mature young might be related to the aforementioned high levels of predation. The young grow rapidly and are weaned in about one month, at which time they are about nine times their birth weight. Although adult size in about five months, they rarely breed in their first year. However, a small percentage of juveniles may breed during the initial stages of a population increase. During the breeding season, males may fight so viciously that they bite each other's fur off. Pregnant females are hostile toward the males. Typically, one male's home range encompasses that of the several females he hopes to breed with.

## WHITE-TAILED JACKRABBIT (*Lepus townsendii*)

Total length: 22 1/4 to 25 3/4 inches; tail length: 2 5/8 to 4 3/8 inches.

Not only is the white-tailed jackrabbit the largest rabbit in the region, it is capable of spectacular leaps and it runs with great speed. It

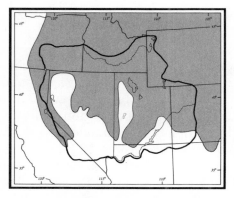

DISTRIBUTION OF WHITE-TAILED JACKRABBIT.

can jump from 12 to 20 feet high, maintaining a stride of 36 miles per hour with spurts of up to 45 miles per hour. During the summer, its fur is pale buffy gray above with a lighter undersurface. Overall, the tail is white but may have a midline of gray or black above. The black on a black-tailed jackrabbit's tail differs by continuing up the rump. In winter, white-tailed jacks molt to a pure white or pale gray except for their black ear tips. Individuals in the far southern portions of the range, including areas in this region, may not molt. Their long ears, from three and three-fourths to four and three-eighths inches, are grayish in front and whitish with a black stripe on the back and, again, have black tips. Proportionate to their body sizes, both the ears and hind limbs are smaller than those of the black-tailed jackrabbit. White-tailed jackrabbits occur through-out the north-central United States, including most of the Intermountain West, with the exception of central and southern Nevada.

Their characteristic habitat is the open plains. They may occur above the timberline on mountains, where they are also found in the open. As with other rabbits, they conceal themselves in forms dug near plants or rocks during the day. They come out to feed in the early morning and throughout the night. They are primarily nocturnal, whereas black-tailed jackrabbits are crepuscular. In summer, the diet consists of grasses and herbs; individuals near farms supplement their intake with clover and alfalfa. Winter is the time for a meager menu featuring dried shrubs and other plants, bark, and some buds and shoots. Haystacks are often utilized where native foods are in short supply. Preyed upon by many of the same animals as other leporids, these jackrabbits also suffer greatly from parasitism and disease. Humans heavily impact their populations through hunting and land clearance for agriculture. Suitable habitat for them has greatly diminished in recent years due to these incursions and their inability to adjust to them. Many hunters consider their meat to be tastier than that of their black-tailed cousin. Their fur is used to make hatter's felt and other goods but is considered too fragile for clothing. One escape that they have from many of these nuisances is an ability to swim; they do a "rabbit-paddle" with all four feet.

White-tailed jackrabbits breed from late February through mid-July, producing two to four litters with an average of three to five young. Early litters appear to contain the most bunnies. Estimates of gestation length range from 30 to 43 days. The precocial young are concealed in forms or burrows rather than nests. Within a month, they are independent, attaining adult weight at four months. They normally breed in the spring following their birth. Adult males, or bucks, fight fiercely during the breeding season, kicking violently with their hind feet and biting one another. Although this jackrabbit is considered to be one of the least social, large winter aggregations have been observed in places with abundant food. It is reported to have a polygynous mating system.

## BLACK-TAILED JACKRABBIT (*Lepus californicus*)

Total length: 18 1/4 to 24 3/4 inches; tail length: 2 to 4 3/8 inches.

The black-tailed jackrabbit is the most abundant and widely distributed North American jackrabbit. Densities of 260 per square mile have been recorded. Visitors to this region are more likely to encounter it than any of the other leporids, especially at dusk. Moreover, it is increasing both in its numbers and range, a shift in fortunes that is related to several factors. As the plains continue to undergo cultivation, black-tailed jackrabbits invade and

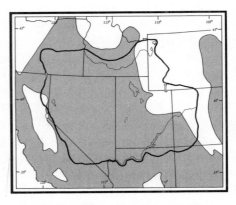

DISTRIBUTION OF BLACK-TAILED JACKRABBIT.

take over what once was white-tailed jackrabbit habitat because of their greater adaptability to agricultural conditions. Another possible reason is that although the black-tailed jackrabbit is primarily a Southwestern species, it has expanded its range northward due to an apparent warming trend in this century. Yet another element in its success may be the effectiveness of anti-predator programs. These have reduced the number of coyotes and other animals which formerly could have checked jackrabbit population growth. This hare is typically smaller than the white-tailed jackrabbit. Its black-tipped ears are very long, measuring from three and seven-eighths to a whopping seven inches. Originally, it was called the jackass rabbit due to these long structures. It is buffy gray to blackish and speckled with black above. The sides are gray and its undersurface is white. The upper part of the tail has a black line along its middle extending up onto the rump. Unlike the other hares in the region, black-tailed jacks molt but once a year and do not undergo a striking winter color change. They occur throughout much of the Intermountain West except where northeastern Utah meets Colorado and Wyoming.

Like the white-tailed jackrabbit, they are a species of the open plains. Here, their preferred habitat has short grasses and herbs to eat and scattered brush for cover. Because overgrazing produces this type of environment, they thrive where it has occurred and may further deteriorate the range condition. Unfortunately, overgrazing is but another aspect of their recent success since many western lands suffer from it. They rest in forms during the day, feeding in the early morning or late afternoon in loosely arranged groups. Summer diets consist of grasses, herbs, and crops, such as alfalfa. In winter, their diet seems more varied than the white-tailed jackrabbit's, consisting of dried grasses, buds and bark of woody plants, small fruits, roots, winter wheat in cultivated areas, and prickly pear cactus. When one spies a freshly eaten prickly pear or tufts of hair on its thorns, it is a likely sign of this mammal. Clustering at haystacks occurs when other food is unavailable.

As is true for many of their relatives, these jackrabbits produce two kinds of feces: hard and soft pellets. The soft ones are reingested, a process called "coprophagy." This probably occurs to enhance digestibility of the nutrients in their largely cellulose diet. In addition, it may save vitamins produced in the intestines. They rarely drink water, obtaining most of what they need from plants; this is also true of most other jackrabbits. Predators, such as coyotes, foxes, various snakes, and birds of prey, attempt to catch these fast-moving mammals. However, it is not all that simple since they move at speeds of 35 to 40 miles per hour, occasionally interspersing their stride with hops of up to 20 feet. Like a cottontail, they flash the white side of their tails when pursued, probably to confuse their chaser or alert other individuals to the danger. They can also swim. They are susceptible to various diseases, such as tick fever and tularemia, the latter of which can wipe out virtually an entire population. This disease can infect humans, and oddly behaving jackrabbits, such as those which do not readily flee, should be given a wide berth.

Their reproductive biology is similar to the white-tailed jackrabbit's, with the possible difference of their breeding season being longer. In Kansas, for example, pregnant females have been found as early as January and as late as the end of August. In Utah, they breed from January through July. The gestation period ranges from 41 to 47 days. Up to four litters of from one to eight young are produced each year; the average litter size is two to four. The young are raised in an open fur-lined ground hollow, not a nest. Interestingly, the mother may place littermates in several such forms, possibly to prevent losing all of them to a predator. Newborn are precocial and hop about after several days. Growth is rapid, and they are almost as large, though not quite as heavy, as their parents in about ten weeks. Breeding generally does not occur during the first year of life. Mortality can be extremely high, even over 90 percent, during this time, so only a small percentage of the new jackrabbits ever reproduce. In Utah, near the northern limits of their distribution, they exhibit a 7-to-10-year population cycle. Several investigators have attributed the existence of this cycle to ongoing changes in the level of coyote predation, which is in turn generated by jackrabbit numbers.

In addition to the problems that humans encounter with diseased animals, these jackrabbits have become pests on farms, in orchards, and in plant nurseries. When this occurs, preventative measures, such as fencing, should be undertaken. Shooting the culprits is also a measure that, unfortunately, needs to be taken at times. Other common names for the black-tailed jackrabbit are the Great Plains jackrabbit and the gray-sided jackrabbit.

## REFERENCES

Campbell, T. M., III, T. W. Clark, and C. R. Groves. 1982. First record of pygmy rabbits (*Brachylagus idahoensis*) in Wyoming. *Great Basin Naturalist* 42: 100.

Chapman, J. A. 1975. *Sylvilagus nuttallii*. Mammalian Species no. 56. American Society of Mammalogists.

Chapman, J. A., and G. R. Willner. 1978. *Sylvilagus audubonii*. Mammalian Species no. 106. American Society of Mammalogists.

Feldhammer, G. A. 1979. Age, sex ratios and reproductive potential in black-tailed jackrabbits. *Mammalia* 43: 473–478.

Green, J. S., and J. T. Flinders. 1980. *Brachylagus idahoensis*. Mammalian Species no. 125. American Society of Mammalogists.

Keith, L. B. 1983. Role of food in hare population cycles. *Oikos* 40: 385–395.

Keith, L. B., and L. A. Windberg. 1978. A demographic analysis of the snowshoe hare cycle. *Wildlife Monographs* 58.

Kuvlesky, W. P., Jr., and L. B. Keith. 1983. Demography of snowshoe hare populations in Wisconsin. *Journal of Mammalogy* 64: 233–244.

Lim, B. K. 1987. *Lepus townsendii*. Mammalian Species no. 288. American Society of Mammalogists.

Pritchett, C. L., J. A. Nilsen, M. P. Coffeen, and H. D. Smith. 1987. Pygmy rabbits in the Colorado River drainage. *Great Basin Naturalist* 47: 231–233.

Vaughan, M. R., and L. B. Keith. 1980. Breeding by juvenile showshoe hares. *Journal of Wildlife Management* 44: 949–951.

Verts, B. J., S. D. Gehman, and K. J. Hundertmark. 1984. *Sylvilagus nuttallii*: A semiarboreal lagomorph. *Journal of Mammalogy* 65: 131–135.

Weiss, N. T., and B. J. Verts. 1984. Habitat and distribution of pygmy rabbits (*Sylvilagus idahoensis*) in Oregon. *Great Basin Naturalist* 44: 563–571.

# The Rodents—Order Rodentia

Rodents are the largest and most diverse group of mammals. The approximately 1,700 species in this order account for close to 40 percent of the world's mammals. Thriving in most reaches of the globe, they are a strong influence in many environments. In this region, there are 77 different rodents, accounting for more than half of the mammal species. They are typically divided into three categories based on jaw musculature: sciuromorphs, the squirrel-like rodents; myomorphs, the mouselike rodents; and hystricomorphs, which includes porcupines and many large South American rodents. Most rodents are terrestrial, but they exhibit a great diversity of life-styles. They occur over a wide range of sizes, from tiny mice to the South American capybara (*Hydrochoerus* spp.), which can weigh over 100 pounds.

Perhaps their most characteristic feature is the presence of upper and lower pairs of persistently growing incisors. Tips of the upper pair wear away those of the lower one, and vice versa, keeping all incisors well honed. These teeth are thus excellent clippers, providing their bearers with access to a wide variety of foods. Together with their powerful jaws and grinding teeth, the rodents are highly efficient herbivores. Even so, many are not solely dependent on plants.

Most rodents have high reproductive rates; they bear large litters and reproduce several times a year. Much of our current understanding of mammalian population ecology is derived from members of this group since they are often accessible as well as numerous. Unfortunately, their high populations commonly create problems by destroying grains, other crops, and ornamental plants.

# CHIPMUNKS, MARMOTS, SQUIRRELS, AND PRAIRIE DOGS—FAMILY SCIURIDAE

The Sciuridae is a diverse family with an almost global distribution. It consists of three types of squirrels: tree squirrels, ground squirrels, and flying squirrels, which actually glide rather than fly. Most tree and ground species are diurnal, but flying squirrels are largely nocturnal. Another way of grouping them is by their food habits. Here, the breakdown differs: whereas most tree and flying species feed on nuts, seeds, and fruits, many of the ground-dwelling forms are grazers. Of the approximately 260 sciurid species, 27 occur in the Intermountain West, with representatives of each type.

## LEAST CHIPMUNK
(*Tamias minimus*)

Total length: 6 5/8 to 8 7/8 inches; tail length: 2 3/4 to 4 1/2 inches.

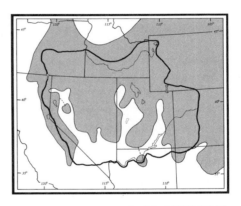

DISTRIBUTION OF LEAST CHIPMUNK.

Least chipmunks, of course, go by that name for a reason: they are the smallest chipmunks of all. Their long tail is light brown above, olive yellow below, and has black-tipped hairs. Somehow this chipmunk seems justified in carrying this colorful structure straight up as it runs about. It is also the lightest colored of the western chipmunks, typically a mixed tawny and ash gray above grading to pure tawny on the sides. It has a blackish midstripe and four additional dark brown to black side stripes which are mixed with a rufous or reddish hue. These stripes are separated by grizzled gray ones. The belly is grayish white. To further complicate matters, the fur color varies with the climate. In dry regions, it is a soft yellow gray with dark tan stripes. In moist environs, it is brownish gray with black side stripes. Some of the distinguishing characteristics are stripes continuing to the base of the tail and the orange-brown sides. As is true for the other chipmunks here, least chipmunks have both a summer and a winter pelage. Sometimes, these are so different that it is difficult to recognize the same species from one season to the next.

The species with which least chipmunks are likeliest to be confused is the yellow-pine chipmunk. In Nevada and California, least chipmunks are smaller, paler, and the underside of the tail is olive yellow rather than red. In other regions, skeletal features are necessary to tell the two apart. Here, however, they coexist only along the southern Idaho border and around northeastern California. Least chipmunks differ from other similar chipmunks in the region, including the yellow-pine, as follows: The ears of the Uinta, yellow-pine, and Colorado chipmunks are dark in front, whereas those of the least chipmunk are tawny. Side stripes in the cliff chipmunk are either indistinct or absent, but are obvious in the least chipmunk. Least chipmunks have both the widest geographic and ecological distribution of any chipmunk, occurring across Canada and throughout the western United States. They have an irregular distribution in the Intermountain West, occupying most of its northern parts and mountains, but are absent in its southern locales.

These little chipmunks often live in sagebrush habitat, regardless of whether conifer trees are present. Alternately, yellow-pine chipmunks are usually only in areas with conifers. Sagebrush deserts, pastures, rocky ravines, alpine tundra, and both conifer and broad-leafed forests are their other homes. They dig burrows either in the ground or in old logs consisting of a tunnel two to three feet long which ends in a chamber a foot underground. Within this chamber are a nest and a winter cache of seeds. They are fine climbers and will nest in trees. They have a cosmopolitan diet of acorns, nuts, seeds, grains, fruits, berries, grasses, flower tops, and vegetables. Such a smorgasbord may be supplemented by fungi, insects, and, rarely, small vertebrates. Pinyon nuts and conifer seeds are among their preferred foods. Often, they carry food in their large internal cheek pouches to a feeding station at a stump or log. They are preyed upon by marsh hawks, red-tailed hawks, weasels, minks, marten, red foxes, and snakes. Perhaps because they are so exposed to predators in their open habitats, they appear more cautious than most other chipmunks.

In areas where snow remains on the ground all winter, least chipmunks hibernate the entire season. They are tough little creatures, though, and may not enter dormancy until well after the first snow. Activity is renewed by March, even if snow is still on the ground, when their attention turns to breeding. In the warmer areas of their range, they are active throughout the winter. They are diurnal, or active during the day.

Only one litter of from three to nine young is born, ordinarily in April or May, after a 28-to-30-day pregnancy. The average litter size is from four to six. The tiny chipmunks are very altricial, with eyes and ears not fully opened for about four weeks. Growth is slow, with nursing lasting for up to 50 days. Independence from the mother is not attained until about two months of age. Although least chipmunks are considered to be rather social as chipmunks go, little has been learned about this aspect of their lives. It is known only that they feed together in small groups.

## YELLOW-PINE CHIPMUNK (*Tamias amoenus*)

Total length: 7 1/8 to 9 5/8 inches; tail length: 2 7/8 to 4 1/4 inches.

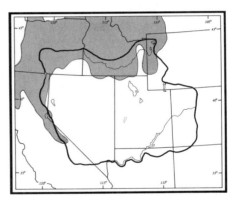

DISTRIBUTION OF YELLOW-PINE CHIPMUNK.

The relatively small yellow-pine chipmunk is one of the most brightly colored chipmunks, varying from tawny to a pretty pink cinnamon. Its stripes contrast sharply and consist of light white or gray lines alternating with dark, usually black, stripes. The inner light stripes are normally broader and more conspicuous than the outer ones. The brownish yellow sides and underside of the tail are among its most distinguishing features. Ears are blackish in front, whitish behind, and possess noticeable white patches behind them. Its facial stripes are dark. Several other chipmunks share its distribution in our region. Of these, Uinta chipmunks are larger with a more grayish head and shoulders and darker brown side stripes. The Panamint chipmunk has tawny ears; its range barely overlaps that of the yellow-pine chipmunk. The edging around the tail in yellow-pine chipmunks is distinctly buffy, but in the cliff chipmunk it is white or only faintly buffy; in our region, the ranges of these two species meet only in far southern Idaho. Differences between the yellow-pine and similar least chipmunks are reviewed in the previous account. Yellow-pine chipmunks occur throughout the northwestern United States into southwestern Canada. In the Intermountain West, they have a limited distribution, chiefly occurring through southern Idaho and adjacent areas.

These appealing creatures are active during the day. Not surprisingly, conifer forests with yellow-pine trees most often are their homes. They prefer the relatively open shrub-seedling-sapling stage of the forest. Shrubs, slash piles, and stumps seem to be required for populations to be successful. Their most important foods are seeds, but they also nibble on berries, insects, fungi, and even thorny thistles. Occasionally, they climb trees for food, but most foraging is done on the ground. In the fall, they become obsessed with storing food for the coming cold months; one cache alone consisted of over 67,000 items, including 15 kinds of seeds. All of this hoarding is likely related to the fact that they probably hibernate for but a small fraction of the winter, if at all. They only put on a little fat prior to the coming of the cold months, which, again, is unusual for a chipmunk that occurs in areas with severe winters. As is the case for other chipmunks, they live in underground burrows. Theirs are in open areas within the forest and are from one and a half to three feet long and up to two feet beneath the surface. Although one opening is most common, several entrances may exist.

Mating begins in April, but they become most active in May and June. The young arrive approximately one month after conception. From four to eight highly altricial young are born in a nest constructed of leaves, grass, lichen, and feathers, including those of the blue grouse. One litter a year is produced. Weaning is accomplished at about six weeks of age.

TOWNSEND'S
CHIPMUNK (*Tamias
townsendii*)

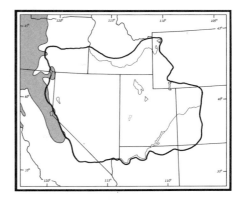

DISTRIBUTION OF TOWNSEND'S
CHIPMUNK.

Total length: 9 to 10 1/8 inches; tail length: 3 3/4 to 4 3/8 inches.

Townsend's chipmunk is a fairly large chipmunk. The species includes several subspecies which until recently were each regarded as distinct species. In fact, research on their alarm calls indicates that it may still be more appropriate to consider them separate species. One of these, commonly called Allen's chipmunk (*T. townsendii senex*), is found in our region. This account is based on it. The top of its head is a mixed pinkish cinnamon and brownish gray sprinkled with grayish white. On each side, the head is bordered with a brownish gray stripe. The characteristic dark stripes on its back are blackish brown with the median one being the darkest. Lighter back stripes are grayish white; the middle pair are occasionally a faint cinnamon. Its underparts are creamy white. In summer, the upper body is typically a reddish yellow. Barely entering the Intermountain West, it occurs here only near the far northeastern corner of California, possibly along the Nevada-California border by Lake Tahoe, and in central Oregon. Most of its distribution is in the mountainous areas of northern California and west-central Oregon.

This chipmunk is widespread in all of the coniferous forests in its range. Its preferred habitat is dense chapparal, an environment characterized by shrub thickets and small trees, as well as forested areas with a thick shrub understory. In a Sierra Nevada study, it was the predominant chipmunk in the closed canopy forest, that in which a dense upper foliage permits little light to reach the forest floor. Its habitat requirements include brush, logs, stumps, snags, and rocks. It does not appear to be an avid climber. Although its food habits are not known, it is probably a seed and berry eater like its relatives. This subspecies of Townsend's chipmunk is diurnal and suspected to hibernate from November through March. Its breeding biology is unknown.

## CLIFF CHIPMUNK
(*Tamias dorsalis*)

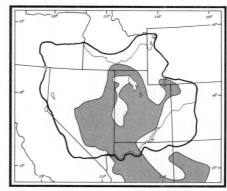

DISTRIBUTION OF CLIFF CHIPMUNK.

Total length: 7 3/4 to 10 7/8 inches; tail length: 3 1/4 to 5 1/2 inches.

The cliff chipmunk is an interesting species because of the lesson it teaches us about stripe patterns in chipmunks. Its stripes, except for the dark center one, are either indistinct or absent; they are only slightly more noticeable on the sides of the head. In winter, even the normally distinct center stripe is not easily seen. In the brushy areas it inhabits, small twigs cast indistinct shadows. Here, the stripe pattern is assumed to have protective value by camouflaging it more than if it had highly visible stripes. Alternately, the yellow-pine chipmunk's rather sharp striping pattern offers concealment in its open forest home where sharp shadows are cast. The rest of the cliff chipmunk's body is grayish except for the bushy tail's underside, which is a rusty red. All other chipmunk species found in this region have relatively distinct striping on their backs. The cliff chipmunk is a Southwestern species which occurs through much of the central Intermountain area, primarily across eastern Nevada and most of Utah.

As the name suggests, cliff chipmunks' primary habitats are rocky areas and cliffs. These are often at higher elevations, around the slopes of pinyon-juniper forests. Foods include seeds, nuts, fruits, and berries, particularly those from junipers. Although these chipmunks are hibernators, they readily emerge from their torpor on warm winter days. They are highly vocal, giving sharp barklike sounds about 160 times per minute, each accompanied by a tail twitch.

UINTA CHIPMUNK

YELLOW-BELLIED MARMOT or ROCKCHUCK

In Nevada, lactating females have been collected during June; little else is known about their breeding habits. Cliff chipmunks are both more aggressive and territorial than another species which occurs within their range, the Uinta chipmunk. In areas with widely spaced trees, cliff chipmunks can chase off these cousins on the ground. But if the forest is dense enough, Uintas have the advantage, for they are more skilled at maneuvering through the branches.

## HOPI CHIPMUNK (*Tamias rufus*) and COLORADO CHIPMUNK (*Tamias quadrivittatus*)

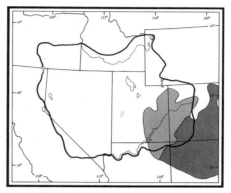

DISTRIBUTIONS OF HOPI CHIPMUNK (LIGHT) AND COLORADO CHIPMUNK (DARK).

Total length: 7 3/4 to 9 5/8 inches; tail length: 3 1/8 to 4 1/4 inches.

The Hopi chipmunk is so close in appearance to the Colorado chipmunk that the two have frequently been considered to be the same species. They are virtually impossible to tell apart based upon external characteristics; it is only recently, using skeletal traits, that they have been distinguished. To separate the two, one can occasionally rely on their distributions; most in the Intermountain West are Hopi chipmunks. But where their populations are near one another, only trained mammalogists can distinguish them.

These chipmunks are found in a section of the south-central Rocky Mountains which encompasses some of this region, primarily along the Utah-Colorado border. Hopi chipmunks occur in eastern Utah, western Colorado, and the northeastern corner of Arizona. Colorado chipmunks are found in a small portion of the region, in southwestern Colorado and adjacent northwestern New Mexico and northeastern Arizona; most of their range is in central Colorado.

Resemblances also occur between Hopi or Colorado chipmunks and two others in the region: the least and Uinta chipmunks. Compared to the least chipmunk, Hopi and Colorado chipmunks may be recognized by their larger size and a tendency to be found in rocky rather than wooded sites. In addition, it should be recalled that the least chipmunk's stripes continue to the base of the tail; those of Colorado and Hopi chipmunks do not. Compared to the brownish Uinta chipmunk, Colorado and Hopi chipmunks are a pale yellowish red shade. Color is not, however, a reliable identification trait since populations show considerable variation in it. In Colorado, Hopi and Colorado chipmunks are found from 4,600 to 11,200 feet. They are usually at lower elevations than Uinta chipmunks and may only occur at higher altitudes if Uintas are not present. Such is the case in southwestern Colorado, where they are found at 10,000 feet. Conversely, when Hopi and Colorado chipmunks are absent, Uintas occur lower than at their usual altitude of 9,000 feet. In Colorado's White River Valley they live at 6,500 feet.

The bright upper bodies of Colorado and Hopi chipmunks are usually reddish buff with distinct stripes of white, black, and reddish buff. In some, the most lateral dark side stripes are indistinct. Hopi chipmunks are said to be in their purest form in western Colorado and southeastern Utah. Here, they are distinguished by back stripes which, except for the median one, are uniformly tawny in color. In both, the head is smoky gray with a reddish cast, and the ears are blackish in front with a white patch behind them. These features should be useful in distinguishing them from other chipmunks. Their undersurfaces are whitish.

They are found on broken rocky terrain in open pine and juniper woodlands. There is nothing unusual about their diets, which consist of seeds, nuts, berries, and invertebrates. Juniper berries, actually the plant's cones, are preferred. Having such a similar appearance and habitat to other chipmunks makes it understandable that they have many of the same predators, such as coyotes and foxes. Their populations may be less dense than those of related chipmunks, perhaps consisting of no more than two or three per acre. So those same predators may not have the same luck in finding them. Burrows are utilized for housekeeping chores, such as food storage, hibernation, and rearing of young.

After a gestation of 30 to 33 days, the young are born. In our region, this typically occurs in April. Newborn are very immature and are not weaned until about two months of age.

## PANAMINT CHIPMUNK (*Tamias panamintinus*)

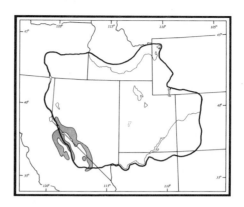

DISTRIBUTION OF PANAMINT CHIPMUNK.

Total length: 7 5/8 to 8 3/4 inches; tail length: 3 1/4 to 4 inches.

Panamint chipmunks are brightly colored, medium-sized chipmunks with reddish or tawny backs and conspicuous gray rumps. Their most lateral dark side stripes are indistinct and the inner ones are reddish or grayish. The crown of the head is gray and the front of the ear is tawny. Whereas the upper eye stripe is black, the lower one is an almost indistinguishable brown. In this region, Panamints may overlap with least and yellow-pine chipmunks. Compared to the least chipmunk, Panamints are slightly larger, more reddish than gray (especially in summer), and the central area of the tail's underside is redder and wider. Relative to the yellow-pine chipmunk, Panamints have slightly shorter feet and ears; are paler, gray instead of brown atop the head; have narrower and less distinct eye stripes, less conspicuous dark back stripes and indistinct lateral ones, and, finally, narrower inner but broader outer stripes. If you could watch one long enough to account for even some of these differences, you would be very lucky, indeed. There may also be some overlap between the Panamint chipmunk and the narrowly delimited Palmer's chipmunk. The latter is larger, has more solid black and white stripes, and is tawny on the tail's underside. For all of the above, it must be confessed that Panamint chipmunks occur in but a thin band along the southern border of Nevada and California.

This chipmunk lives in pinyon-juniper forests in semiarid rocky areas. It makes its home on rock ledges, in bushes, or among the lower limbs of pinyon trees. Conclusive studies are lacking, but it is suspected that its habits are similar to those of the yellow-pine chipmunk, including the possibility that it does not hibernate.

## UINTA CHIPMUNK
(*Tamias umbrinus*)

Total length: 7 3/4 to 9 5/8 inches; tail length: 2 7/8 to 4 1/2 inches.

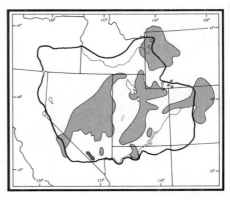

Uinta chipmunks are a medium-sized chipmunk, similar to the Colorado chipmunk in both length and coloration. Uintas are dark above, including the crown area, and have

DISTRIBUTIONS OF UINTA CHIPMUNK (LIGHT) AND PALMER'S CHIPMUNK (DARK).

wide, dark brown side stripes and outer, pure white light stripes. They are white below and tawny on the sides. Their pretty tails are black-tipped, bordered with white, and tawny below. One may use their ears as an identifying character: they are blackish in front and whitish behind. Differences between the Uinta and Colorado chipmunks are described in detail in the account of the latter species. In essence, Uintas are grayish brownish rather than the paler yellowish red of the Colorado chipmunk. As well, their distributions vary altitudinally, with Uintas occurring at higher locations when they are found in the same area. However, it is extremely difficult to tell the two apart and skeletal features are often needed to do so. It is considerably easier to distinguish them from the other chipmunks which share their range here. Least chipmunks are smaller, have grayer underparts, and ears that are tawny in front. The yellow-pine chipmunk is recognizable by its distinct black side stripes, and the cliff chipmunk is easy to pick out by its indistinct side stripes. Uinta chipmunks are one of those species for which almost their entire distribution falls within the Intermountain West. It is a discontinuous distribution, though, broken up into several large areas of Utah, Nevada, Wyoming, Colorado, and Arizona. In the forests of the North Rim of the Grand Canyon, this is the large chipmunk that is observed in campgrounds and many scenic spots.

Many different habitats are suitable for this species, including conifer forests, mixed woods, open areas, and rocky slopes up to timberline. Such areas are often dominated by one or more of the following: yellow pine, white pine, juniper, and scrub oak. Uintas are tree-dwellers, commonly occurring in the same vicinity as golden-mantled ground squirrels. There is nothing strikingly different about their food habits; they eat the usual array of nuts, seeds, fruits, and berries. Not only do they hibernate, they accumulate much body fat before doing so for warmth and energy during the long winter. Their reproduction is unstudied although it is known that the young arrive in summer.

## PALMER'S CHIPMUNK (*Tamias palmeri*)

Total length: 8 to 9 1/8 inches; tail length: 3 1/2 to 4 inches.

Of all the chipmunks in our region, it is Palmer's about which the least is known. Similar to the Uinta chipmunk, its dark dorsal stripes are browner; those of the Uinta may be redder. Further, the underside of Palmer's tail is tawnier, and the rostrum is shorter. In winter, its stripes are so indistinct that they are reminiscent of those of the cliff chipmunk. This obscure chipmunk is found in a small, isolated area of the Charleston Mountains of southern Nevada. There, it resides in conifer forests of yellow pine or pinyon-juniper and on rocky slopes from 7,000 feet to the timberline at about 12,000 feet. Based on its activities beneath the conifers, it is likely that seeds make up much of its diet.

## YELLOW-BELLIED MARMOT or ROCKCHUCK (*Marmota flaviventris*)

Total length: 18 1/2 to 27 5/8 inches; tail length: 5 1/8 to 8 3/4 inches.

The yellow-bellied marmot is an amusing and highly visible component of our fauna. The only marmot in the region, it is a close relative of the familiar woodchuck of the eastern United States and Canada. It is heavy bodied, yellowish brown to tawny, and has brown feet. Considerable color variation exists, but most look frosted due to their light-tipped guard hairs. Of course, another distinguishing feature is the yellow belly, which may actu-

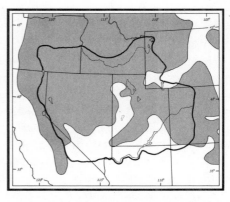

DISTRIBUTION OF YELLOW-BELLIED MARMOT OR ROCKCHUCK.

ally be yellow, orange, or reddish brown. There are whitish spots between the eyes and buff colored patches from the ears to the shoulder. Partial or complete melanism, resulting in black individuals, is common in the southern Rockies. The tail is long and bushy. Males are slightly longer and heavier than females. Yellow-bellied marmots occur in most of the western United States, extending far into the Pacific Northwest. They range throughout the Intermountain region except for southern Nevada and some of western and southeastern Utah.

These marmots usually inhabit rocky places on mountain slopes or in meadows. They may be found in semidesert areas in the Great Basin, woodland and forest openings, and the alpine zone. In the south of their range, they occur at higher altitudes. Rocks serve many functions for them, acting as support structures for burrows as well as sunning and observation decks. Their digging habit is regarded as semifossorial, meaning that they spend some but not all of their time underground. Burrows, which can be spotted by their surrounding dirt mounds, go down to about 2 feet and extend into the hillside for 10 to 15 feet. These are crucial to the marmots, serving as nurseries, hiding spots from predators and each other, and hibernacula. Moreover, burrow temperatures are stable, permitting those inside to save energy by avoiding extreme conditions. This has special importance during hibernation. In one area of Colorado, it was determined that the marmots spend about 80 percent of their time in burrows. Oddly, a Montana population (which uses hollow trees as homes and tree limbs as sunning spots) has recently been discovered in a cottonwood grove.

Yellow-bellied marmots are almost entirely herbivorous, consuming grasses, alfalfa, flowers, forbs, and in the late summer, large quantities of seeds. In one report, an individual filled itself up on sphinx moth caterpillars. Despite extensive field studies, little predation has been observed. Predators include coyotes, bobcats, and birds of prey. Along the Columbia River, these mammals were found to be the main food source for golden eagles. Overall, though, it is suspected that predation is a minor cause of mortality. More are believed to lose their lives from the stress of hibernation or during emigration from their home areas.

Yellow-bellied marmots are most active in the morning and late afternoon. They are sun worshippers, spending most of their time aboveground sunning themselves. Communication between individuals is both auditory and visual, but they also scent mark with cheek glands. There are scent glands around the anus as well, but it is not known if these are used in marking. Territorial males patrol their areas with their tails "flagging," a waving movement that goes in an arc from above the body to its rear. At this time, the anal glands might be used to let intruders know about the male's presence at a distance. There is considerable social interaction among the individuals in a marmot colony, including play, grooming, and greeting behaviors. Friendly behaviors occur between burrow mates, but nonburrow mates are often antagonistic. Hibernation takes up much of their existence, lasting from September through May at high altitude locations. Those living at lower elevations may come out of hibernation several months earlier. During hibernation, young marmots can lose up to 50 percent of their body weight. It should thus be easy to comprehend why mortality is so high at this time, especially for those which did not put on sufficient weight earlier in the year.

Reproductive activity takes place in the first few weeks after arousal from hibernation. Few, if any, breed in their first year; in one study only 25 percent of the two-year-old females bore young. After a 30-day pregnancy, from three to eight yellow-bellied babies are born, typically in June. The average litter size is between four and five. When the young first venture forth from their burrows, 20 to 30 days after birth, they are nearly weaned. All males and most females disperse from the natal area, usually as yearlings. In alpine colonies, yearlings may stay with their parents for an additional year. Dispersal does not necessarily result in the finding of a suitable habitat and, thus, is a common cause of mortality. These marmots may live singly, in pairs, or, most commonly, in colonies. Within the colonies, individuals are members of harems consisting of an adult male, several adult females, and their offspring.

In a classic study, J. F. Downhower and K. B. Armitage discovered that the average harem size in a Colorado site tended to be two to three females per male. The number of yearlings produced per female decreases with the number of females she has to share the male with. Thus, if a male keeps adding females to his harem beyond a certain point, he does not necessarily enjoy a higher reproductive output. This is because his reproductive success is equal to the number of females in his harem multiplied by each of their reproductive success. A male with two females, each of which has three young, would have a higher fitness than one with four females, each of which only had one young. Hence, this study uncovered a principle involved in the regulation of harem size; that it is, in a sense, determined through a compromise by the two sexes.

## WHITE-TAILED ANTELOPE SQUIRREL (*Ammospermophilus leucurus*)

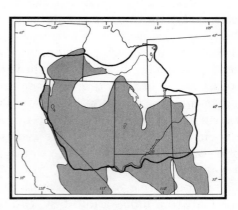

DISTRIBUTION OF WHITE-TAILED ANTELOPE SQUIRREL.

Total length: 7 5/8 to 9 3/8 inches; tail length: 2 1/8 to 3 1/2 inches.

An antelope squirrel is distinguished from other ground squirrels by the way it holds its tail when running. Whereas ground squirrels of the genus *Spermophilus* hold their

WHITE-TAILED ANTELOPE SQUIRREL

relatively horizontally, antelope squirrels hold theirs more vertically, exposing the white undersurface. While in this position,
the tail may be nervously twitched. Holding the tail in such a
manner looks similar to a pronghorn antelope lifting its tail and
flashing its white rump to warn others of danger; thus, the
name. The white-tailed antelope squirrel is the only squirrel of
this type in our region. In summer, its upper body varies from
buffy to cinnamon brown, molting to gray in the winter. Its
underparts are white. This pale coloration provides concealment
in its typically arid habitat. On each side of the body is a narrow white stripe extending from the side to the hip. The white
hairs on the bottom of the tail have black tips, creating a narrow black border. Antelope squirrels are found throughout
much of Nevada and Utah and several adjacent areas in the
Intermountain West. Their range extends to the southern tip of
Baja California in Mexico.

Habitats of this squirrel include low deserts, plateaus,
foothills, and places with sparse vegetation and hard gravelly

surfaces. Often it is spotted along highways. Its main food items are seeds and fruit, including those from greasebush plants and cacti. Insects are occasionally taken, and there is a report of one preying on a pocket mouse. It readily climbs in yuccas, cacti, and other vegetation. Food may be stored in caches. Interestingly, as is the case for many desert mammals, it does not require much drinking water but instead metabolizes water from its food. It probably requires some moisture as it cannot subsist entirely on this metabolic water. These squirrels are preyed upon by rattlesnakes and several mammalian and avian predators. One of their sure signs is a subterranean burrow with radiating pathways and no mounds at the entrances. They also live in rock crevices and the abandoned burrows of other animals. In the northern parts of their range, they may hibernate, but this is not necessarily the case in their southern homes.

Even in the blistering environments they inhabit, they remain active during the daytime. They accomplish this, in part, by having a nearly constant metabolic rate when outside temperatures are between 90° and 107° F. Such constancy in this temperature range, gives them what may be the highest "thermal neutral zone" of any nonsweating mammal. A thermal neutral zone is that range of temperatures within which an animal hardly alters its metabolism to cope with either warmer or colder conditions. In addition, this mammal can cool itself off on very hot days by washing its head with saliva. Though much water is lost from this behavior, little else is lost in the highly concentrated urine it produces. Naturally, it returns to the burrow should temperatures become unbearable.

In early spring, a litter of 5 to 14 young is born. Occasionally, second litters are produced. The newborn are raised in a nest constructed from grass, fur, bark, and other available material. In Nevada, where jackrabbits have been caught in coyote traps, the squirrels clean off their fur, ostensibly to use it in their nests. They appear to be solitary. White-tailed antelope squirrels are mistakenly referred to as chipmunks. But anyone looking at them should not be fooled by the stripes. They are members of the fascinating antelope squirrel group.

TOWNSEND'S
GROUND SQUIRREL
(*Spermophilus
townsendii*)

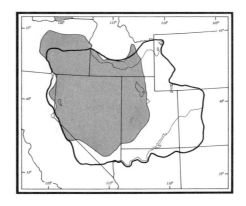

**DISTRIBUTION OF TOWNSEND'S
GROUND SQUIRREL.**

Total length: 6 5/8 to 10
3/4 inches; tail length: 1
1/4 to 2 3/4 inches.

Because this is the
first ground squirrel to
be discussed, a few
introductory remarks
are in order. Ground
squirrels differ from
chipmunks and antelope squirrels in that almost all lack body
stripes. When stripes are present, they do not occur on the head.
Their genus name, *Spermophilus*, means "seed loving"; John J.
Audubon referred to them as "spermophiles." Actually, many
are more appropriately described as generalist herbivores, eating
the wide variety of plant items available on their open, grassy
habitats. Several texts place the ground squirrels in the genus
*Citellus*, but the name used here is currently more accepted. All
ground squirrels are burrowers, most hibernate, and a good
number are colonial.

Townsend's ground squirrel is plain, somewhat dappled gray
above and tinged with a pinkish cast. The underside is white or
buff. Individuals from the Escalante Desert of southern Utah
tend to be much redder than those from the northern part of
their range. One of this squirrel's distinguishing marks is a short
tail which is either reddish or tawny below and edged with
white. Both the face and hind legs are also reddish. Some
appear to have pale dots on the upper body. There are several
similar species in the region which differ as follows: Wyoming
and Belding's ground squirrels are larger; Uinta ground squirrels, which cross into the northeastern portion of Townsend's
range, are larger, have a brown streak down the middle of the
back, and a tail with a blackish shade above and below. Each of
these other ground squirrels have larger ears and darker fur.

Townsend's ground squirrels occur in much of the western two-thirds of the Intermountain region. Largely restricted to this area, they also inhabit a small segment of Washington.

These squirrels have been exceptionally important to the Piute Indians of Nevada, who used them for food throughout much of their history. They would travel miles to find areas where the squirrels were numerous. A common way of capturing them would be for the women to pour water into the burrows, with the men grabbing the squirrels by their necks as they ran out of the holes. J. R. Alcorn, in the paper cited in the rodent reference list, provides a lengthy account of the Piutes' utilization of this squirrel.

The habitat of Townsend's ground squirrels is usually arid, high, open sagebrush or greasewood communities, or occasionally grasslands. Their numbers are also high in irrigated lands and at desert springs due to the high food productivity in such places. In Utah's Delta Valley, they can be extremely numerous, and go by the local name of "quimps." Where both Townsend's and Wyoming ground squirrels occur together, as they do in northeastern Nevada, Wyoming ground squirrels typically inhabit meadowlands and lower bottomlands. Townsend's ground squirrels occupy the more arid sagebrush benches above the bottomlands. Preferred foods are seeds and green parts of grasses, forbs, and other plants. To reach the succulent part of grasses, they will even dig through the snow. Often, they are regarded as pests because they plunder crops, such as alfalfa and sprouting corn. Badgers are probably their most common predator, which is not surprising given the amount of time they spend underground. Others include coyotes, long-tailed weasels, western rattlesnakes, and birds of prey, particularly prairie falcons and Swainson's and red-tailed hawks.

They are diurnal, with most aboveground activity taking place in the early morning. Although they may form colonies, they are not highly social; they may live together but keep their distance. An intriguing behavior is that adults dig two burrows. The first, a small one, is dug in the feeding area. It is probably used as an escape hatch for quick getaways from avian predators. The other burrow is their home and is much larger, up to 50 feet long and 6 feet deep. Tunnels often extend from the sagebrush into nearby rocky ridges. Burrow openings are

rimmed with four-to-six-inch piles of dirt, one of their distinctive signs. They are excellent swimmers and climbers.

Where summer temperatures are relatively high, adults begin
to estivate in June or July. Young of the year usually do not
become fat enough to estivate until August. Estivation is the
summer equivalent of hibernation, in which animals enter a
state of torpor to avoid activity during the warm months. The
ground squirrels go from this state directly into hibernation,
emerging in midwinter or early spring. Hence, most of their
lives are spent in a dreamlike state.

Breeding occurs between late January and early March.
From 4 up to possibly 17 altricial young are born after about a
24-day pregnancy. A single litter of 7 to 10 is typical. During
severe drought years with insufficient food at the start of the
breeding season, females may be unable to breed. Rather than
being used to produce young, food is converted into fat to prepare for hibernation. This is probably the only desert ground
squirrel that engages in such a cessation of reproduction. Young
are weaned about a month after birth. Males of the subspecies
(*S. townsendii mollis*) which occupies most of their range can
breed as yearlings; those of a southwestern Idaho subspecies (*S.
townsendii idahoensis*) do not mature until two years old. Males
do not appear to be involved in parental care and even cannibal-
ize their own young or those of other males.

## WYOMING GROUND SQUIRREL
(*Spermophilus elegans*)

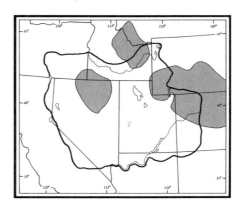

DISTRIBUTION OF WYOMING GROUND
SQUIRREL.

Total length: 10 to 12
inches; tail length: 2 3/8
to 3 1/8 inches.

The Wyoming
ground squirrel is a
small-to-medium-sized
ground squirrel with big
ears and a relatively
long tail. Above, it is a
light drab shade, flecked
with pinkish buff to pinkish cinnamon. Its belly is a deep cinna-

mon. Its tail is edged with white to pale buff and is buff to light brown underneath. In this region, Wyoming ground squirrels are occasionally sympatric, or occur in the same area, with some similar ground squirrels. Although they may be slightly smaller than the Uinta ground squirrel, they can be better distinguished by the color of the underside of their tails: the Wyoming ground squirrel's is pale buff rather than gray. They are also about the same size as Belding's ground squirrel, but the latter has a shorter tail. Furthermore, Belding's ground squirrel has a tail that is reddish on the underside, and it lacks the deep cinnamon color on the nose and underparts possessed by the Wyoming ground squirrel. Where sympatric with Townsend's ground squirrels, Wyoming ground squirrels are again distinguishable by their cinnamon underparts, whereas Townsend's are whitish. Other differences between these two species include the buffy white border around the tail and the larger size of the Wyoming ground squirrel. One should also assess whether the ears are proportionately long; those of the Wyoming ground squirrel are.

These squirrels occur as three different subspecies in separate places in the region. The first, *S. elegans elegans*, is found in mountain meadows from about 5,000 feet to above timberline in an area encompassing northern Colorado, southern Wyoming, and northeastern Utah. A more gold-colored subspecies, *S. elegans aureus*, occurs in valley bottoms and foothills around southeastern Idaho. In this area, it appears to have been displaced from mountain meadows by the Uinta ground squirrel. Finally, a larger, grayer subspecies, *S. elegans nevadensis*, is found in north-central Nevada, where it occupies sage and grassland habitats. Until recently, all three of these were regarded as Richardson's ground squirrel (*Spermophilus richardsonii*), which inhabits a large area in south-central Canada and the north-central United States. But it is now accepted that Wyoming and Richardson's ground squirrels are distinct. They are still both referred to by the nickname "picket pin," as are some other ground squirrels, because their habit of standing on their hind legs, surveying the surroundings, likens them to the stakes to which cowboys tied their horses. It is suspected that the Wyoming ground squirrel "complex" became separated from Richardson's ground squirrels by forest barriers which developed in a glacial period some 11,000 years ago. Due to their own genetic differences and isolation, it is conceivable that the Wyoming ground squirrel subspecies could also become separate species, themselves, in the future.

Typical habitats of these ground squirrels include sagebrush and bunchgrass rangelands on well-drained soils. In addition to the aforementioned places, they occur on subalpine talus slopes and reclaimed surface mines. Their burrows are found along the edges of open marshes, cultivated fields, railway embankments, and on rocky hillsides. Burrows are marked by a bare soil mound from which the entrance descends at a steep angle. Each burrow system has a central nest chamber. Their preferred foods are forbs (herbaceous plants other than grasses) and grasses. Plant parts, such as seeds, stems, roots, flowers, leaves, and even shrub bark, are gobbled up. They also eat members of their species that have been killed by motor vehicles. Various grasshoppers are devoured as well. Their predators consist of the usual collection of coyotes, foxes, badgers, and hawks. They are highly vocal, warning each other of predators with special alarm calls. Sylvatic plague takes a heavy toll and they are also a host of Colorado tick fever virus. Because they carry these transmissible diseases and can compete with livestock for food, they have been the subject of widespread control efforts. Yet, the natural hazards they face are so severe that often fewer than one of four survives to reproduce the following year.

As with most other ground squirrels, they are completely diurnal, with most activity in the midmorning and early evening hours. Much of their year is spent hibernating since they enter torpor as early as July, if they have put on enough fat, remaining in it until March. Prior to hibernation, many are so fat that it actually is difficult for them to walk. Entering the relative safety of the hibernaculum must be more adaptive than being too fat to move away from predators aboveground. Males begin to hibernate before juveniles and females who have nursed their young the preceding spring. Females emerge from hibernation about two weeks after males as well.

Mating takes place about five days after both sexes have stopped hibernating. One litter, of 1 to 11 young with an average of 6, is produced after a pregnancy which lasts for some 23 days. The newborn are so altricial at birth that their digits are still fused. Even after two days, the blood vessels and internal organs remain visible beneath the skin. Their eyes remain closed for 24 days. Weaning does not take place until from four to six weeks of age, and the young still follow their mother around for several more weeks outside of the burrow. Although Wyoming ground squirrels may live in dense colonies, they are not especially social. Female offspring tend to remain in or near the mother's burrow in "kin clusters," but males disperse and live separately. Each kin cluster is not sociable with other such groups. Some males may only breed with two females, but others do so with several more; they are thus polygynous. Males as well as females do not breed until they are yearlings.

## UINTA GROUND SQUIRREL
(*Spermophilus armatus*)

Total length: 11 to 11 7/8 inches; tail length: 2 1/2 to 3 1/4 inches.

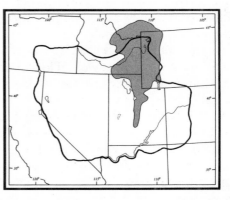

DISTRIBUTION OF UINTA GROUND SQUIRREL.

The Uinta ground squirrel is another species with strong similarities to several other ground squirrels. It is brownish to buff above, with paler sides, and a buffy belly. A noteworthy feature is the buff-colored tail, mixed with black above and below and edged with pinkish buff. Its head, front of the face, and ears are cinnamon, but the crown is sprinkled with gray. The sides of the face and neck are pale gray. Finally, its limbs are colored as follows: the forelegs and forefeet are cinnamon and pinkish buff, respectively; the hind legs are cinnamon; and the hind feet are buff. Where they overlap, a Uinta ground squirrel can be distinguished from a Townsend's ground squirrel by the tail of the latter species, which is usually shorter and reddish or tawny below. The Wyoming ground squirrel also has a different tail; it is edged with light buff or white and is buff to light brown underneath. It also lacks the black wash and pinkish edge of the Uinta's tail.

UINTA GROUND SQUIRREL

Although their ranges cross only near Utah's far northwestern corner, it is still useful to know that Uintas may be told apart from Belding's ground squirrel by the brown streak down the back of the latter species. Uinta ground squirrels have a fairly small range, most of which is in the Intermountain West. From a narrow strip in Utah's Wasatch Mountains, their distribution broadens northward into eastern Idaho and western Wyoming, up into southwestern Montana.

Typical habitats of these ground squirrels are dry sage, sage-grass areas, field edges, and lawns. They occur in mountains, foothills, and high valleys up to 8,000 feet, favoring well-drained places. Major foods are various seeds, but they also eat other plant parts as well as invertebrates and small vertebrates. Badgers appear to be their most common predator, but weasels nab a few, too. Adults go into summer torpor, estivation, as early as July, with juveniles following several weeks or even months later. Estivation continues unabated into hibernation, from which males emerge first in late March to mid-April. They are followed in succession by adult females, yearling females, and yearling males. Hence, Uintas are another ground squirrel which spends but a small fraction of its existence awake. Adults are only active for an average of 90 days a year.

Breeding occurs shortly after the adults emerge from hibernation, although copulation takes place underground. Females then become aggressive and establish territories around their nesting burrows. David Balph, who has studied Uinta ground squirrels in northern Utah, suggests that female territoriality has several functions. First of all, it may ensure a nutritious source of food during pregnancy and nursing. This is because the grass that females crop around their terrritories sends up new shoots with more nutrients than the older leaves. In effect, they are tending a garden. Territoriality may also protect the young against intruders, including other squirrels in the population. Males also establish territories, which they mark by wiping the ground with glandular secretions from the sides of the head. Apparently, they mate with more than one female, but females, too, may be bred by more than one male. Yearlings have four or five young, but may not breed at all when the population density is high. After their second year, females produce about six or seven young. Gestation is approximately 26 days. About 24 days after birth, the newborn emerge from their burrows to explore the outside world. From this time on, mothers exhibit little parental care. Dispersal of young into new areas is common and is an important population regulatory factor. Although colonial, Uintas are remarkably intolerant of one another. Female kin may live near each other, but they do not share burrows. Sibling groups dissolve only a few weeks after they come aboveground.

## BELDING'S GROUND SQUIRREL
(*Spermophilus beldingi*)

Total length: 10 to 11 3/4 inches; tail length: 2 1/4 to 3 inches.

Belding's ground squirrel is easily distinguished from others in the region by the broad brown streak running down the middle of its back. Overall, it is gray, washed with a reddish or pinkish shade above. It is pinkish atop the head and reddish brown on the belly. The tail is distinctive due to its combination of being pinkish gray above, reddish to hazel below, edged with pinkish buff, and tipped with black. It is also moderately

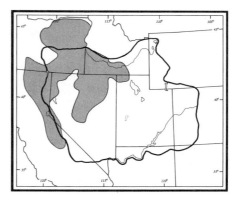

DISTRIBUTION OF BELDING'S GROUND SQUIRREL.

bushy and somewhat flattened; there's no mistaking this squirrel's tail. Other differences between this and similar sympatric species in the region are discussed in the previous accounts. To review briefly: The tail of the Wyoming ground squirrel is buff to light brownish below; that of Townsend's ground squirrel is not only smaller, it is whitish to buff below. For Belding's ground squirrels, one need only spot the brown back streak to recognize them. They occur in the western portion of the Intermountain West through central and northern Nevada, southwestern Idaho, and neighboring southeastern Oregon. Their range extends from the region into the northeastern segments of both Oregon and California.

This species primarily occurs in meadows and on open wooded slopes at elevations up to at least 10,000 feet. It also inhabits old fields, roadsides, and other grassy areas, especially where the vegetation is short. In addition, it is found in hay and alfalfa fields. Where colonies are large, Belding's ground squirrels can inflict substantial damage on pastures and grainfields. They are strictly diurnal, feeding on weed and grain seeds, leaves and stems, bird's eggs, and insects such as grasshoppers, crickets, and caterpillars. Food is not put in caches for the winter, as is so for many other squirrels, but is stored as fat. Predators include hawks, snakes, coyotes, bears, badgers, and weasels. When predators approach, some individuals give alarm calls, a dangerous behavior since more callers are killed by predators than are noncallers. However, it should be worth the risk for callers to be exposed to predators if their behavior results in an increase in the survival of several close relatives. Such altruistic behavior is the result of what is called "kin selection." Seemingly contrary to this, yearling males and adult females kill and eat juveniles. But in these cases, the victimized squirrels are the offspring of unrelated females. Such infanticide accounted for almost a third of all juvenile deaths prior to winter in one high Sierra population.

Despite this internecine warfare, the major cause of death in this species often is severe weather. Over 90 percent of the juveniles and close to 70 percent of the adults may die during hibernation. And more may perish after they emerge, by freezing or starving following a spring snowstorm. Hibernation and estivation can last for eight months. A study in the southern Sierras of California revealed that males hibernate alone but females often remain with close relatives. As with other ground squirrels, adult males emerge first, followed by adult females one to two weeks later, then yearling females, with yearling males last.

Just four to six days after emerging from hibernation, breeding occurs. Females are receptive to the male's amorous advances for only three to six hours. One might suspect that this puts undue pressure on the males. It undoubtedly does, for they will fight fiercely for mates — so much so that they interrupt one another while copulating — injuring and frequently killing each other. Males do not defend territories which are attractive to females as they do in related species; they simply follow a female around when she is in heat. The female's behavior at this time reveals that she actively selects her partners, with heaviest males being chosen the most. On the average, females mate four times with three different males in rapid succession. The first male is usually the one that sires the offspring. But a fascinating result of this mayhem is that many litters are actually multiply sired; that is, there is multiple paternity of offspring in the same litter. This is known through an analysis of blood proteins of potential fathers and their offspring. Much is known about the reproductive behavior of Belding's ground squirrels because courtship and mating occur aboveground, which is unusual for a ground squirrel. Just why this is so is not known. Certainly, it should make them more vulnerable to each other and to predators.

A single litter with an average of five to seven altricial young is born in a grass-lined burrow nest following an approximately 25-day gestation. After being nursed for about a month, the young appear aboveground in midsummer. The males in a litter disperse after weaning, but the females may remain together for several generations. Not only do related females share parts of territories, they even chase away intruders from each other's unguarded burrows. By the time the young are weaned, many adult males have already begun their torpor. The young, however, keep putting on fat, not hibernating until the first snowfall. Yet, they may not put on enough to meet the demands of both hibernation and breeding. Unlike the males of many other ground squirrels which breed as yearlings, a male Belding's does not breed until two years of age. Females, however, do breed as yearlings, although slightly later in the season than adult females. Whereas almost all older females are impregnated, only about two-thirds of the yearlings are. Yearlings usually give birth to several fewer young than do adults as well.

## THIRTEEN-LINED GROUND SQUIRREL (*Spermophilus tridecemlineatus*)

Total length: 6 3/4 to 11 3/4 inches; tail length: 2 3/8 to 5 3/4 inches.

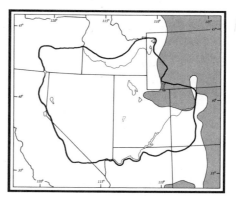

DISTRIBUTION OF THIRTEEN-LINED GROUND SQUIRREL.

There is no mistaking the thirteen-lined ground squirrel for any other species. The pattern on its back is so unnatural looking that it appears to have been designed by an op artist. On the upper body there is a series of dark brown or blackish stripes which alternate with pale longitudinal ones. Particularly striking are the almost square white spots, regularly spaced along each of the dark stripes. As the name reveals, there are 13 stripes in all; the term *tridecemlineatus* is Latin for "thirteen-lined." The lowermost stripes along the sides may not be as well defined as those on the upper back and are even broken up into spots. So do not discount the possibility that an individual belongs to this species if you cannot count 13 stripes. The sides, feet, and belly range from nearly white to yellowish orange, depending on the subspecies and habitat. In the arid West, individuals tend to be paler. Of small to moderate size, these ground squirrels are slender compared to most others. Their eyes appear large, especially in the young, and their ears are small. Although they are the most widely distributed ground squirrel in North America, they occur in but a small portion of the Intermountain West, primarily around the northern border between Utah and Colorado. This is only part of the western extension of a range that covers most of the continent's central portion.

Animals with broad distributions are typically common in a variety of habitats and this one is no exception. Thirteen-lined ground squirrels tend to occur in grasslands with well-drained soils, but are also found along roadsides, in pastures, and even on golf courses. In Colorado, they prefer low bunchgrasses and inhabit semidesert shrublands. They are omnivorous, eating a variety of items, such as grass, leaves, seeds, roots, insects, mice, small chickens, young cottontails, and road-killed animals. In the spring, insects may account for over two-thirds of their diet. Where abundant, they can wreak havoc on a great variety of crops. And they are not merely putting about on the golf courses they inhabit. There, and in cemeteries, their burrowing is not appreciated. Yet their habits are not totally negative to humans due to their prodigious insect eating and soil-aerating ability. Surely, this animal, which Audubon called the "leopard-spermophile," is so unique-looking that it is aesthetically pleasing to many as well.

These ground squirrels are so strictly diurnal that they rarely come aboveground on overcast days. On sunny days, they sit erect by their burrows, alert to any predators lurking about. Their litany of enemies includes predatory birds, feral or wild house cats, badgers, weasels, coyotes, and snakes. Other significant mortality agents are floods and motor vehicles. In some areas, juvenile mortality can be over 95 percent for males and nearly as high for females. An individual might build several burrows, some for temporary shelter and others as more permanent structures. A burrow is usually one to two feet below ground and has several entrances. During hibernation and at other times, the entrances are blocked with dirt plugs. It is difficult to detect an opening in any case since it is often hidden under a clump. There is no mound to mark it either; excess dirt is spread evenly around the entrance. In fields, one can observe runway systems connecting the entrances that are similar to those created by smaller rodents. These ground squirrels usually enter hibernation in late September or early October, emerging in late March or April. Males are aroused about a week earlier than females.

Upon emerging, they are ready to breed. Ovulation only takes place in females that have copulated, a phenomenon known as induced ovulation. Pregnancy lasts for about 28 days, ending with the birth of 5 to 13 altricial young as early as May. An average litter has 8 or 9 young; second litters are occasionally produced. By the time they are a month old, the young are weaned but may continue to use the burrows for a few weeks. These ground squirrels occur in loose colonies, but individuals are essentially solitary. Families break up just several weeks after the young emerge from the burrows.

## SPOTTED GROUND SQUIRREL
(*Spermophilus spilosoma*)

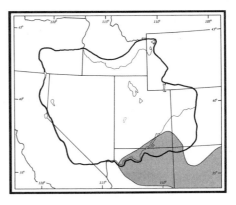

DISTRIBUTION OF SPOTTED GROUND SQUIRREL.

Total length: 7 1/4 to 10 inches; tail length: 2 1/4 to 3 5/8 inches.

Although the spotted ground squirrel is the closest relative in the region of the thirteen-lined ground squirrel, the two are easily distinguished. Spotted ground squirrels are grayish beige to cinnamon brownish above, whitish below, and have small, inconspicuous, squarish, light spots randomly sprinkled across the back. Their black-tipped tail is sparsely haired and buffy below. Of course, thirteen-lined ground squirrels have stripes as well as spots.

Moreover, the two are not sympatric in this region. Whereas thirteen-lined ground squirrels enter the Intermountain West only around the northern Utah-Colorado border, spotted ground squirrels occur in the region's southeast corner. Their overall distribution takes them across the south-central United States, extending throughout central Mexico.

These ground squirrels are a high-desert species whose most common habitats have dry, sandy soils and sparse, shrubby vegetation. They will occur in grassy areas and pine woods. Active in the late morning and early afternoon, they feed on green vegetation, seeds, cacti, grasshoppers, and beetles. They also prey on kangaroo rats and lizards. From the limited information available, they do not seem as carnivorous as the more blood-thirsty thirteen-lined ground squirrel. They are feasted upon by birds of prey and predatory mammals. In Colorado, bull snakes have been observed visiting their burrows. During the heat of the day, they seek refuge in the burrows. These are about 2 inches wide and 18 inches below ground; entrances are often under bushes or overhanging rocks. At the end of the burrow, there is a round chamber lined with grass. Although they hibernate in their northern range, it is warm enough in their southern homes for them to remain active almost year-round. In some southern locales, however, they may estivate in the warmer months. Curiously, the young are reported to be more active than their parents in the winter. This is difficult to explain. The cold should have a greater impact on the young since they would not have had the time or opportunity to put on as much fat as the adults would have had.

During the mating season, males repeatedly approach females and seem to entice them into their burrows. Most breeding occurs in May or June, with some stragglers waiting until July. The latecomers are probably yearling females reproducing for the first time. An average litter size is 7; the range is 4 to 12. Two litters per year are reported to be common, especially in the south, which is unusual for a ground squirrel. Such observations, however, might be due to adult breeding preceding that of the yearlings. Pregnancy, which lasts approximately 28 days, results in the birth of highly altricial young. About six weeks after birth, the newborn are weaned and on their own. Unlike many of their relatives, these ground squirrels are of little economic importance. They mostly occur on barren land, where they do not present problems for farmers.

## ROCK SQUIRREL
(*Spermophilus variegatus*)

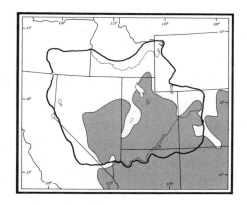

DISTRIBUTION OF ROCK SQUIRREL.

Total length: 16 7/8 to 20 3/4 inches; tail length: 6 3/4 to 9 7/8 inches.

Rock squirrels are easy to recognize since they are the largest ground squirrels in their range. To make matters even simpler, there are no sympatric ground squirrels that resemble them. Both their markings and similar appearance to tree squirrels make them unique. The long bushy tail has a distinctively mottled pattern of buff and brown surrounded by a white edge. This is why *variegatus* is part of their scientific name; "variegated" means having discrete markings of different colors. The upper body is also dappled, grayish brown in front and reddish brown toward the back. On the belly, the fur is whitish to pinkish buff. In some races, however, the entire back and head are black. For a ground squirrel, its head and ears are large. Rock squirrels occur in most of northern Mexico, up into Texas and the southwestern United States. In the Intermountain West, the major areas of their distribution include most of Utah, southern Nevada, and neighboring spots.

The typical habitat of rock squirrels is broken canyon country with open rocky areas. Where slopes support stands of juniper and brushy oak, they may be easily spotted perched on rocks. They are not populous in areas without ample rimrock or other rocky habitats. However, they are frequently found in areas of human habitation, where they den under sheds, in lumber piles, and even junked cars. They are identified by a sharp, trembling whistle. Most active in the early morning and late afternoon, they feed on seeds, nuts, insects, eggs, and carrion,

ROCK SQUIRREL

depending upon seasonal availability. Efficient climbers, they search for food in trees and bushes. After the food is gathered, it is stored in a den. Unfortunately, they have a taste for fruit and can damage orchards. They suffer death at the claws or teeth of bobcats, badgers, coyotes, golden eagles, and hawks. Predation, however, may not be a major cause of mortality. One can locate their burrows, which are lined with grass, shredded bark, or leaves, beneath rocks, bushes, and trees. They occasionally den in trees. In their southern range, they remain active all year. But even in their northern range, where hibernation can last for up to six months, they are not deep sleepers, waking about once a week.

Unlike most other ground squirrels, males become capable of breeding only after hibernation, rather than emerging from their slumber already in breeding condition. Females become receptive about a week after the males are ready. Following a pregnancy of 30 days, an average of about five altricial young are produced between May and July. Individuals have two litters a year in some warmer regions. After approximately eight weeks, the young come out of their burrows, but do not disperse for another month. Rock squirrels seem to be moderately social, and will defend a small personal space. In a Texas population, adult females became territorial toward each other near the burrows containing their young. The territories of several females may overlap that of one male; they thus seem to have a polygynous mating system. Males try to actively exclude other males from the colony during the breeding season, defending an area of about an acre. Most males end up with scars or wounds from these encounters. But the females are not turned away during this most important of times.

## CALIFORNIA GROUND SQUIRREL (*Spermophilus beecheyi*)

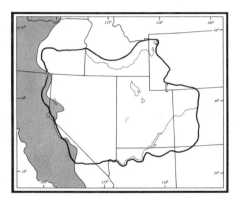

DISTRIBUTION OF CALIFORNIA GROUND SQUIRREL.

Total length: 14 1/8 to 19 3/4 inches; tail length: 5 3/4 to 8 7/8 inches.

Primarily a West Coast species, California ground squirrels occur in but a tiny portion of the Intermountain West in western Nevada and northeastern California. With their long bushy tails and otherwise similar appearance to tree squirrels, these animals resemble their relative, the rock squirrel. Nevertheless, they do not occur in the same area and are differently colored. The body is brown, flecked with buffy white to buff spots. Along the sides of the neck and shoulder region is a whitish shading with a distinctive brown or black triangular pattern between the shoulders. The undersurface is buff. The tail, which is colored like the rest of the body, is edged with white. All of the other ground squirrels in the same range are smaller.

This species occupies a variety of habitats, tending more toward humid regions than do other ground squirrels. California ground squirrels are abundant in the Sierra Nevadas; around Lake Tahoe, they are common up to 7,100 feet. Open areas, such as rocky ridges, pastures, grainfields, roadsides, and hills with scattered trees, are preferred. Places with thick tree or shrub growth are avoided. Although almost all of their food is plant material, they also eat insects and an occasional small vertebrate. In winter, food is stored at high elevations; in summer, it is placed in lower altitude dens. Because they readily forage on fruit, grains, and nuts, they are pests in many areas. Furthermore, as is true of many ground squirrels, they carry bubonic plague. Burrows are dug under rocks or trees if present; if not, they are constructed out in the open. Usually, these squirrels remain on the ground, feeding near their burrows. However, they are fine climbers and will go 20 feet up a cottonwood tree to feed on its catkins, the tree's male reproductive structures. They also regularly hoist themselves up trees or shrubs to warm themselves on sunny mornings. Most adults take it easy during the hot months, estivating through July and August. Hibernation lasts from approximately November until February, but, oddly, first-year individuals may remain aboveground at this time.

A single litter of five to eight altricial young is born after a 25-to-30-day gestation. Most births occur in early spring although young may arrive in summer and fall. The little squirrels dig their own burrows about two months after birth. Although California ground squirrels are colonial, individuals are not particularly sociable. Adult males are aggressive toward each other during the breeding season. Experimental fieldwork by Steve Dobson indicates that the young of each sex disperse from the natal area for different reasons. Young males leave their birthplace before reproducing; avoidance of both inbreeding and competition with other males for mates seems to be involved in their dispersal. Dispersal rates by young females are much lower. But when dispersal does occur in this group, it is likelier due to population density pressures rather than the tendency to avoid inbreeding. Such findings may have implications for the significance of dispersal in related species.

ROUND-TAILED
GROUND SQUIRREL
(*Spermophilus
tereticaudus*)

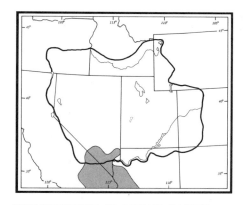

DISTRIBUTION OF ROUND-TAILED
GROUND SQUIRREL.

Total length: 8 to 10 1/2
inches; tail length: 2 3/8
to 4 1/4 inches.

Compared with all
of the bushy-tailed
ground squirrels just
described, round-tailed
ground squirrels appear
most unusual. Rather
than the hairy tail found on the other species, that of the round-
tailed ground squirrel is pencil-like. This animal has an upper
surface that is pinkish cinnamon with a grayish cast; the belly is
slightly paler. Such coloration enables it to blend in with the
sandy desert soil it inhabits. No contrasting markings, such as
stripes or spots, highlight the body, as is the case for so many
other ground squirrels. Instead, this relatively small ground
squirrel resembles an antelope squirrel without the stripes. The
feet, particularly the hind ones, are large and broad with soles
covered by long, stiff hairs. It barely enters the Intermountain
region, occurring only in Nevada's far southern corner. Its overall distribution is limited to the southwestern corner of the
United States and Baja California.

The habitat for round-tailed ground squirrels is flat, sandy,
low-desert areas characterized by creosote and mesquite bushes,
palo verde, and cacti. They often inhabit sand dunes. They usually dig burrows under bushes, although they also use the burrows of kangaroo rats and other rodents. Although they are
diurnal, it is so hot in the middle of the day in their range that
activity is normally limited to mornings and evenings. A siesta in
the burrow or shade of a bush gets them through the most
extreme part of the day. Major foods include green vegetation,
seeds, and insects, the proportion of each changing seasonally.
Seed consumption is greater in winter. They have been observed
to prey on English sparrows and, undoubtedly, would not hesitate to kill other birds if given the chance. They have good

climbing skills in the bushes and short trees near their homes.
Predators do not differ from the ground squirrel's usual wrecking crew: birds of prey, coyotes, badgers, and bobcats. But in
their range, round-tailed ground squirrels are faced with another
enemy; their remains have been found in Gila monsters. Even in
their warm surroundings, they hibernate for a substantial
amount of time, from about late September until early January.
Nevertheless, some are spotted aboveground during every month
of the year. Thus, it is likely that their torpor is not a deep one.

Unlike most of their relatives, they do not mate immediately
after emergence from hibernation. Some populations of these
patient squirrels wait until late March or early April to breed. In
some areas, however, evidence suggests that breeding occurs as
early as January. After a gestation of about 27 days, the
altricial young appear. Litter size is correlated with the amount
of precipitation and resultant vegetation. In dry years, they may
produce as few as an average of 3 young, whereas in wet, more
productive years, the number of young may increase to 12. An
average litter consists of 6 or 7 young. At three weeks the newborn are completely covered with hair; by four weeks their eyes
are open and they can run. Weaning occurs at five weeks. Both
males and females are sexually mature at ten to eleven months.
Round-tailed ground squirrels have a "semicolonial" social
structure, although individual burrows are used much of the
time. Their social system is based on a matrilineal kin group in
which the daughters and even granddaughters inherit the
mother's homesite.

## GOLDEN-MANTLED GROUND SQUIRREL
(*Spermophilus lateralis*)

Total length: 9 1/8 to 12 1/8 inches; tail length: 2 1/2 to 4 5/8
inches.

The brilliantly colored golden-mantled ground squirrel is
perhaps the most attractive ground squirrel of all. Its common
name is derived from a deep coppery red area that drapes the
head and shoulders, forming a "golden" mantle. Its back may
be gray, brownish, or buffy; the sides and abdomen are buffy
brown to creamy whitish. Although its short tail is well haired,
it would not be described as bushy. On the sides of its body

there is a characteristic pattern of one broad white stripe bordered on each side by black ones. These attractive animals closely resemble chipmunks, but without the facial stripes. Actually, they are no more closely related to chipmunks than is any other ground squirrel. Males are usually more brightly colored than females. They

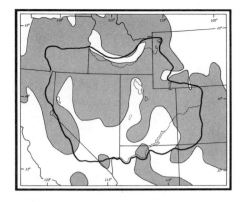

DISTRIBUTION OF GOLDEN-MANTLED GROUND SQUIRREL.

occur in each of the Intermountain states, but not throughout the region due to their habitat requirements. They are broadly distributed throughout the western United States and a small part of Canada along the Alberta-British Columbia border.

These ground squirrels generally inhabit moist conifer forests. They typically reach their highest densities in open forests lacking dense understories. They occur as well in mixed forests, above timberline, and in chapparal country, which is characterized by dense stands of shrubs. They are also found around rockslides and have thus been dubbed "rock squirrels" by some. Technically, however, this common name is reserved for *Spermophilus variegatus*. On my first hike in the Tetons, I was delighted to meet several of these energetic animals in the high-country terrain. They amuse many visitors to our national parks; they are often the seemingly tame ground squirrels around the campsites. Beware, though, for they can inflict painful bites. Most of their diet consists of seeds, nuts, and fruit, but they also eat green vegetation and insects. They use their large internal cheek pouches to transport food to their dens so they can fuel the body during periodic arousals from torpor and emergence from hibernation. Hibernation lasts from October through as late as May; the duration varies with the location. Much of it is under deep snow, and the squirrels put on considerable fat in order to survive the extreme winter conditions. Burrows are not dug deeply, but they can extend for 100 feet. Their openings are usually located by logs, tree roots, bushes, or boul-

GOLDEN-MANTLED GROUND SQUIRREL

ders. Golden-mantled ground squirrels are preyed upon by a variety of hawks and mammalian carnivores.

In the early summer, one litter averaging four to six altricial young is delivered. The young are similar in appearance to the adults, but with softer and silkier hair. Unlike most of their relatives, golden-mantled ground squirrels do not appear to be colonial. Because they tend not to occur in agricultural areas, they are not considered pests, as are so many of their relatives.

## WHITE-TAILED PRAIRIE DOG (*Cynomys leucurus*)

Total length: 13 3/8 to 14 5/8 inches; tail length: 1 5/8 to 2 3/8 inches.

Prairie dogs are familiar to most of us, but probably only a few people know that there are four different species in North America above Mexico. In this region, we are fortunate to have three of them. Of course, these animals are rodents not dogs. Their common name is derived from early settlers' mistaking

WHITE-TAILED PRAIRIE DOG

BEAVER

their chirping bark for that of a dog. As one would expect, white-tailed prairie dogs are distinguished from their relatives by a tail that looks as if it had been dipped in white paint. This tail is also short compared with those of the other prairie dogs; it is only two inches long. Overall though, they are the largest of the prairie dogs in the region. On the upper body, they are a yellowish to pinkish buff, streaked with black. Other identifying features include spots above the eyes and patches on the cheeks, all a dark brown. The nose is yellowish. The bulk of their distribution falls across western Wyoming and northwestern Colorado, spilling over into sections of eastern Utah. Where the Intermountain West extends into these areas, we may find populations of these amusing creatures. Our understanding of their precise occurrence in the southern part of their range is incomplete and hampered by the many attempts to eradicate them.

The prairie dog has long been thought of as a competitor with livestock for food on grasslands. Furthermore, cattle and horses can stumble into burrow entrances, often breaking a leg when doing so. In such instances, the livestock would usually have to be destroyed. For these reasons, prairie dogs have been the subject of intense eradication campaigns by public and private interests. Although too late to save most populations, there now is mounting evidence that they are not as harmful to agricultural enterprises as was once believed. Because they tend to be most numerous on ranges that have already been overgrazed by livestock, they could be a symptom rather than a cause of poor range conditions. In fact, they may actually hasten the recovery of poor rangelands, for they tend to feed on plants typical of a range's early stages. This practice ultimately encourages the growth of climax plant species, those appearing at the end of the successional sequence. It is these climax plants which provide high-quality livestock forage. Recently, there has also been evidence indicating that few livestock are lost due to stumbling into prairie dog holes. What a shame that the settlers did not know that these animals could have been providing benefits for them.

Most of these studies were done on black-tailed prairie dogs (*Cynomys ludovicianus*), a grassland species which does not occur here. The typical habitats of white-tailed prairie dogs include high-elevation sagebrush plains and mountain meadows.

However, one might take into consideration the findings on their black-tailed brethren before efforts are made to persecute them based on time-worn rationales.

These prairie dogs are active only during daylight hours. After emerging from the burrow, they look around for a while before foraging. At first, they stick close to the burrow entrances, which are surrounded by three-foot mounds. As the day progresses, they gain courage and feed farther away from them. In the hot days of summer, they usually retreat to the burrow during midday, going back out to feed only after it cools off in the late afternoon. Major predators are golden eagles, badgers, and rattlesnakes. Predation, however, is not suspected to significantly affect their populations. Emigration usually accounts for some losses, and plague is believed to be the most important factor in their declines. In a Wyoming colony where plague was suspected to be rampant, close to 90 percent of the population was lost between June and September of one year. By late August, most adults have put on enough weight to begin hibernating. Some juveniles do not start their slumber until early November. The emergence date varies with location. Near Laramie, Wyoming, most are aboveground by mid-March.

Following a 30-day gestation, an average of five to six altricial young are born by about the beginning of May. Only one litter is produced annually. A month after birth, the young make their first appearance aboveground. The social system of white-tailed prairie dogs is unlike the oft-described colonial life of their black-tailed cousins. White-tails do not live in densely populated "towns," nor do they engage in elaborate mutual grooming and cooperative burrow-building behaviors. Although individuals in the colony are visually aware of each other and responsive to each other's sounds, the only functioning social unit is that of the nursing mother and her young. And this disappears once the young are weaned. Another difference is that white-tailed prairie dogs usually breed during their first spring, unlike the black-tailed prairie dog, which normally does not reproduce until its second year. There appears to be a relationship between delayed breeding and communal care in mammals, although the reasons for it are not well understood. It may be that the presence of "helpers" in the society somehow permits, in an evolutionary sense, a slowing down of the juvenile's development.

These differences in social behavior have been the subject of some intriguing discussions. It has been suggested that the high degree of coloniality in black-tailed prairie dogs evolved in response to both vegetation characteristics and predation pressures. The short-grass prairies which they commonly inhabit are surely able to support higher populations than the sparsely vegetated, high altitude environments of white-tailed prairie dogs can. Furthermore, only such large populations could provide enough food for the voracious black-footed ferret, an endangered species, which was a specialist predator on black-tailed prairie dogs. The ferret's energy demands require a diet of large numbers of animals of prairie dog size. Thus, coloniality could have evolved in the dense black-tailed prairie dog populations to aid in the detection and warning of ferrets. Further, in areas inhabited by the black-tailed prairie dogs, plant cover is less dense and thus not as protective as it is in white-tailed habitat. Greater visibility to both predators and individuals within the population has been associated with increased sociality throughout the species of ground squirrels.

## UTAH PRAIRIE DOG
(*Cynomys parvidens*)

Total length: 12 to 14 1/8 inches; tail length: 1 1/5 to 2 3/8 inches.

The Utah prairie dog is a multicolored mammal restricted to a colorful part of the Intermountain West: south-central Utah. Its upper body is cinnamon clay to buff, darker on the rump, with each hair composed of many colors. From base to tip, the hairs are black,

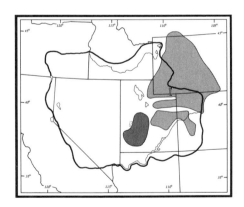

DISTRIBUTIONS OF WHITE-TAILED PRAIRIE DOG (LIGHT) AND UTAH PRAIRIE DOG (DARK).

pale buff, cinnamon, and tipped with either dark brown or pale buff. This harlequin appearance is heightened by a whitish mouth and chin area. The first time I saw these prairie dogs, off of Interstate 15 in southern Utah, I was struck by their chocolate-colored cheek patches, which make them look as if they are wearing rouge. Compared with other prairie dogs, they are small, only about a foot long including the tail. Like white-tailed prairie dogs, they have a white-tipped tail. The two are assumed to be more closely related than either is to any other species. Yet, it is difficult to confuse them due to their differences in body color and facial markings and the fact that their ranges do not overlap. A subspecies of Gunnison's prairie dogs (*C. gunnisoni zuniensis*), referred to as "zunis," resembles Utah prairie dogs in color but lacks their distinctive dark eyebrows. Once again, their ranges do not overlap. Nevertheless, each of these species occurs near at least one of the others, so we need to be aware of their differences to recognize them.

Although Utah prairie dogs were once widely distributed throughout the southern part of the state, now they occur in substantive numbers only in a few places. These include the Awapa Plateau along the East Fork of the Sevier River and in eastern Iron County. Due to extensive poisoning, with disease as an added ingredient, their populations have precipitously declined. Whereas there were about 95,000 in 1920, less than 3,500 remained in 1976. In one year alone, 1970, their numbers dropped from 8,800 to 5,700, a 35 percent decrease. Due to their low numbers and uncertain future, they have been classified as an endangered species by the U.S. Bureau of Sport Fisheries and Wildlife. The northward expansion of their range appears to be inhibited by dense vegetation and possible competition with Uinta ground squirrels.

Diurnal in activity, they primarily feed on grasses and forbs. Burrows resemble those of the white-tailed prairie dog, with tunnels descending from the entrance at about a 45-degree angle. One litter per year is produced in early spring. Litter sizes are comparable to those of the other prairie dogs, averaging about five altricial young. Although Utah prairie dogs are colonial, the large towns typical of black-tailed prairie dogs have not been reported.

GUNNISON'S
PRAIRIE
DOG (*Cynomys
gunnisoni*)

Total length: 12 1/8 to
14 3/4 inches; tail
length: 1 1/2 to 2 5/8
inches.

Although Gunnison's
prairie dog is similar to
the others in our region,
it is sufficiently different
in its markings and

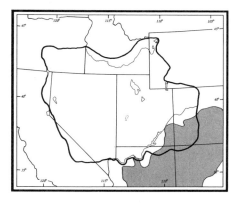

DISTRIBUTION OF GUNNISON'S
PRAIRIE DOG.

coloration to be easily recognized. It is cinnamon buff mixed
with black on top and is streaked toward the rump. The top of
the head, cheeks, and "eyebrows" are clearly darker than the
rest of the body. The subspecies in this area, *C. gunnisoni
zuniensis*, is cinnamon rather than the yellowish buff which is
typical of the subspecies in the eastern part of its range. The tip
of a Gunnison's tail is grayish white. White-tailed prairie dogs
are larger, Utah prairie dogs are slightly smaller, and the ranges
of the three species do not overlap. Other ways of separating
them are discussed in the previous accounts. The distribution of
Gunnison's prairie dog has its center near the Four Corners
region where Utah, Colorado, Arizona, and New Mexico meet;
it is also where this species occurs in the Intermountain West.
Its distribution extends southward into substantial portions of
Arizona and New Mexico.

These prairie dogs are ordinarily found in the open grassy
and brushy areas of high mountain valleys and plateaus from
6,000 to 12,000 feet. In our area, they also occur in lower, dry
habitats commonly associated with white-tailed prairie dogs.
Strictly diurnal, they confine most of their activity to mornings
and afternoons. While feeding, they are constantly on the alert
for predators. Their preferred food is grasses; forbs, shrubs,
and sedges are also taken. Insects are eaten, but constitute a
small part of the diet. Predators, which include badgers, coyotes, rattlesnakes, and birds of prey, probably do not have much
of an impact on their populations. However, diseases, such as

plague, can have drastic effects. In one area of Colorado, plague virtually eliminated them from over 650,000 acres in less than four years. Attempts at eradicating them because of their reputation as agricultural pests also have dramatically influenced their fate. They, too, have been placed on the list of endangered species by the United States government.

Their burrows have been likened more to those of ground squirrels than those of prairie dogs. The mound around the entrance is not modified; rather, dirt is just randomly kicked about. As a protection from flooding, burrow entrances are typically positioned on slopes or small knolls. There is no evidence that they store food in their burrows, as do most ground squirrels. Although it is highly likely that hibernation occurs, little direct evidence for it exists. Whether they become dormant or simply remain inactive, they do so in burrows which can be under several feet of snow. In early spring, often with snow still on the ground, they emerge to the surface.

When they are a year old, females are capable of bearing young. In our area, the altricial pups arrive in late April or early May after a 30-day pregnancy. Average litter size is slightly lower than that of the white-tailed prairie dog, typically between four and five. Only one litter per year is produced. Approximately a month after birth, the pups are aboveground. As soon as they are weaned, the mother abandons them and moves to another burrow. The young then disperse to other empty burrows. This behavior is precisely the opposite of that in most ground squirrels in which the young remain with the mother through the first year and often beyond. The colonies are usually smaller than those of the other species, ranging from 50 to 100 individuals. Denser populations arise in more open habitats. Gunnison's prairie dogs are loosely organized, with a social structure like that of many ground squirrels, despite the differences in pup rearing. Adult males live apart from the females and their young.

## ABERT'S SQUIRREL (*Sciurus aberti*)

Total length: 18 1/4 to 23 inches; tail length: 7 1/4 to 10 inches.

Abert's squirrel is the only large tree squirrel in the Intermountain West. If there had to be just one, we are indeed fortunate that it is this attractive mammal. It has long, broad ears that bear distinctive tufts at their tops. From these, we get another of its names, the tassel-eared squirrel. The remarkable tassels rapidly grow to as much as one and a half inches by late winter, after which they shorten. Ordinarily, the tassel increases the

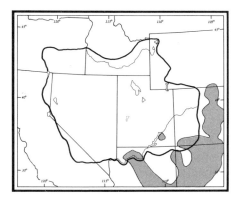

DISTRIBUTION OF ABERT'S SQUIRREL.

length of an ear that is one and three-fourths inches by another three-fourths of an inch. The upper body, including the tail, is a dark, grizzled gray with even darker sides. The hind region is reddish and the underparts are white. The Kaibab squirrel (*S. aberti kaibabensis*), a subspecies of Abert's squirrel, has dark underparts and a beautiful, completely white tail. Previously regarded as a separate species, Kaibab squirrels are found only on the North Rim of the Grand Canyon in Arizona. Abert's squirrel is polymorphic in color, meaning that it exists in several varieties. Individuals are gray, brown, or black. For a tree squirrel, the broad tail is surprisingly short, only about eight inches. In this region, Abert's squirrels are usually rare and found in only a few areas. This is characteristic of their entire distribution, which is discontinuous throughout the Southwest and Mexico. Their occurrence in southwestern Colorado is part of the largest intact area they inhabit. An isolated population of another subspecies, *S. aberti navajo*, was discovered in 1947 in Utah's San Juan County.

Their range is fragmented because Abert's squirrels largely occur from 6,000 to 10,000 feet in ponderosa pine forests, which have a discontinuous distribution in the Southwest. They are highly dependent on this tree for both shelter and food, and might even prevent red squirrels from inhabiting them. Red squirrels are rare in ponderosa pine forests when Abert's is present, but are often found in them when Abert's is not. Nests of pine needles, grass, sticks, and bark are constructed high in a tree's foliage. Most tree parts are eaten, including the inner bark, seeds, terminal buds, and staminate or male flowers. Other foods are fleshy fungi, carrion or dead flesh, bones, and antlers. Although food is not stored in caches, these squirrels bury individual cones in shallow pits. Their feeding seems to be destructive, given that they may remove up to 75 percent of a forest's cone crop in a single year. However, this seldom causes mortality to mature trees. Furthermore, feeding activities knock down twigs and other material from the trees. This is important in the transfer of nutrients, such as carbon and nitrogen, to the forest floor. Strictly diurnal, Abert's squirrels stay out all day, returning to their nests before sunset. They do not hibernate.

During the spring breeding season, a dominant male and several of his subordinates follow a female in heat. This behavior, known as a "mating chase," lasts for about 11 hours and is common in other tree squirrels. After such a long day, one might guess that both sexes would be too tired to breed. But litters, typically of three or four young, are born in April or May following a 40-to-46-day pregnancy. The young are so altricial at birth that membranes still cover the ears and eyes. Their eyes do not open until they are about six weeks old. Although they venture from the nest at this time, they do not descend from the tree for a few more weeks. Weaning occurs at about ten weeks. Second litters may be produced in the southern parts of this squirrel's range.

## RED SQUIRREL or
## CHICKAREE (*Tamiasciurus hudsonicus*)

Total length: 10 5/8 to 15 1/4 inches; tail length: 3 5/8 to 6 1/4 inches.

The red squirrel is the smallest tree squirrel in its range. Although it spends a fair amount of time on the ground, it is a tree squirrel nonetheless. Its name also seems to be a contradiction since its summer pelage is often brownish; some individuals are not even reddish in the winter. Usually, though, the summer coat is rust-red on the back and sides and white on the bottom. A distinctive black band separates the back from the belly. The

pretty tail is reddish
above, gray to yellowish
below, and outlined with
a broad black band
edged with white. In
winter, the hair is simi-
larly colored but has
become longer and
denser. At this time,
there is usually a bright
red stripe from the neck
to the tail, which has
become redder on top.
Other differences in the

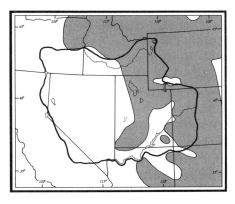

DISTRIBUTION OF RED SQUIRREL OR CHICKAREE.

colder months are that the sides are yellowish gray and the belly
may become grayer. Like those of an Abert's squirrel, the ears
bear tufts, which become apparent in winter. To top off this
fancy look, there is a prominent white eye ring. Red squirrels
have a vast distribution, occurring across the northern part of
the continent from Alaska to Labrador and through the northern tier of the West, Midwest, and Northeast. In the
Intermountain West, they largely reside in the Rocky Mountain
states, inhabiting much of central Utah, western Colorado, and
most of Idaho and Wyoming.

Their preferred habitats are spruce-fir and lodgepole pine
forests in far northern boreal and montane areas. They nest in
any available tree cavities, but more often construct nests of
grass, shredded bark, and twigs close to the trunk. Major foods
are seeds of conifers, such as spruce, pine, and hemlock. Visitors of conifer forests may find evidence of this in the pieces of
cones that are left at feeding stations, which are chiefly tree
stumps, and all over the forest floor. To harvest the seeds, a
squirrel will cut off the cone before the seeds can ripen and
thus disperse. The seed-bearing cones are then cached in heaps
or middens, which often consist of several bushels of seeds.
One midden in western Colorado was 33 feet long and close to
4 feet wide. Especially large middens are probably several
decades old and thus must be the work of several generations of
squirrels. Located on stumps, logs, or in tree hollows, middens
are positioned well within the squirrel's territory. They also are

RED SQUIRREL or CHICKAREE

typically located in moist places, which helps in keeping the cones closed. Smaller caches have even been found in ponds and streams.

When the seeds are cached, mostly in summer and autumn, the squirrels are highly aggressive and chase away intruders of several species, including their own. Undoubtedly, this behavior evolved because the caches are crucial to survival, serving as larders during winter and early spring. Despite a seeming obsession with seeds, these squirrels have eclectic tastes during the warmer months, eating buds, flowers, fruits, inner tree bark, fungi, insects, small mammals, and birds and their eggs. They are diurnal and do not hibernate. Marten are considered to be their chief predator. Others include coyotes, red foxes, lynx, and bobcats. Unlike the situation for most ground squirrels, diseases are not a major mortality factor.

The breeding season is long, lasting from February to September. Males cross through one another's territories as they pursue females in heat. As many as 10 males might move into a female's territory, but only one of them usually establishes dominance and usurps the mating privileges. The altricial young are born after a 31-to-35-day gestation. An average litter has 3 to 5 young, but litters of 10 occur. The mother raises the young by herself on an area which is usually unshared with another female. After about a month, the young's eyes open and it leaves the nest. Development is slow, and weaning is not accomplished until they are about ten weeks of age. Up to two litters per year are produced in some regions, but only one is common in the north. What appears to be a second litter in northern areas is more likely to be one produced by a yearling female. Red squirrels are occasionally hunted and frequently trapped for their attractive fur. Their common name of chickaree is due to the "chr-r-r-, che-e-e-e" chattering sound they make as danger approaches.

## DOUGLAS' SQUIRREL
(*Tamiasciurus douglasii*)

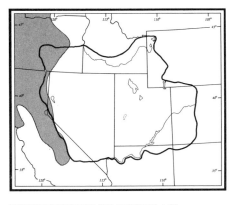

DISTRIBUTION OF DOUGLAS' SQUIRREL.

Total length: 10 5/8 to 14 inches; tail length 3 7/8 to 6 1/8 inches.

In the same genus as the red squirrel, Douglas' squirrel resembles it in many ways. Indeed, the two species are even suspected of interbreeding in the Blue Mountains of northeastern Oregon. If this is so, this squirrel would be classified as a red squirrel, taking the older scientific name. Thus far, though, it is considered a separate species. On the upper body, it is a dark olive brown to brownish gray, grading into rust or chestnut halfway down the back. The distinctive undersurface is gray to orangish washed with black. The winter pelage is grayer overall. In this species, too, the ears develop small tassels in the winter.

Most of the tail is colored like the back with the last third usually blackish. On its bottom, the tail is rusty in the center and bordered by a black band with a whitish edge. This squirrel may be readily told apart from its red relative by its different undersurface shades. Moreover, although their ranges slightly overlap in some places, the two squirrels are not sympatric in the Intermountain West. This squirrel barely occurs in our region, crossing only the extreme northwestern border in California and Oregon. Its distribution is through southwestern British Columbia and the northern Pacific Coast states.

These squirrels are widespread in most of the conifer forests in their range. Large trees with substantial crowns are preferred; areas with heavy shrub understories are avoided. Foods include seeds, new conifer shoots, green vegetation, acorns, nuts, mushrooms, and fruit. Their foraging habit on conifer cones differs from that of the red squirrel. They also cut down cones from limbs in late summer and fall. However, they usually eat the seeds in the trees rather than at stumps. This is likely a difference of degree, not of kind. Because they are smaller than the red squirrel and have a weaker jaw musculature, they are usually found more in areas with smaller cones that are easier to manipulate. They also deposit scales with seeds in piles or middens, and like the red squirrel, defend their food sources. Humans harvest seeds from the middens of both species for the planting of nursery trees. Green cones are stored in moist places, which keeps them tender. Mushrooms, of all things, are cached in tree forks. Predators of this epicure include bobcats, owls, and humans, who consider it a game species. Summer tree nests, which resemble large balls, are composed of mosses, lichens, twigs, and shredded bark. These squirrels do not hibernate, but try to find tree cavities in which they can remain warm in winter. Being diurnal, they have a large repertoire of sounds which makes the forest a noisy place during the day.

Breeding takes place in the early spring, lasting until October. Litters averaging four or five altricial young arrive in May or June following a 36-to-40-day pregnancy. The range of litter sizes is from three to eight. Second litters may occur. Although the young descend from the nests in August, the family remains together for most of the first year. During the breeding season in the Sierra Nevada, males extend their territories into female home ranges. The males exhibit territorial behavior toward one another using vocalizations called "rattle calls." Dominant males act territorially in an area; they are the ones which enjoy the greatest mating success.

## NORTHERN FLYING SQUIRREL (*Glaucomys sabrinus*)

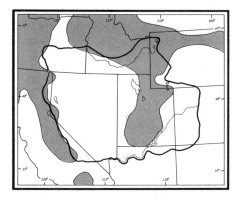

DISTRIBUTION OF NORTHERN FLYING SQUIRREL.

Total length: 10 3/8 to 14 1/2 inches; tail length: 4 1/2 to 7 1/8 inches.

Flying squirrels are mammals whose forelimbs and hind limbs are connected from the wrists to the ankles by loose folds of fully haired skin. Each skin fold, or patagium, is internally supported by a slender cartilaginous rod which is attached to the wrist. The folds are stiffened as they spread their legs, turning them into gliding surfaces. Hence, their name is a misnomer since they actually glide rather than fly. While gliding, they can turn and even change the angle of their descent. Just before stopping, they drop the tail and raise their forequarters. This slackens the flight membranes so that they serve as air brakes, allowing a gentle landing on a tree trunk. To determine if one is present, tap on a tree with a woodpecker hole; it will peer out if at home.

In North America, there are two species: northern and southern flying squirrels. The one inhabiting our region is the larger northern species. On the upper surface, its color ranges from cinnamon to light brown with a darker, even blackish tail. Its belly is creamy white washed with a buffy or yellowish shade. Again, the tail's undersurface is darker. Its head is usually gray to brown with large, dark eyes surrounded by black rings. It is a relatively small mammal. The tail, which accounts for close to half the body length, is flattened from top to bottom and has a rounded tip. These squirrels inhabit the forests of the northern

NORTHERN FLYING SQUIRREL

part of our continent. In the Intermountain West, they occur in several disjunct or separate areas of Utah and Idaho and across northwestern Wyoming.

Their habitat is dominated by mature conifer trees, but they also occur in mixed conifer-deciduous and even purely deciduous forests. In southwestern Utah, they have been found in Engelmann spruce forests from 7,900 to 10,300 feet and along stream bottoms surrounded by cottonwood and white fir. Nests occur inside tree cavities or on limbs, where they are built from twigs, bark, and roots. In winter, most seek refuge in tree cavities, including those abandoned by woodpeckers and red squirrels. Inside, they line their nests with insulative materials, such as finely shredded bark, lichen, moss, feathers, and fur. Foods include acorns, nuts, conifer and hardwood seeds, flowers, insects, and baby birds. They do not store food for the winter. At times, fungi may be an important food. Tree sap, which they increase the flow of by chewing away bark between sapsucker holes, is also favored. Although they are clumsy walkers, much of their foraging is done on the ground.

Avian predators include owls and hawks; a pair of spotted owls can devour about 500 flying squirrels annually. Marten, wolves, foxes, and house cats are among their mammalian foes. The legendary naturalist Ernest Thompson Seton even reported a case of a flying squirrel in the stomach of a trout. Members of this species have a biphasic nocturnal activity pattern; they are active at two separate times during the night: right after dark and just before daylight. Apparently, they do not enter torpor in the winter.

The young arrive in late May or June after a 37-to-42-day gestation. The average size of the litter is from two to four. Second litters are not uncommon. Although the young are extremely altricial, the gliding patagium is already present. At birth, their skin both lacks hair and is transparent. They are able to walk at about 40 days and emerge from the nest at this time. Weaning occurs at two months, but the young remain with their mother for much of the year. Mothers raise their young without any direct assistance from the males.

## POCKET GOPHERS—FAMILY GEOMYIDAE

Pocket gophers are a group of similar animals which are all supremely adapted for a subterranean existence. These adaptations are so comprehensive that the gophers rarely come aboveground. Their name is derived from the large, external, fur-lined cheek pouches, each having an opening independent of the mouth. Within these pouches, they carry food and nesting material to their burrows. Items are squeezed out of the pouches by moving their forepaws forward against them. The pouches are then neatly returned to their original position by special muscles. Interestingly, the name "gopher" is from the French *gaufre*, meaning "honeycomb," in reference to the burrow networks. Some of their other specializations include a thickset body with a short muscular neck, powerful shoulders, reduced ears and eyes, and a nearly naked tail with a sensitive tip that is useful when its owner scurries in reverse. This movement is facilitated by the hair, which is smooth lying either backward or forward. The lips, as is so of other rodents, close behind the incisors, permitting the gopher to move dirt and eat without swallowing soil.

Two types of burrows are constructed. The one near the surface is used to gather food, whereas the deeper one functions as a storage depot, shelter, and nursery. Construction involves cutting through the earth and removing obstacles with the incisors, digging with the crescent-clawed forepaws, and sweeping dirt back under the body with the hind feet. The tunnels are lateral to slightly inclined toward the surface. Soil is deposited in fan-shaped mounds rather than in the rings or volcano-shaped mounds of moles. Gophers can be highly destructive: devouring crops, killing seedlings of fruit and timber trees, and altering the soil so that it is difficult to use farm machinery. Alternately, their burrowing aerates and enriches the soil and makes water more accessible to plants. There are about 40 species in this family; the 6 in this region are all in the genus *Thomomys*.

## NORTHERN POCKET GOPHER (*Thomomys talpoides*)

Total length: 6 1/2 to 9 1/4 inches; tail length: 1 5/8 to 3 inches.

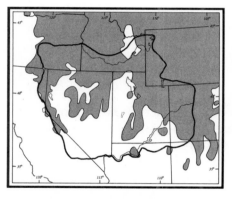

DISTRIBUTION OF NORTHERN POCKET GOPHER.

There are many subspecies of the northern pocket gopher and they vary widely in size and color. Often, they simply match the color of the soil, but most are rich brown or yellowish brown. The feet are whitish, and the top yellowish orange incisors are often tipped with white. There are white markings beneath the chin. The small, rounded ears have large, dark patches behind them, each of which is about three times the size of the ear. Another species here, the mountain pocket gopher, can be distinguished by its long and pointed ears. Northern pocket gophers have a complicated spring molt, with hair replaced from snout to rump in "waves," resulting in a series of bands across their width. They enjoy a wide distribution across the northern portion of the western United States and bordering areas of southern Canada. In the Intermountain West, they are found throughout large portions of most of the states.

Many different environments are inhabited by these gophers, from cultivated fields to mountain meadows. They show preference for deep, soft soils which can be easily worked for burrow excavation. This is important since their tunnels are extensive, ranging up to 500 feet in length. As with most of their relatives, they keep burrow entrances plugged except for an occasional airing on a sunny day. Plugging has several important functions. First of all, it keeps out unwanted guests, particularly those which will eat them. Also, it alerts them to disturbances; a plug is replaced within several hours of its removal. To determine if a burrow is occupied, simply remove a plug and return the next day to see if it is replaced. Finally, plugging helps to stabilize the burrow temperature and moisture level. In some places, the gophers live in an area of elevated ground called a "mima mound," which extends for about 30 feet. These mounds tend to be more productive of food for the gophers than the areas between them.

They are vegetarians, with most of their food, such as the succulent roots of forbs, tubers, and bulbs, coming from their subterranean surroundings. They will eat the leaves and stems of plants close to the burrow, and have a fondness for prickly pear cactus. Major predators are great horned owls, badgers, and coyotes. Other significant mortality factors include poor food availability and extreme weather. Spring flooding can devastate a population. But their swimming ability and the construction of tunnels leading to higher ground enable some to survive. Pocket gophers do not hibernate, but have inactive periods during the winter and summer. In winter, they make tunnels in the snow in which to deposit the dirt excavated from their burrows. When the snow melts, these dirt cylinders, known as "eskers," sink to the soil. They are well-known evidence of the presence of pocket gophers.

From March to mid-June, these solitary creatures tolerate each other just about long enough to mate. The young are born in a grass- or fur-lined nest after an 18-to-20-day gestation. Females possess the remarkable capability of having their pubic bones separate while giving birth, allowing the young to pass through a birth canal otherwise constrained by slender hips. This is also a characteristic of other pocket gophers. From four to seven young are born in the only litter of the year. They are weaned after 40 days and forced to disperse from the nest just two weeks later. However, they do not reach adult size until they are about six months old.

## IDAHO POCKET GOPHER (*Thomomys idahoensis*)

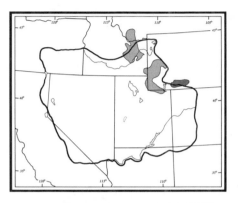

DISTRIBUTIONS OF IDAHO POCKET GOPHER (LIGHT) AND WYOMING POCKET GOPHER (DARK).

Total length: 7 3/8 to 8 9/10 inches.

The Idaho and Wyoming pocket gophers have only recently been classified as distinct species from the northern pocket gopher. Idaho pocket gophers are usually smaller than the northern species. Their yellowish brown or buffy hair is tipped a dark brown. Reddish individuals are rare. Their feet are whitish, and they have dark gray fur around the nose. In southwestern Wyoming and adjacent areas, they are sympatric with a northern pocket gopher subspecies (*T. talpoides bridgerii*). Here, the Idaho pocket gopher favors shallow, stony soils, whereas the other appears more suited to deep soils with fewer rocks. Neither, though, is totally restricted to any one habitat. Areas occupied by Idaho pocket gophers include open sagebrush, grasslands, and mountain meadows. They are found in two locales: southeastern Idaho and southwestern Wyoming.

## WYOMING POCKET GOPHER (*Thomomys clusius*)

Total length: 6 1/3 to 7 1/4 inches.

Wyoming pocket gophers are small, pale rodents which lack the patches behind the ears typical of northern and Idaho pocket gophers. They, especially the young, are distinctly yellow-ish. Surrounding the ear is a fringe of white or whitish hairs. In northern and Idaho pocket gophers, this fringe is dark. Wyoming pocket gophers seem limited to the southern portions of Carbon and Sweetwater counties, Wyoming. Areas from which they have been collected are characterized by well-drained, gravelly soils along either ridgetops or the edges of stream-cut, eroded washes. They are found around stands of greasewood rather than sagebrush.

## MOUNTAIN POCKET GOPHER (*Thomomys monticola*)

Total length: 6 5/8 to 10 3/4 inches; tail length: 1 3/4 to 3 7/8 inches.

Mountain pocket gophers are a relatively large species with a range that overlaps that of both the northern and Botta's pocket gophers. Although they

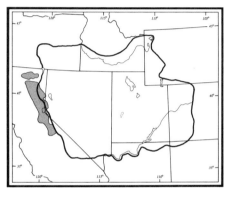

DISTRIBUTION OF MOUNTAIN POCKET GOPHER.

only meet the northern species in a small area of the region and do not overlap Botta's at all here, some tips are provided to distinguish them. One of the best methods is to notice the ears: northern pocket gophers have rounded ears, whereas mountain pocket gophers have longer, pointed ones. Furthermore, mountain pocket gophers are generally reddish brown to black as opposed to yellowish brown to grayish brown. Finally, the large black patches behind the ears are more prominent in mountain pocket gophers, and their lips and snout are dark. Some of the tail, the wrists, and the feet are white. They may be differentiated from Botta's pocket gopher also by the ear region. Botta's pocket gopher's ear is rounded and the patch is about the same size as the ear. Barely an Intermountain species, mountain pocket gophers slip into our region in far west-central Nevada and neighboring California. Almost all of their range is in northeastern California.

Comparatively little is known about their ecology or life history. They are widespread in meadows and rocky slopes in pine, spruce, fir, and hemlock forests above 5,000 feet in the Sierra Nevadas. In all habitats, they prefer the grass-forb stage of forest succession. Their food habits are much like those of other pocket gophers; they eat the roots, tubers, and bulbs in their burrows and the stems and leaves of aboveground forbs and grasses. They can damage young conifers in commercial plantations by feasting upon the roots and seedlings. Active throughout the year, they build nests above the snow in winter. Many invertebrates and some vertebrates inhabit their burrows, which are from 20 to 120 feet long. Mating may occur from May through September, typically resulting in an average of three to four altricial young in July and August. Litter sizes range from two to eight and only one litter is produced a year.

## BOTTA'S POCKET GOPHER (*Thomomys bottae*)

Total length: 6 5/8 to 10 3/4 inches; tail length: 1 3/4 to 3 3/4 inches.

Botta's pocket gopher is another species containing many subspecies; several hundred are recognized. Its classification is problematic. Hall referred to it as the southern pocket gopher (*Thomomys umbrinus*) in his last edition of *The Mammals of North America*. However, I call this mammal *Thomomys bottae*, following the more accepted usage. This may seem overly technical, but it is important to understand which one is being discussed, particularly when several works refer to an animal by different names. Botta's pocket gophers are dark brown, buffy, or grayish above, and purplish on the sides. The belly is slightly lighter. The tail is tan to grayish. As in other pocket gophers, the ear area is used for identification. The ears are small and rounded, with a similarly sized patch behind them. The ear and patch are each less than three-eighths of an inch. Noting these traits may be useful, but it can still be difficult to distinguish these gophers. They range throughout the southwestern United States and Mexico. Common in the southern Intermountain West, they inhabit most of Nevada and Utah.

As with their northern relatives, Botta's pocket gophers occur in a wide range of habitats. They may live in mountain

BOTTA'S POCKET GOPHER

meadows, but are likely to be found in areas with sandy soil, including deserts. The type of soil, however, does not determine their presence. These gophers are found in various areas as long as the soil can support the burrow and provide ample forage. Information suggests that they are similar to northern pocket gophers in regards to their ecology, reproduction, and behavior. In most areas, they prefer the grass-forb stage of plant succession. They have a taste for prickly pear cactus and, unfortunately, crops and the roots of fruit and timber trees. Due to their destructive potential, pocket gophers have been the subject of intensive research. Weasels are a significant predator in some Nevada locations.

The average litter size in a northern Arizona population was about three. From a study made of a central California group, it was learned that females begin to breed within their first three months. Males, however, are not sexually mature until the following season, at six to nine months of age. The notion that the males continue to grow throughout their lives was recently questioned by J. C. Daly and J. L. Patton, the biologists in the California study. They discovered that heavier adult males were not necessarily older than lighter ones. One difference between Botta's pocket gopher and the others in our region is that, in parts of Nevada and Texas, it breeds throughout the year. This could imply a greater tolerance among individuals and would thus affect social behavior. Pocket gophers, particularly this species, are considered to be polygynous, with most populations consisting of more adult females than males. As is typical of polygynous species, there is a relatively high variability in male reproductive success; only a few probably do most of the breeding.

## TOWNSEND'S POCKET GOPHER (*Thomomys townsendii*)

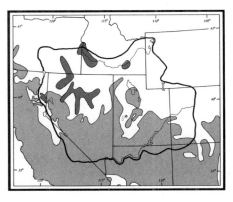

DISTRIBUTIONS OF BOTTA'S POCKET GOPHER (LIGHT) AND TOWNSEND'S POCKET GOPHER (DARK).

Total length: 9 to 13 3/8 inches; tail length: 2 1/16 to 4 7/16 inches.

Townsend's pocket gopher is closely related to Botta's pocket gopher. In fact, the two have even been found to reproduce. Yet, this occurs so rarely that their designation as separate species is considered to be appropriate. Where Townsend's pocket gophers occur, they are usually the largest pocket gopher present. They typically vary in color from a light cinnamon buff to a dark brown; most are grayish brown. Their bottoms are a lighter shade of the upper body. Typically, they have white on the upper feet, tail, and chin. In addition, the patches behind the ears are usually a sooty black.

These gophers occupy several widely separated areas of the Great Basin in southern Idaho, northeastern California, north-central Nevada, and southeastern Oregon. Their distribution pattern suggests that they once had a more continuous range. Apparently, they are more limited than the other gophers in the region by soil conditions; they exhibit a strong preference for deep and moist soils, such as those around lakes and river bottomlands. The historical decrease in the area's precipitation and the great reduction in the size of its lakes have thus been implicated as causes of their range fragmentation.

## POCKET MICE, KANGAROO MICE, AND KANGAROO RATS – FAMILY HETEROMYIDAE

The heteromyids, which include pocket mice, kangaroo mice, and kangaroo rats, are more closely related to the geomyids than to the true mice and rats. This relationship is revealed by members of both groups possessing external cheek pouches and by many shared skeletal characteristics. In fact, *Perognathus*, the genus name of the pocket mice, means "pouch-jawed." Food is collected in and removed from these pouches similarly in each group. Many species in this family are representative of the region and all occur west of the Mississippi River. They are often difficult to tell apart. All are nocturnal, burrowing forms that rely on seeds and some green vegetation. Most live in arid areas and can exist without drinking water; they are the dominant rodent group in most of the deserts on this continent. Like the geomyids, they construct complex burrows with separate chambers for nesting, sleeping, rearing of the young, and food storage. Frequently, the stored seeds are neatly sorted according to species. Heteromyids also plug their burrows, creating a safer, more stable environment. Their enemies include rattlesnakes, hawks, coyotes, foxes, bobcats, weasels, badgers, and skunks.

There is a trend in this family, beginning with the pocket mice and culminating with the kangaroo rats, toward a better jumping ability and a reliance on bipedal locomotion. Kangaroo rats, many of which have beautiful markings, are differentiated from the others by their long hind legs and large, powerful hind feet. When in danger, they use them to make enormous jumps, up to nine feet long in the larger species. Since they rarely venture far from their burrows, they can return to safety in but a few leaps. Pocket mice also have large hind feet although their jumps are not as spectacular. All 75 species in this family are from the Western Hemisphere; 16 occur in the Intermountain West.

## OLIVE-BACKED POCKET MOUSE
### (*Perognathus fasciatus*)

Total length: 4 1/2 to 5 5/8 inches; tail length: 2 1/4 to 2 5/8 inches.

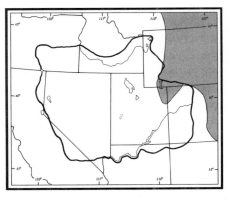

DISTRIBUTION OF OLIVE-BACKED POCKET MOUSE.

The olive-backed pocket mouse is one of several soft-furred pocket mice. As the name suggests, it is a grizzled olive-gray above, particularly along the top, where it is marked by a prominent olive and black band. It is buffy to pure white below. On the side, there is a yellowish buff lateral line; its specific epithet, *fasciatus*, means "banded" and refers to it. Behind the ear is a buffy patch which is smaller than the ear itself. The only similar species in the region, the Great Basin pocket mouse, is much larger. Their ranges barely overlap only in northeastern Utah. Olive-backed pocket mice also resemble the smaller silky and plains pocket mice, but are not sympatric with them in this region. The olive-backed's occurrence in northeastern Utah and neighboring Colorado and Wyoming is the only part of its distribution in the Intermountain West. Most of its range extends northeast of the region into the Plains states.

These mice are inhabitants of open country, often on sandy soil with either moderate or sparse vegetation. They are also found at the edge of ponderosa pine forests in patches of yucca and cacti and on shortgrass prairies. In sparsely vegetated areas, they manage to subsist on the seeds of such plants as foxtail grass, needlegrass, Russian thistle, and tumbleweed. Insects are also eaten, although seeds are their items of choice. In most areas, there are probably too few of these pocket mice for them to serve as a staple food source for predators. They are active burrowers, and one of their telltale signs is a burrow opening surrounded by a small sandpile, typically under a plant. Tunnel systems can cover areas of about 20 feet. Burrows containing storage chambers are some 12 to 15 inches underground. During the extreme parts of the summer and winter, the mice remain inactive in chambers as much as six feet below the surface. This inactivity is not regarded as true hibernation.

Pregnancy lasts about four weeks, producing an average litter of five altricial young. It seems likely that the females have two litters per season, with a breeding lull in June. Adults are solitary most of the year.

PLAINS POCKET MOUSE (*Perognathus flavescens*)

Total length: 4 3/8 to 5 1/8 inches; tail length: 1 7/8 to 2 3/8 inches.

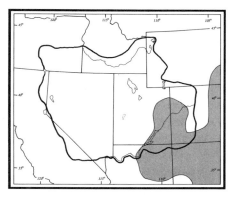

DISTRIBUTION OF PLAINS POCKET MOUSE.

Another soft-furred species, the plains pocket mouse is pale grayish to yellowish buff overlaid with dark or black hairs above. It is white below. Unlike the olive-backed and silky pocket mice, there is either a tiny yellow buff patch behind the ear or none. Many have a buffy lateral line, but it is much less distinct than that of the similar-sized olive-backed pocket mouse. Plains pocket mice are essentially mammals of the Central Plains, ranging from northern Mexico to east-central North Dakota and bordering Minnesota. In the Intermountain West, they are found in most of eastern Utah and adjacent western Colorado and in portions of the states south of this area.

Their habitats are places with sandy soils covered with grasses either alone or mixed with sagebrush and yucca. In the Plains states, they are also found in grainfields. Little is known about their natural history, but it is believed to be similar to that of the other pocket mice. They are active at night. Seeds are their most common food item and insects are also taken. They plug most of their burrow entrances but leave some of the less conspicuous ones open. Owls can be significant predators in some areas. In one Nebraska study, they constituted 2.7 percent of the diet of Great Horned owls.

Reproduction occurs from April to August. Litter sizes range from two to five young, with an average of four. Females probably have two litters a year.

## GREAT BASIN POCKET MOUSE
(*Perognathus parvus*)

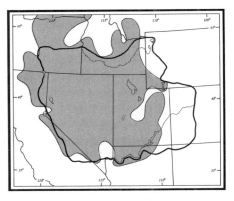

DISTRIBUTION OF GREAT BASIN POCKET MOUSE.

Total length: 5 3/4 to 7 3/4 inches; tail length: 3 to 4 1/4 inches.

The Great Basin pocket mouse is a moderately sized species that occurs over a wide area. It is soft-furred, pinkish, yellowish, or even olive-buff, washed with brown or black above. The belly is white or buff. It has tiny, round ears and a buff or olive-green lateral line which is indistinct in most individuals. The tail is unique; it is long—dark above and whitish below—and has a slight tuft of hairs toward the tip. It may be separated from similar species in the region as follows: the little pocket mouse is smaller, and the long-tailed pocket mouse has a tufted tail which is much more heavily crested. It is truly a mammal of the Intermountain West. The borders of its distribution are similar to those of the region itself. It occurs on some of the islands of the Great Salt Lake, where populations have the opportunity to exchange individuals with mainland groups across sandbars when the lake level recedes. It ranges north from the Intermountain area up through Washington into a small section of British Columbia.

Great Basin pocket mice inhabit arid, sparsely vegetated grassy plains and brushy saltbush and greasewood flats. Often, they occur on the talus slopes of mountains; they may be locally abundant in rocky areas far from easily accessible soil. In

GREAT BASIN POCKET MOUSE

Nevada, they have been found among scattered stands of juniper and pinyon pine. They appear to occur closer to streams than do other pocket mice in this state. Active at night, they feed on a variety of insects and the seeds from such plants as Russian thistle, wild mustard, sunflowers, and bitterbrush. Much of the food is stored in specific burrow chambers. Occasionally, they are locally abundant and create problems for farmers and ranchers. But most of their habitat is unsuitable for agriculture. Predators include snakes, owls, hawks, weasels, skunks, and badgers. One of their signs is packed piles of soil near the burrow entrances, often located at the base of a sagebrush plant. In Washington, burrows are usually less than four feet long, branching from two to four times, a description that may be valid in this region as well. This is one pocket mouse for which hibernation has been documented. These creatures are inactive from about October through April, remaining in a nest within a chamber three to six feet deep.

Mating takes place in April following emergence from hibernation. After about a 24-day pregnancy, a litter of two to eight young arrives in May. The mean litter size is about five; a second litter is commonly produced in August.

SILKY POCKET
MOUSE (*Perognathus
flavus*)

Total length: 3 7/8 to
4 3/4 inches; tail length:
1 3/4 to 2 3/8 inches.

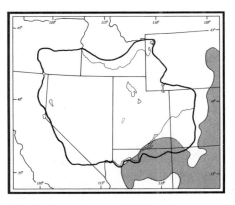

DISTRIBUTION OF SILKY POCKET MOUSE.

As suggested by the name, the small, silky pocket mouse is another of the soft-furred species. In its case, though, this term takes on special meaning; the hair is extremely soft and silky. It is pale reddish to yellowish buff above, interspersed with much black in northern populations, and it has white undersides. There is a distinctive large yellow patch behind the ear and frequently a white spot below it. Although there is a lateral stripe, it is usually inconspicuous. Similar species are distinguished as follows: the plains pocket mouse lacks the ear patch; little pocket mice, ironically, are larger. The tail is usually shorter that the head and body, which is another diagnostic trait. On the average, these mice are the smallest member of their genus. They have a large distribution through the south-central portion of the United States and northern Mexico. In the Intermountain West, however, they occur only in southeastern Utah and the adjacent areas of the Four Corners region.

They inhabit semidesert grasslands and, occasionally, areas with rocky soils. Little is known about their natural history in this region. In eastern Wyoming, they are found on loamy or moistened claylike soils occupied by such grasses as grama and needlegrass. Neighboring populations of the plains pocket mouse are more prevalent in shrub communities. Around the Grand Canyon, silky pocket mice prefer open deserts with sparse vegetation. In Colorado, their burrows have been found beneath yucca, prickly pear cactus, and low shrubs. Their diet is composed almost entirely of seeds, in contrast to many of the other pocket mice which supplement their diet with insects.

Knowledge about their reproduction is scanty. One or two litters of two to six young appear to be the norm; an average litter has four young. Gestation lasts approximately four weeks. When the altricial young first put on hair, the coat is gray and remarkably thin. It is molted off by the time they attain sexual maturity.

## LITTLE POCKET MOUSE (*Perognathus longimembris*)

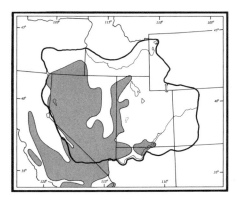

DISTRIBUTION OF LITTLE POCKET MOUSE.

Total length: 4 1/4 to 5 7/8 inches; tail length: 2 1/8 to 3 3/8 inches.

Little pocket mice are soft-furred rodents that are pinkish yellow to buff, with dark hairs interspersed, on the upper body. Coloration is highly variable, often approximating that of the local soil. Undersurface color also varies; it is either buff, brownish, or white. Distinguishing markings are the two small whitish patches at the base of each ear. The tail is typically a uniform light brownish, but this is not always the case. Other similar species sympatric with little pocket mice in our region are differentiated as follows: the long-tailed and Great Basin pocket mice are larger, and the latter is dark olive-gray. The silky pocket mouse is usually smaller. Their distributions barely overlap. In Utah, little pocket mice are the palest member of the genus. In Nevada, they are the smallest. Naturally, though, size is not always a reliable identification aid since individuals vary considerably in this regard. Their distribution is largely within the Intermountain West, specifically the western two-thirds of Nevada and around the western and southern boundaries of Utah. In addition, they inhabit most of southern California.

A characteristic habitat of this species is a desert or valley slope which has gravelly soils underlying a sandy surface. Such areas support widely spaced, low-growing shrubs, such as sagebrush and creosote. Little pocket mice can be the most abundant mammal in these places, reaching up to 400 per acre in parts of Nevada. In the far southeastern Sierra Nevadas, they occur in open grasslands and in forest clearings bordering the Mojave Desert. Their diet is similar to that of other pocket mice, largely consisting of the seeds of annual or perennial grasses and forbs. Some food is stored in the burrow for later use. They have the uncanny ability to become dormant for a few nights when food is scarce. In the laboratory, they become torpid, rather than starve, if food is withheld for over 24 hours. In this way, energy is conserved because their metabolic rate is much lower while in torpor. Predators include those of their relatives; but in Nevada, a relatively uncommon one, the kit fox, is another enemy. They are suspected of hibernating for fairly lengthy periods where winters are rough. In parts of California, they are inactive from October through January. The timing of dormancy, however, is unpredictable, as indicated by their ability to slip into it so easily during harsh periods. Excluding bats, the little pocket mouse is the smallest mammal known to hibernate.

Breeding occurs from April through September, resulting in an average litter of four or five young. The range of litter sizes is from three to seven and there is a likelihood of two litters per year. Gestation lasts for about 23 days. There is a record of one individual living for over seven years in captivity.

## LONG-TAILED POCKET MOUSE
(*Perognathus formosus*)

Total length: 6 3/4 to 8 1/4 inches; tail length: 3 3/8 to 4 3/4 inches.

The long-tailed pocket mouse clearly stands out from its relatives in the region. It is easily identified by a long, approximately four-inch tail, which is

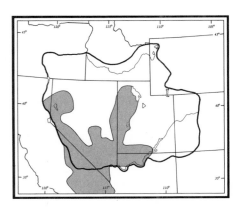

DISTRIBUTION OF LONG-TAILED POCKET MOUSE.

grayish above and whitish below, with a distinct crest of dark tufted hairs over the last third. In this region, the Great Basin pocket mouse is similar, but its tail is only slightly crested. The little pocket mouse is yellowish and its tail is not crested. Long-tailed pocket mice have the largest hind feet of any of the "soft-furred" species, with a length of over three-quarters of an inch. They also have long ears, at the front of which are lengthy hairs that nearly reach across them. Gray or brown above, they have a white belly frosted with yellow. Their color may match that of the local soil. Their distribution in the Intermountain West is similar to that of the little pocket mouse, covering southern Nevada and Utah's western and southern borders. They extend south into Baja California.

Areas inhabited by this species include rocky or gravelly soils along slopes and in desert canyons up to 8,000 feet. In Nevada, a tendency to select stony ground is most evident in the north. Occasionally, long-tailed pocket mice occur along rivers, on hard-packed sandy surfaces, and in open mesquite-juniper communities. They may be locally abundant; in black sage communities in the ancient Lake Bonneville basin, they can account for over 20 percent of the entire mammalian population. Their presence is revealed by small piles of dirt or sand at rock bases. Undoubtedly, they are seed eaters with a natural history much like that of their relatives. Like the little pocket mouse, they become torpid when temperatures are either too high or too low for them. They also share the kit fox as a predator.

Breeding lasts from at least May to July. Litters range in size from four to six young, with an average of five.

## DESERT POCKET MOUSE
(*Perognathus penicillatus*)

Total length: 6 3/8 to 8 1/2 inches; tail length: 3 1/4 to 5 1/8 inches.

The desert pocket mouse is one of two rough-haired pocket mice in the region; the rock pocket mouse is the other. Its pale yellowish brown to yellowish gray upper body is interspersed with black hairs. Both the belly and bottom of the tail are white. The long tail is over half the total length and its end possesses a crest of tufted hairs. Unlike some other rough-haired species, desert pocket mice lack spines on their rump. Some individuals have inconspicuous bristles, but these should not be confused with the heavier spines. These mice occur only in the extreme southwestern corner of the Intermountain West, mostly in the southern tip of Nevada, where they are the largest

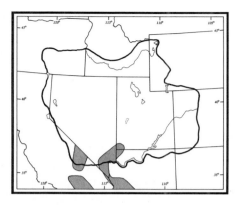

DISTRIBUTION OF DESERT POCKET MOUSE.

pocket mouse. They have a wide distribution through the southwestern United States and north-central Mexico.

They occur among cacti and mesquite on the sandy desert floor. In these places, they are often found along streambeds or washes. Active at night, they feed on the seeds of grasses, broomweed, mesquite, and creosote bush. As with other pocket mice, they store seeds in their burrows.

After a pregnancy of about 26 days, from two to five young are born. An average litter has four young, produced between May and September.

## ROCK POCKET MOUSE (*Perognathus intermedius*)

Total length: 6 to 7 1/8 inches; tail length: 3 1/4 to 4 1/8 inches.

The rough-haired rock pocket mouse differs from all other related species in the region by having weak, spinelike hairs that project beyond the coat

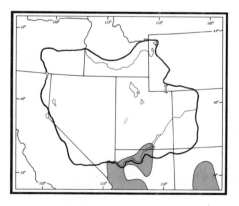

DISTRIBUTION OF ROCK POCKET MOUSE.

on its rump. Usually, it is yellowish gray slightly mixed with black above, but is almost totally black where it occurs on lava flows. On the undersurface, it is white. The long tail is bicolored, gray above and white below. At its end, the tail is crested with a tuft of hairs. A rodent of the deep Southwest, it enters the Intermountain West only at the central portion of Utah's southern border.

Rock pocket mice occur in rocky areas and lava flows in sparsely vegetated desert habitats. In the Grand Canyon, they prefer steep rocky slopes. One of their signs is a small burrow, located under rocks, with tiny trails leading from it. Their burrows are highly insulative from the desert heat. In the Grand Canyon area, the temperature in one burrow, a foot beneath the surface, was 82°F at 9 a.m. following a day when the ground-level temperature was a sizzling 144°F. Nocturnal, they feed on the seeds of weeds and other desert plants. Their predators include owls, snakes, and carnivorous mammals, such as the ringtail.

From three to six young are born in either May or June. The average litter size is four and a half. By mid-July, the half-grown young are weaned. It is not known if there are second litters.

## DARK KANGAROO MOUSE
(*Microdipodops megacephalus*)

Total length: 5 3/4 to 7 inches; tail length: 2 7/8 to 3 7/8 inches.

The kangaroo mice are, in a sense, intermediate between pocket mice and kangaroo rats. Like species in the latter group, they have long

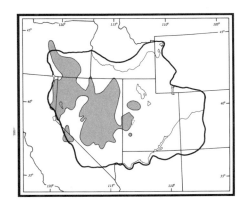

DISTRIBUTION OF DARK KANGAROO MOUSE.

hind legs modified for jumping. However, their short-haired tails are much different from those in either group by being broadest in the middle. It has been speculated that this thickening is due to the tail's functioning as a balancing device while they hop about on their hind legs. Another notion is that the swelling, which contains large fat cells, serves as an energy source during torpor. The tail is darker toward the rear and lacks the terminal tuft characteristic of kangaroo rats. A kangaroo mouse's tail averages slightly longer than its total body length. One last note-worthy characteristic is that the soles of the hind feet are densely covered with long hair. The dark and the pale kangaroo mice are the only members of this genus; both occur in the Intermountain West. In his book *Mammals of Nevada*, E. R. Hall provided an account of the ecological factors involved in the speciation of these two mammals.

Dark kangaroo mice are either brownish, dark grayish, or blackish above with hairs that are gray at the base. Their belly hairs are lead-colored and have white tips. The tail is usually darker toward the back with a blackish tip. No other species closely resembles them; the pale kangaroo mouse, discussed next, has a much lighter coloration; the Great Basin pocket mouse lacks the swollen tail. A subspecies, *M. megacephalus leucotis*, found in the basin of Pleistocene Lake Bonneville in western Utah, has relatively lighter upper parts, extensive white areas atop the head, and a tail lacking the dark tip; it might be mistaken for the pale species. However, pale kangaroo mice do not occur in this particular area, so the two should not be con-fused. Dark kangaroo mice are essentially restricted to the Intermountain West, with most of their distribution in Nevada and southeastern Oregon.

They live in the Upper Sonoran sagebrush desert, where they are associated with sage, shadscale, and fine, gravelly soils from 3,900 to about 8,000 feet. Sand dunes are also occupied. In their preferred habitat, they may be locally abundant. They dig unbranched burrows from two to four feet long and one foot deep in which they sequester seeds. Individuals defend small ter-ritories around their burrows but have considerably larger home ranges. Those of the males are about 8,000 square yards; the females' are approximately 4,600 square yards. They are noctur-nal, with most activity occurring within the first two hours after sunset. Although the reason is not known, they are particularly active under partly cloudy skies. In southeastern Oregon, they prefer the black seeds of desert star plants. Other seeds and insects are also eaten, especially during summer. Predators include owls, foxes, badgers, and weasels. Although kangaroo mice can walk on all fours, they more commonly hop about on their hind limbs. They assume an upright posture when defending nest areas. One may determine their presence by their almost round footprints, with each pair of feet leaving side-by-side impressions. They are suspected of hibernating, although firm evidence for this is lacking.

Pregnant individuals have been found from the end of April through September; most young are born in May and June. Average litter size is about four young; the range is two to seven. If fall and winter precipitation levels are low, resulting in poor germination of winter annuals, reproduction declines.

## PALE KANGAROO MOUSE (*Microdipodops pallidus*)

Total length: 5 7/8 to 6 3/4 inches; tail length: 2 7/8 to 3 3/4 inches.

The pale kangaroo mouse is so similar to the dark kangaroo mouse that it is suspected they diverged from one another fairly

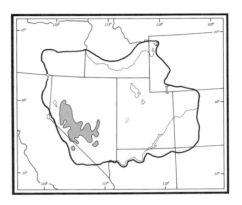

DISTRIBUTION OF PALE KANGAROO MOUSE.

recently. It is slightly smaller than its relative and is easily distinguished by its coloration; it is pale pinkish cinnamon above and lightly marked with buff or a blackish wash. On the belly, the underside of the tail, as well as the feet and legs, the hairs are white from tip to base. There is a pure white patch behind each ear. Its tail lacks a tuft and any distinct markings, such as the black tip of the dark kangaroo mouse's. Its hind foot is a little more than an inch in length, slightly longer than that of the dark kangaroo mouse. The pale kangaroo mouse occurs in south-central Nevada and a small area of eastern California; its entire distribution lies within the Intermountain West.

This species is associated with the Upper Sonoran sagebrush desert from 3,900 to 5,700 feet. Pale kangaroo mice were thought to be restricted to scattered brush habitats on fine, wind-blown sand, but they also can occur on gravelly soil. They are abundant in the lower parts of valleys where fine sand tends to accumulate. Desert kangaroo rats and Merriam's kangaroo rats are often found in the same habitat. The kangaroo mice are nocturnal and most active shortly after sundown. Although they largely subsist on seeds, insects are taken. As with the other heteromyids, they do not rely on free water. Burrows are remarkably similar to those of their dark relative: two to four feet long and one foot under the soil. Apparently, they are capable of torpor and perhaps even hibernation since the former state can be induced by reducing temperature and food intake. Nevertheless, they are active on cold nights. To move around, they rely mostly on a ricochetal or hopping movement employing all four legs. A bipedal jump is occasionally employed as well.

Pregnant individuals are found from the end of March through September. Litters range from two to six young, with an average size of four.

## ORD'S KANGAROO RAT (*Dipodomys ordii*)

Total length: 8 1/8 to 11 1/8 inches; tail length: 3 7/8 to 6 3/8 inches.

Kangaroo rats are truly striking animals. They have a sleek, silky fur which is often exquisitely marked. Most have a narrow white stripe running across the thigh that

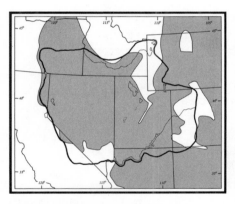

DISTRIBUTION OF ORD'S KANGAROO RAT.

joins the white underside of the tail, thus creating an isolated patch of darker hair on each hind leg. Their facial markings also result in appealing combinations of black and white on the light brown fur. As mentioned in the introduction to this family, their name is derived from the large, powerful hind limbs that can produce spectacular leaps. In the Intermountain West, we are indeed fortunate to have six different kangaroo rat species.

Ord's kangaroo rat is deep yellowish buff with a blackish wash above and white below. There are distinct white spots at the base of the ears and above the eyes. Some kangaroo rats have four toes per foot and others have five; Ord's kangaroo rat belongs to the latter category. Perhaps its most distinguishing external feature is the striping pattern on the tail. On kangaroo rats, there are four tail stripes: a dark stripe on top, one on the bottom, and a white stripe on each side. In Ord's kangaroo rat, the white stripes are typically narrower than the dark ones. Furthermore, the bottom dark stripe tapers to a point near the tip of the tail. Usually, the end of the long, bushy-tipped tail is not white. The lower incisors are rounded on top. In this region, there are two other five-toed kangaroo rats. The Panamint kangaroo rat, which overlaps Ord's only in extreme western Nevada, is larger and its tail and hind feet are longer. Chisel-toothed kangaroo rats, sympatric with Ord's across much of the region, are distinguished by the flat edge of their lower incisors. Ord's is typically lighter colored than either of these other species. Clearly, it is not that simple to distinguish live animals by counting toes and assessing teeth. But with repeated observations and attention to ranges and habitats, it becomes easier to recognize them. Ord's kangaroo rat has the widest range of any member of the genus, occurring from southern Canada to north-central Mexico over most of the western United States. It is absent from this region in but a few isolated areas.

Ord's kangaroo rats commonly inhabit areas with sandy soils. In Nevada, most occur in the Upper Sonoran Desert from 3,900 to 7,000 feet, although some have recently been discovered in greasewood and big sagebrush-shadscale communities in the northeastern part of the state. No one vegetation type is critical to their occurrence; they occupy various grasslands and shrublands as long as the soil is suitable. Sandy habitats permit dust bathing, which keeps their oily fur from becoming matted. During this behavior, they dive into the sand, writhe about with forefeet held to the chest, pushing along with their hind feet. These nocturnal rodents are largely granivores or seed eaters. In Idaho, they eat seeds of shadscale, lupine, grasses, prickly pear, and Russian thistle. Seeds are gathered by sifting the sand with their forepaws. They then stuff them into their cheek pouches and carry them to the burrow. The seeds are husked before being eaten. In some locations, almost 20 percent of the spring diet consists of insects, such as carabid beetles, moths, and butterflies. As with other heteromyids, they manufacture their own water by metabolic processes, such as the burning of fat. Predators include owls, badgers, coyotes, and snakes. By jumping erratically, flashing their white rump marks, and even kicking sand in a snake's face, they manage to foil some predation attempts. In warmer locales, they are active throughout the year.

The burrows of this species may be rather complex; they usually open at the bottom of a shrub or clump of grass or in a cut in the landscape. Although these kangaroo rats cannot dig as well as a pocket gopher, they create burrows similarly, using their forepaws to pile sand beneath the body and then move it back with the hind feet. In their burrows, they build nests from plant material that they shred by grasping an end of it with their incisors while jerking the head. They can walk on all fours, but their basic style of locomotion is a bipedal hop that produces leaps about the length of their bodies. Efficient and versatile in their bipedality, they also can walk on two legs and change directions in midair during big jumps. In all types of movement, the tail functions as a balancing device. If falling, they flail it about in order to right themselves.

As with many aspects of their life, reproduction is highly variable over their range. In northeastern Colorado, the breeding season probably lasts from February through August. In Utah, there are two distinct breeding periods, one from January to March and another from late August to October. Breeding occurs later in the year farther to the south. After a lengthy courtship, a successful mating results in a 29- or 30-day pregnancy. Nests for the young are built just before the birth of an average of three altricial young. Litter sizes range from two to five. Their extreme immaturity at birth is exemplified by a lack of cheek pouches. Adult size is attained at five to six weeks, and they can reproduce in their first year. Ord's kangaroo rats are solitary, and individuals can be highly antagonistic toward one another. Their fighting involves pushing, clawing, shoulder butting, and much kicking with those powerful hind limbs. It appears that they resemble kangaroos in more ways than one.

## CHISEL-TOOTHED KANGAROO RAT
### (*Dipodomys microps*)

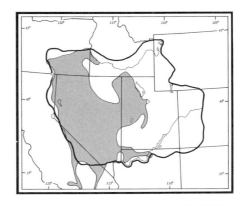

DISTRIBUTION OF CHISEL-TOOTHED KANGAROO RAT.

Total length: 9 5/8 to 11 3/4 inches; tail length: 5 3/8 to 6 7/8 inches.

The chisel-toothed kangaroo rat is a five-toed species that could be easily identified if it would only open its mouth. This is because its most distinguishing trait is the flat front surface of its lower incisors, which makes them resemble chisels. Both five-toed species that it is sympatric with, the Panamint and Ord's kangaroo rats, have lower incisors which are rounded in front. Pinkish buff to dusky, mixed with black above, chisel-toothed kangaroo rats are whitish on the belly. They are slightly darker than average for this genus. As in Ord's kangaroo rat, the white side stripes on the tail are narrower than the dark ones. But the chisel-toothed's bottom tail stripe does not taper toward its tip. The ears are white on the outside with a brownish black front margin. White spots are found both above the eyes and behind the ears. Chisel-toothed kangaroo rats are slightly larger than Ord's and their tail has a smaller brushy tip. Where the two species occur together, the Panamint kangaroo rat has a larger hind foot, usually at least one and three-fourths inches long. Chisel-toothed kangaroo rats are almost entirely restricted to the Intermountain West, particularly Nevada. Their distribution extends slightly out of the area into southern California.

They inhabit sagebrush and shadscale scrub communities; they are rarely found in pinyon-juniper clearings. In Nevada, over 90 percent of the individuals are at elevations of 3,500 to 6,500 feet. Panamint kangaroo rats are usually at higher altitudes. It is likely that the chisel-toothed's natural history is similar to that of Ord's kangaroo rat, given that these animals are close relatives with corresponding life-styles. In contrast to that of most kangaroo rats, however, the chisel-toothed's diet consists largely of leaves rather than seeds. Burrow entrances are along banks and other raised areas. In far southwestern Utah, the mounds are built at the bases of blackbrush and creosote bushes that are about a foot high and several feet across. The chisel-toothed occupants keep the vegetation surrounding these mounds closely trimmed; they also eat the leaves and new shoots of nearby bushes.

Although their breeding habits are not well documented, they also are probably similar to those of Ord's. In a Nevada study, the range of litter sizes was 1 to 4 young, with an average of 2.3. To attract a female's attention, a male drums on the sand with its hind foot. Males compete for females, fighting and growling as they roll in the sand with one another.

## PANAMINT KANGAROO RAT
(*Dipodomys panamintinus*)

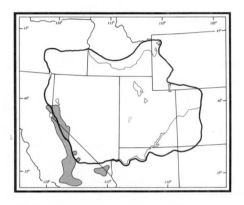

DISTRIBUTION OF PANAMINT KANGAROO RAT.

Total length: 11 1/4 to 13 1/8 inches; tail length: 6 1/8 to 8 inches.

The Panamint kangaroo rat is another attractive rodent of the western United States. On the upper body, it is dark brownish gray with cinnamon sides, and the belly is white. The dark bottom tail stripe tapers to a point, as is true of Ord's kangaroo rat. Like Ord's and chisel-toothed kangaroo rats, Panamints are five-toed. But unlike their chisel-toothed relative, their lower incisors are rounded in front, not flat. Their cheek patches are lightly shaded, but may be hidden by dusky-colored whisker patches; there is a large white spot behind each of the small ears. They are a fairly large kangaroo rat and have a pro-portionately long tail. In Nevada, the only larger one is the desert kangaroo rat. Most of the limited range of the Panamint kangaroo rat is in southern California. It enters the Intermountain region only in far western Nevada.

Panamints typically occur on sandy or gravelly soils occupied by Joshua trees, cholla, and prickly pear. Scattered sage and creosote scrub and pinyon-juniper woodlands are also inhabited. Of all the Nevada kangaroo rats, they are the only ones regularly caught within open spaces surrounded by trees. In the northern part of their range in Nevada, they occur at elevations of 3,950 to 8,900 feet. Their nocturnal foraging bouts likely result in locating many of the same seeds and insects eaten by other kangaroo rats in the region. Although their habitats are generally not as sandy as those of their relatives, they still engage in dust bathing to prevent the fur from matting.

Following a 29-day gestation, females give birth to an average of 3.5 young. The account of Ord's kangaroo rat should provide clues about other aspects of their reproduction.

## BANNER-TAILED KANGAROO RAT
(*Dipodomys spectabilis*)

Total length: 12 1/4 to 14 3/8 inches; tail length 7 1/8 to 8 1/4 inches.

This large, four-toed kangaroo rat is easily recognized by its unique tail; the last one and a half inches of it are completely white, giving it the appearance of a

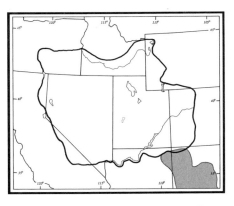

DISTRIBUTION OF BANNER-TAILED KANGAROO RAT.

banner or flag. This image is enhanced by a black band on the tail just in front of the banner. White side stripes are only present on the section of the tail proximal or closest to the body. These are the only kangaroo rats in our region with such an elaborate appendage. Yet they are hardly present here; most of their range is throughout New Mexico, west Texas, and southeastern Arizona. They become an Intermountain mammal only in the northwest corner of New Mexico and adjacent Arizona.

They inhabit scrub- or brush-covered slopes on gravelly soils often occupied by creosote or acacias. They are found as well in arid or semiarid grasslands. They create extensive burrows with up to a dozen openings, providing them with a fine retreat system from predators. It is not known if they suffer particularly high predation rates, which may induce such burrow-building behavior. The flashing of a white tail in such mammals as white-tailed prairie dogs and white-tailed deer distracts predators and alerts group members to their presence. It could be that the tail of this kangaroo rat serves the same function, making one wonder if there are indeed high levels of predation. Large mounds, composed of soil and vegetation, up to 4 feet high and 15 feet wide, surround the burrows. These banner-tailed rodents are nocturnal, feeding and collecting seeds at night. Seeds are stored; over 12 pounds were found in one den alone. Through laboratory experiments it has been found that they prefer slightly moldy seeds. They seem to promote mold growth on seeds by placing them in areas selected for their humidity. Nourishment is also found in the green parts of plants.

The young are born between January and August after about a 27-day gestation. From one to four are produced per litter; they may have up to three litters a year. An average litter is comprised of about three young.

## MERRIAM'S KANGAROO RAT
(*Dipodomys merriami*)

Total length: 8 3/4 to 10 1/4 inches; tail length: 4 3/4 to 6 1/4 inches.

Merriam's is, on the average, the smallest kangaroo rat of all. Usually, it is a light yellowish buff above, although some individuals may be dark brownish; it is white below. The facial markings are comparatively

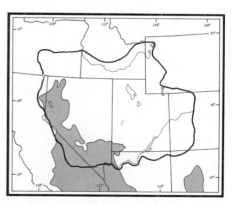

DISTRIBUTION OF MERRIAM'S KANGAROO RAT.

MERRIAM'S KANGAROO RAT

pale, consisting of a dark line on each side of the nose which
does not connect across it. The slender tail is distinguished by
white side stripes that are wider than the upper or lower black
ones and by a dusky to dark brown tufted tip. The dark hip
patches, each separated from the body by a white stripe, are
relatively small. In this region, the other similar four-toed species is the desert kangaroo rat, which overlaps with Merriam's in
southern Nevada. The two can be told apart, for desert kangaroo rats are larger, lack facial markings, and have a white rather
than a dark-colored tail tip. In the Intermountain West,
Merriam's kangaroo rat is primarily found in southern and
western Nevada and some neighboring areas. It has a large
range encompassing the Southwest, much of central Mexico,
and almost all of Baja California.

These rodents are found in a wide variety of habitats,
including sagebrush, shadscale, creosote bush, and other desert
scrub communities. Most commonly, they inhabit low desert
areas with scattered vegetation. Their habitat at the base of the
Sierras in Nevada consists of low-lying sinks and alkali flats

alternating with sandy areas. They are often the most common mammal in the deserts of California. Foods include the seeds of mesquite, creosote, mustard, locoweed, and ocotillo. They have two nocturnal activity peaks, one beginning at about 9 p.m., the other near 4 a.m. Burrows systems, which usually contain one territorial individual, have an opening at the base of a shrub. Male and female territories do not overlap.

Up to two litters are produced; their arrival time corresponds with spring and fall periods of new vegetation growth. A litter averages two to four altricial young; the range is from one to five. Gestation length is approximately 33 days; early reports erroneously gave values of about half that period. In the laboratory, females become mature after about two months.

## DESERT KANGAROO RAT (*Dipodomys deserti*)

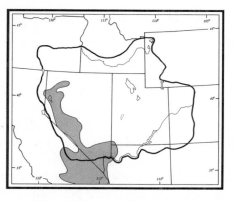

DISTRIBUTION OF DESERT KANGAROO RAT.

Total length: 12 to 14 3/4 inches; tail length: 7 1/8 to 8 1/2 inches.

These large kangaroo rats are pale yellowish buff on top and white below. The crested tail has a white tip, preceded in some individuals by a short, dusky cinnamon stripe along the top. No other species in their range has a tail with a white tip. Further, the dark bottom tail stripe is either absent or poorly defined. Also four-toed, desert kangaroo rats are differentiated from Merriam's kangaroo rat by the tail, a lack of facial markings, and their considerably greater size. They occupy the far southwestern corner of the continental United States and adjacent Mexico. In the Intermountain West, they are found in western Nevada. They are the largest, lightest colored kangaroo rat in this state.

Their habitats include areas with deep, fine sand, such as dunes, with sparse vegetation. Creosote and shadscale scrub communities are also home to these kangaroo rats. In the extreme southwestern corner of Utah, they occur only in the bottoms of washes with loose, shifting sand. Occasionally, these areas become heavily flooded and the rats must escape to higher ground or drown. Their diet consists of the seeds of creosote bush, shadscale, and lupine as well as green vegetation. Often, one can make out the conspicuous, nearly straight trails across the sand which connect their burrows. They are nocturnal, tending to be most active on cloudy, humid nights.

Breeding is from February through June. From two to five altricial young are born following a 29-to-30-day gestation. The average litter size is between three and four.

## BEAVERS—FAMILY CASTORIDAE

The Castoridae consists of only two living species, the familiar beaver of North America and the similar Eurasian beaver. In prehistoric times, this family had several interesting members. *Paleocastor*, from the Miocene, has been found in and seems to have excavated elaborate corkscrew-shaped burrows. A more recent beaver from the Pleistocene, *Castoroides*, was the size of a bear.

BEAVER (*Castor canadensis*)

Total length: 35 1/2 to 46 inches; tail length: 11 3/4 to 17 3/8 inches.

Except for humans, no other animal has the capacity to alter its environment to the extent that beavers can. They have also had a tremendous impact on our continent's history. For

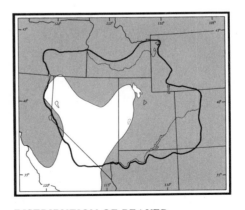

DISTRIBUTION OF BEAVER.

these and many additional reasons, it is important to learn why they are considered such remarkable animals.

Beavers are the largest rodents in North America; some adults weigh over 60 pounds. Usually, they are reddish brown, although individuals vary from yellowish brown to black. Their distinctive tail, which stores fat, is basically hairless, scaly, and flattened from top to bottom. Beavers are built for their aquatic existence in many ways. Their large hind feet are webbed and provide propulsion for swimming. In the water, their much smaller forefeet are usually balled up, acting as bumpers. The eyes are protected by watertight membranes; water is also prevented from entering the body through the nostrils and ears by valves which shut behind them. Although they usually remain underwater for 1 to 2 minutes, they can stay submerged for at least 15 minutes. The genus name *Castor* comes from their paired anal scent glands, the "castors," which they use to mark mud mounds in their territories. Beavers occur throughout the entire continent except for the arctic tundra, most of Florida, and the southwestern deserts. They are restricted from most of the Intermountain West due to their reliance on aquatic habitats.

They may be found wherever there is both permanent water and enough woody vegetation; ponds, lakes, streams, and rivers all provide potential habitat. When arriving in an area without suitably deep water, they build dams across shallow portions of streams. The dams, constructed from logs and sticks, are covered with mud. The grooved, gnawed marks on the trees they cut for dams and lodges are one of their well-known signs. The pond, which forms behind a dam, serves many functions. First of all, it protects the lodge, which is eventually built within the pond, from potential predators. Deep water also confers protection on beavers living in bank dens. The water is now more suitable for moving about food and building materials and for swimming if ice should cover the pond in the winter. Moreover, saturation of the soil is conducive to the growth of food supplies, such as aspen, willows, alders, and cottonwood. Many other plants are eaten; green vegetation, such as water lilies, is favored in the warmer months. Tree branches may be stored for winter food. Beavers can cause extensive flooding and thus destroy farmlands, but many landowners still encourage their presence. This is not only due to their appeal as a mammal with interesting talents but is also because of the host of wildlife species, such as waterfowl, songbirds, fish, and muskrats, which are attracted to their ponds.

Anyone who has seen a beaver lodge knows just what a sophisticated engineer this animal is. Lodges are started with a ring of sticks that ultimately becomes the door. As the lodge is built upward, a hollow space is maintained inside. Large tree limbs are used for the major supports and smaller branches add strength and fill space. Finally, the entire structure is cemented together with mud. Several inches above the water level within the lodge, a mud floor is constructed for the nest chamber. It is lined with soft plant parts. Although this fortresslike home and their aquatic habits grant beavers considerable protection, otters and mink can get to the lodge and prey on them. While feeding on land, they are susceptible to a host of predators, including wolves, coyotes, feral dogs, bobcats, lynx, and mountain lions. Therefore, they feed close to the water's edge so they can easily escape. The slap of a beaver's tail on the water warns others in the colony of danger and could even scare off some uncertain foes.

Mating typically begins in the dead of winter during January or February. After a 107-day pregnancy, which is extremely long for a rodent, an average of three or four "kits" is born. Litter sizes range from one to six. Some reports suggest that the young are mature at birth, perhaps because they are fully furred. But firsthand observations reveal their altriciality; they require several weeks before they exhibit many locomotor and predator-avoidance behaviors. They are not weaned until they are about two months of age. Growth is slow; they do not breed until at least their second winter or reach adult size for several more years. They normally disperse from the natal area during their second year. Beaver colonies are usually based on that hallowed entity, the nuclear family, consisting of the monogamous parents, the yearlings, and the kits. The father contributes to his family by constructing and maintaining the lodge and dams and by watching and warning for predators. Several families can coexist in a colony, and adults may travel from one colony to another.

In a revealing Alaska study, Mark Boyce demonstrated that beaver life histories differ depending upon whether the population is subject to trapping. In trapped areas, young prereproductive beavers had relatively higher survivorship, most likely because better quality colony sites became available to them after adults were removed. Furthermore, in these trapped populations, females first bore young as three-year-olds; in an unexploited population, they did not give birth until four years of age. In the area where females bred earlier, they did not become as big as those which reproduced later in life, probably because more of their energy was allocated to reproduction instead of growth. Finally, the smaller individuals had higher mortality over the winter; they had proportionately less fat to rely on. This analysis illustrates how individuals in separate populations can respond differently to the environmental pressures they face.

Pursuing the beaver for its luxuriously thick pelt was responsible for much of the continent's exploration in the nineteenth century. Several of America's wealthiest men, including John Jacob Astor, made their fortunes from beaver pelts. In the Intermountain region, trappers, such as Peter Skene Ogden, for whom Ogden, Utah, is named, collected many beavers in Utah and northern Nevada in the early nineteenth century. By 1900, beavers were drastically reduced in number. They have now been reintroduced and are thriving in much of their original range. One may learn much about the history of the fur trade in the museum adjacent to the headquarters of Grand Teton National Park in Moose, Wyoming. Beaver hides are worth substantial sums, and these remarkable animals are still heavily trapped.

## CRICETID RODENTS—FAMILY CRICETIDAE

Cricetids are the largest family of mammals both here and in the world. Overall, they include more than 650 species, 25 of which occur in this region. They range in size from the tiny western harvest mouse to the muskrat. They occur in every continent, except Australia and Antarctica, and are found in a great range of habitats. Although they are highly diverse, certain dental and skeletal features unify them. They lack external cheek pouches, most use burrows, and few hibernate.

This family is divided into two groups or subfamilies, cricetines and microtines. Most are cricetines, including harvest mice, deer mice, grasshopper mice, and wood rats. These generally have long tails, large eyes and ears, and cheek teeth with well-developed cusps. In addition, most are nocturnal and omnivorous. All of the microtines in this region are voles except for the muskrat. Lemmings also belong to this group, but do not occur here. Microtines are differentiated from cricetines in having stouter bodies, shorter legs and tails, beady eyes, and smaller ears. Their cheek teeth are flattened on top with surfaces that have distinctive patterns of loops and triangles. These provide an effective surface area for grinding the fibrous grasses and leaves which account for most of their diets. Microtines are usually active day and night. Most live in areas with extreme seasonality and substantial snow accumulation. They are also characterized by reaching sexual maturity earlier than most other mammals and by their marked population fluctuations.

## WESTERN HARVEST MOUSE
(*Reithrodontomys megalotis*)

Total length: 4 1/2 to 6 3/4 inches; tail length: 2 to 3 7/8 inches.

In this region, the western harvest mouse is the only one of a group whose members are recognized by a deep groove running down

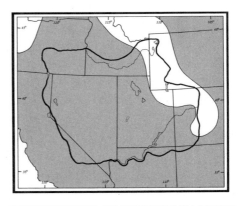

DISTRIBUTION OF WESTERN HARVEST MOUSE.

the middle of the front surface of each incisor. This is where the name *Reithrodontomys* comes from. These mice are small, grayish brown above yet slightly darker along the upper body's midline, buff along the sides, and white to deep gray below. The epithet *megalotis* is derived from two words referring to their large ears. Their long tail is bicolored, slender, and sparsely haired. Western harvest mice have the largest distribution of any of the five harvest mice on the continent north of Mexico, occurring from southwestern Canada to southern Mexico and across the western and midwestern United States into Indiana. They range throughout almost all of the Intermountain West except for the area where Utah, Colorado, and Wyoming meet.

Their predominant habitats are grassy and weedy areas, such as overgrown pastures, meadows, brushy zones along rivers and streams, and around farms and ranches. They are often one of the most numerous mammals in these places. Other habitats include shrublands, yucca-grass communities, deserts, and salt marshes. They are commonly sympatric with meadow and montane voles and use their runways. But because the harvest mouse is strictly nocturnal, it does not "overlap" much with the voles which, although active at any time, are basically crepuscular (active at dawn and dusk). Most of its diet consists of seeds, such as those of grasses, legumes or members of the pea family, and mustards. It also eats grains, including oats and wheat, but populations are rarely dense enough to cause farmers much concern. Additional foods are leaves and insects, particularly moth larvae and beetles. Some of its predators are owls, jays, snakes, badgers, coyotes, and scorpions.

Most of the time, western harvest mice stay put in their distinctive spherical nests. These are about five inches across and located within dense ground vegetation or under logs. Some have been discovered in shrubs up to three feet high. The nest is constructed of loosely woven fibrous matter, with an inside lined with soft items, such as cottonwood or milkweed "down." At its base are one or more half-inch openings. Any holes are immediately repaired. Breeding females, naturally, are especially attentive to their nests. Some accounts state that these mice are active throughout the year, although individuals in Nevada are reported to hibernate.

In warmer areas, they reproduce throughout the year, with a respite during the hottest months. Elsewhere, breeding occurs from early spring to late fall. Fecundity is impressive, accounting for their occasional high numbers. By four months of age, females are sexually mature and they can have several litters a year; up to five are common. After about a 24-day gestation, from one to seven highly altricial young are born. Usually, the litter size is either four or five. At 5 days, the young begin to crawl; weaning is at about 24 days. Few live very long. Typically, an entire population is replaced by the succeeding generation every year. Such a life history is similar to that of many small rodents: it is characterized by a short life expectancy and a high reproductive potential which compensates for it. In this case, much energy goes into the production of the young. A litter usually weighs more than 50 percent of the mother's weight. Each male attempts to mate with several females. Social behavior in the wild is not well documented, but those in captivity are remarkably tolerant of each other. Females with newborn young accept males and even individuals from other rodent species. The need for these small mammals to huddle for warmth might override the usual healthy wariness of outsiders.

CACTUS MOUSE
(*Peromyscus eremicus*)

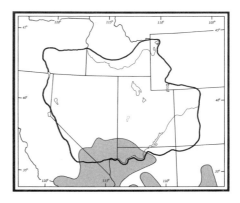

DISTRIBUTION OF CACTUS MOUSE.

Total length: 6 3/4 to 8 5/8 inches; tail length: 3 5/8 to 5 inches.

Rodents in the genus *Peromyscus*, known as deer or white-footed mice, are the most common mammals in many North American habitats. The species are often so similar that only experts can tell them apart. Many have internal cheek pouches and most are excellent climbers.

Cactus mice have long, silky fur which is yellowish buff to cinnamon buff with a blackish wash on top, a yellowish buff line along the sides, and a whitish belly and feet. However, their color is highly variable; for example, very dark individuals are found on lava flows. Females are usually slightly paler than males. The slightly bicolored tail is virtually hairless and normally longer than the head and body combined. The sides and top of the head are grayish. The large ears are also comparatively hairless and quite thin. Internal cheek pouches are lacking. A relative, the canyon mouse, is differentiated by having a tuft of hairs at its tail's tip. Further, where the two species occur together, canyon mice usually inhabit rocky areas whereas cactus mice occur on shrubby, flat desert floors. The brush mouse is also distinguished by the long hairs toward the tip of its tail. Piñon mice have larger ears than those of cactus mice. Even mammalogists, however, often have to rely upon comparisons involving sets of characters to tell apart the sympatric *Peromyscus* species in our region. Cactus mice, nevertheless, are unique in having a life history which appears markedly influenced by their desert existence, with a reproductive output, density, and metabolic rate all usually lower than those of most of their close relatives. They are a Southwestern species with only the northernmost extension of their range entering the Intermountain West around southern Nevada and southwestern Utah.

They occur in various arid habitats, such as desert mountain ranges, mesquite-grass communities, and rocky outcroppings with stands of cacti and yucca. In Utah, they may inhabit riparian zones; in southern Nevada, they are found in creosote and desert shrub regions. Preference is shown for either sandy or loamy soils, those with a mix of clay, silt, and sand. They spend a good bit of time climbing shrubs and have been observed feeding in hackberry and mesquite trees. They are most active on moonlit nights, and their major foods are fruits and flowers of shrubs and desert annual seeds. Green vegetation and insects are also consumed. More so than their relatives, they are food hoarders. Predators include barn and screech owls and king snakes.

Studies indicate that cactus mice often have low population densities, although they may be numerous in the Grand Canyon area. Small population sizes contrast with the norm for many members of the genus, and could be attributed to low food availability. In addition, individuals are generally intolerant of each other, a behavior that might also be a function of the low level of available resources. To conserve water and prolong food supplies, they estivate during the summer. However, they can tolerate higher temperatures and do without water for longer than most related forms. To cool off, they spread saliva over their bodies. Their metabolic rate is as much as 20 percent lower than that of the deer mouse.

Associated with their low population densities, these mice have a comparatively low reproductive potential. After about a 21-day pregnancy, an average of only slightly over two altricial young are born. They may breed throughout the year, but seem to be most active in early spring, mating less frequently during hotter periods. A litter of cactus mice newborn equals less than 15 percent of their mother's weight. Reported weaning periods range from 20 to 44 days. Cactus mice reproduce during their first year. Nesting occurs in rock heaps, stone walls, and abandoned pocket gopher and kangaroo rat burrows. They construct nests from grass, feathers, stems, and leaves.

## DEER MOUSE
(*Peromyscus maniculatus*)

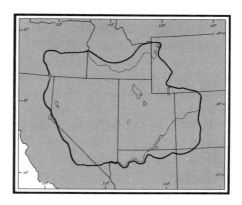

DISTRIBUTION OF DEER MOUSE.

Total length: 4 3/4 to 8 3/4 inches; tail length: 1 3/4 to 4 3/4 inches.

Deer mice are one of the most successful and widespread mammals in North America. In the continental United States, they are absent only from the Southeast, where they are replaced by the oldfield mouse (*Peromyscus polionotus*), a relative that does not occur in our region. Deer mice exhibit a great degree of geographic variation in their characteristics. Color ranges from pale grayish to deep reddish brown above with white on the belly and feet. A distinguishing trait is their relatively short, sharply bicolored tail; it is dark brown to black above and white on the sides and bottom. The tail's appearance is often useful in telling them apart from closely related species, most of which in the region have tails that are either longer, less sharply bicolored, or bear tufts at the tip. Their ears are large and edged with light hairs. Woodland subspecies have longer tails and larger feet than those of prairie forms. Many subspecies occur in the Intermountain West; as a group, they are found throughout the entire region.

Deer mice inhabit a tremendous number of environments, from deserts to grasslands to woodlands. Usually, they are absent from wetlands, but along the Colorado River in Nevada, they occur in riparian zones. Here, the cactus mice are their neighbors among the nearby creosote bushes and cacti. They are

DEER MOUSE

often harmful to human interests, devouring food stores and nesting in furniture and clothing. Although their teeth are well adapted to seed eating, they consume a veritable cornucopia of items. Over half of their summer diet may consist of insects, such as grasshoppers, beetles, and caterpillars. In western forests, they eat the larvae of various insects which are harmful to trees. Seeds become more important in colder months when insects are less available. Water intake is also variable; if present, they lap it up, but they can survive on the moisture in their food. In many places, they store seeds and nuts in hollow logs or other protected spots. Such a common and plentiful animal ends up being an important food source for a host of predators. Deer mice can account for almost half the diet of certain owls. And they fall prey to another small rodent, the grasshopper mouse. Garter snakes follow them into their holes, killing the nestlings. They are active throughout the year, largely remaining beneath the insulative and protective snow cover in winter.

When it comes to choosing a home, they are not terribly particular. They may construct a burrow, but often live in one abandoned by another animal. Within their home, they build a cup- or ball-shaped nest from finely shredded plant material. Nests may be constructed aboveground when burrows are not utilized.

Deer mice breed at any time, although major reproductive periods are in the spring and early fall. Gestation lasts for 23 days in females which are not nursing. It is slightly longer for those still nursing young from the previous litter. Females have a "postpartum heat"; they are receptive to the male right after birth. Litter sizes range from one to nine young, with an average of about four. The extremely altricial young do not open their eyes for around two weeks. Growth progresses quickly, though, and newborn females are usually ready to breed at just seven weeks. Males are also sexually mature as youngsters, at around eight weeks. Autumn population densities can be quite high due to the contributions the spring young and their offspring make to the total number.

## CANYON MOUSE
### (*Peromyscus crinitus*)

Total length: 6 1/4 to 7 5/8 inches; tail length: 3 1/4 to 4 3/4 inches.

The canyon mouse is a small, secretive species about which much basic biology remains to be learned. Its long, soft fur is grayish or yellowish brown, often sprinkled with a blackish

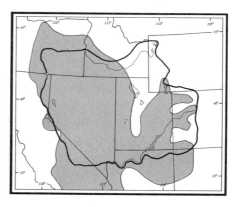

DISTRIBUTION OF CANYON MOUSE.

wash above, and whitish to grayish below. The sides are brighter than the back. In Grand Canyon National Park, it is the most brightly colored *Peromyscus*. Yet in the lava and rimrock country of southeastern Oregon, some populations are composed of entirely black individuals. Perhaps the most distinguishing trait is the tail; it is longer than the head and body, weakly bicolored, well furred, and has a distinctive tufted tip. Another useful characteristic for recognition concerns the size of the ears. They are rather small, only approximately the size of the hind foot. In our region, similar species are differentiated as follows: the tail of the cactus mouse is almost naked and lacks a tuft; that of the deer mouse is usually shorter and also without a tuft; and the rock mouse, piñon mouse, and brush mouse all have noticeably longer ears. Brush mice are usually browner as well. The canyon mouse is a typical Intermountain species with most of its range restricted to the region. Populations also occur in surrounding areas, notably southern and Baja California.

Canyon mice live among the rocks and crevices of canyon walls, from those in hot deserts at sea level to cool mountains over 10,000 feet high. They are also found on old lava flows. In southern Idaho, they are often associated with deer mice, which are found on nearby sagebrush plains, and bushy-tailed woodrats, which occupy cavelike formations. In Nevada, they are common where mountain canyons open up into the valleys. They are nocturnal, searching for seeds amidst the sparse canyon vegetation. Because they occur in the same habitats, rattlesnakes are presumed to prey on them.

Nesting occurs within the rocks or, more commonly, in burrows beneath them. Litter sizes range from two to five, with an average of three to four altricial young. Compared to other members of the genus, canyon mice have exceptionally high birth weights. In addition, they are weaned relatively late, at about 28 days after birth. This is roughly a week later than when the deer mouse is weaned. Such reproductive traits may be a response to the harsh environment in which they live. Larger young should have higher survival on the unproductive steep slopes they inhabit. Mothers may have to travel farther for food, which could cause the delay in the young's growth and, thus, the later weaning age. They are born in the spring and perhaps summer as well.

## BRUSH MOUSE (*Peromyscus boylii*)

Total length: 7 1/8 to 9 3/8 inches; tail length: 3 5/8 to 4 3/4 inches.

The brush mouse is a relatively large *Peromyscus*. Its upper surface coloration is highly variable, ranging from grayish brown to dark brown or cinnamon; the underside is whitish. The sides are typically buff or tawny. Although the ankles are a darker, dusky shade, the feet are white. Once again, tail and ear char-

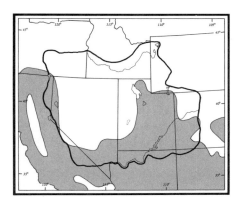

DISTRIBUTION OF BRUSH MOUSE.

acteristics are used for recognition. The tail is clearly bicolored, brown above and whitish below, sparsely haired so that the rings on its skin are evident, and slightly longer than the rest of the body. The ear is approximately three-quarters of an inch. Other species are differentiated as follows: deer mice have shorter tails; the nearly one-inch ears of piñon and rock mice are longer and those of cactus and canyon mice are shorter. Furthermore, the canyon mouse is usually a lighter color, either pale gray or buffy. Brush mice inhabit a large segment of the southwestern United States and range throughout central Mexico into El Salvador. In the Intermountain West, they occur primarily across the eastern two-thirds of Utah and southern Nevada.

Typical habitats are arid to semiarid rocky areas with brushy vegetation. They are not restricted to these spots; in Grand Canyon National Park they are found in pinyon-juniper flats, cottonwood-willow stands, brushy-weedy habitats, and on rocky slopes. In the Sierra Nevadas, they are common in shrubby areas. Habitats in Colorado include rough rocky plateaus, mesas, and canyons with pinyons and junipers. A variety of foods are eaten: conifer seeds, acorns, berries, and fungi. They have a taste for cactus fruit. In addition, they eat and occasionally serve to control insects, including some forest pests. Although subject to predation by snakes, other mammals, and birds of prey, they are excellent climbers and elude their enemies by scurrying up shrubs or trees. They neither store food nor hibernate.

Their grass-lined nests are located under rocks, brush piles, rotting logs, or within the crevices of canyon walls. Breeding occurs throughout most of the year but is pronounced during spring and late summer. As many as four litters are produced per year; the average litter size is three or four and the range is two to six. Pregnancy lasts from 22 to 25 days.

## PIÑON MOUSE
(*Peromyscus truei*)

Total length: 6 3/4 to 9 1/8 inches; tail length: 3 to 4 3/4 inches.

The piñon mouse is a medium-sized species with exceptionally large ears; each is close to an inch long. Such large pinnae could be an adaptation for detecting predators at great dis-

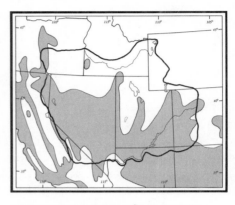

DISTRIBUTION OF PIÑON MOUSE.

tances in the open country inhabited by these mice. Indeed, individuals of this species occupying areas of dense cover have shorter ears. In piñon mice west of the Sierra Nevadas, the tail is longer than the body, whereas in those east of these mountains, it is shorter. Both populations may occur in this region. Piñon mice have a long, silky fur that is pale yellowish brown to brownish black above and whitish below. The tail is bicolored and bears a distinct tuft. They differ from brush mice in the size of the ear; those of the latter species are only about three-quarters of an inch. Further, the piñon mouse's tail is heavily furred, making it difficult to see the rings or "annulations" on its skin. Piñon mice can be separated from rock mice by color differences; the rock mouse is grayish black above and grayish atop the head. Finally, canyon and cactus mice both have smaller ears. The piñon mouse is another denizen of the southwestern United States and central Mexico. It also occurs along California's coast and in central Oregon. In the Intermountain West, it is found across most of Nevada and Utah and in several adjacent areas.

In almost all of its range, this species occurs on rocky slopes in stands of pinyon and juniper trees. No other small rodent is as dependent on and abundant in pinyon-juniper communities. Not only do these mice live in hollow junipers and use its shredded bark for nests, their principal foods are pinyon and juniper seeds. A characteristic sign of theirs is a small pile of remains from these seeds lying at the base of a tree. They are superb climbers and perhaps the most arboreal, or tree-dwelling, of all the mice in this group. Another major habitat type is chaparral, thickets of shrubs and dwarf trees. To a lesser extent, they are found in cedar, yellow pine, and bristlecone pine forests and cottonwood-sagebrush stands in riparian zones. Besides their reliance on pinyon and juniper seeds, they may heavily utilize insects and spiders. The stomach of an individual in western California was more than half filled with mammal remains. Late summer diets may include a reliance on acorns. Although they contend with a diversity of predators, their rocky habitat and climbing abilities afford them some protection.

The breeding period varies with location. In southwestern Colorado, reproduction occurs from April to September. Yet, in Arizona, they breed from mid-February through mid-November. Litter sizes range from one to six; usually three or four young arrive after a 25-to-27-day pregnancy. Newborn piñon mice are highly altricial, with eyes and ears remaining closed for 16 to 21 days. They are fully grown after about three months. Males, however, are capable of breeding a few weeks before that. Undoubtedly, it is crucial for them to breed early, for few live long. Only 2 to 3 percent of the adults in a study in Mesa Verde National Park in Colorado lived to breed in two consecutive years.

## ROCK MOUSE (*Peromyscus difficilis*)

Total length: 7 1/8 to 10 1/4 inches; tail length: 3 5/8 to 5 3/4 inches.

The large rock mouse has long, soft fur that is brownish to blackish above and usually white below. Its undersurface, however, ranges from white to even blackish mixed with silver; its bottom may be uncharacteristically dark for a mouse. Its long tail is more than half the length of the body. The ears are large as well, about the size of the hind foot. Similar to the piñon mouse, it usually is less gray, has a longer tail, and a proportionately longer rostrum. Here, these two species overlap only around far

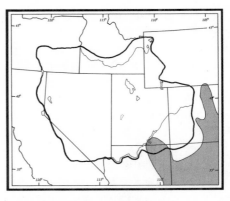

DISTRIBUTION OF ROCK MOUSE.

southeastern Utah, the sole portion of the Intermountain West inhabited by the rock mouse. Yet where they coexist, they are often in the same habitat and difficult to tell apart. Brush and canyon mice may be distinguished by their longer tails and shorter ears. The remainder of the rock mouse's distribution lies to the east and south of our region, largely through Colorado, New Mexico, and central Mexico.

Rock mice are found in brushy habitats within rock outcrops, canyons, cliffs, and lava flows, where they exhibit excellent climbing skills. Vegetation in these areas includes Gambel's oak, skunkbush, and snowberry. Like the piñon mouse, they often occur among pinyon and juniper trees which they, too, rely on for food. As insects become more available in summer, they compose a larger part of the diet. Fungi and green vegetation are other foods. Any food item may be stored for future use in their dens, located under boulders or in woodrat dens. Even those presently occupied by woodrats are shared by rock mice. They are nocturnal and active in all seasons. As with other species in rocky environments, predators probably have low success with them.

Males can breed by March or April, and females come into breeding condition at the same time or shortly thereafter. Following a three-to-four-week gestation, usually three or four young are born. Litter sizes range from one to six young, and several litters are produced in the same year. Females from first litters probably breed later in the year they are born.

# NORTHERN GRASSHOPPER MOUSE (*Onychomys leucogaster*)

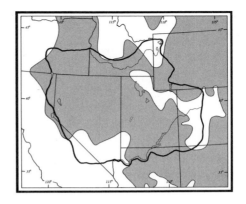

DISTRIBUTION OF NORTHERN GRASSHOPPER MOUSE.

Total length: 5 1/8 to 7 1/2 inches; tail length: 1 1/8 to 2 3/8 inches.

The stocky, short-tailed grasshopper mouse is unique both in appearance and habits. In the northern species, the upper body fur has at least three color phases. The mice are grayish as juveniles, become buffy to reddish brown as adults, and revert to their juvenile coloration in old age. Below, they are pure white. The short, thick tail is less than half the length of the body. It is bicolored with a bottom white portion often extending to the tip. The forefeet are large and have long claws; *Onychomys* means "clawed mouse." In our region, the northern grasshopper mouse overlaps with the southern grasshopper mouse in Nevada, a smaller species with a tail that is greater than half the length of the body. Furthermore, they have different ecological preferences, with the northern species often in moister areas at higher elevations. Northern grasshopper mice have an enormous distribution, extending from the south-central Canadian provinces through the midwestern United States into northern Mexico. They occur in much of the West and throughout the Intermountain region except for a section encompassing northeastern Utah.

Major habitats include semiarid grasslands, shrublands, deserts, and low valleys. Because these mice are dustbathers like the kangaroo rats, they occur largely on fine sandy or silty soils. However, suitable soil must exist over a wide area, given their large distribution. They are commonly found along farm fencerows since such areas support large numbers of prey and provide them with cover. It is their predatory nature which sets them apart from their relatives. Their food habits are closer to those of insectivores or carnivores than those of rodents. About three-quarters of their diet is animal material, with the most taken in spring and early summer. Common victims include larval beetles, caterpillars, crickets, spiders, and scorpions. These vicious little beasts easily kill other rodents up to three times their size by firmly grasping them with their claws and biting through the skull. Not surprisingly, given such bloodthirsty habits, they engage in cannibalism. Although they are also victimized, especially by owls, they rarely compose a large part of any predator's diet. Surely, this is a function of their population size, which is usually small relative to those of most rodents in the region.

Burrows are excavated in open areas. Males dig a U-shaped burrow which goes into the ground for about six inches before enlarging to form a nest chamber. It is sealed, thus providing moisture retention and temperature stability. For protection when away from the nest, they dig "retreat burrows." Individuals also may simply live under rocks or clumps of vegetation. They are quite noisy, emitting long, high-pitched sounds that resemble the call of a wolf or a coyote. Made at night, the "calls" may be used to detect the presence of each other. They are highly territorial, and males aggressively defend their sites. Fights can be avoided if a subordinate mouse assumes a defensive posture. But any individual failing to do so in another's territory is often killed with a bite to the skull or upper neck. This is not a haphazard arrangement; males clearly mark their territory borders with scent glands.

Breeding is from late spring to early autumn, with births reaching a peak from June through August. After a pregnancy of about four weeks, females give birth to an average of three to four altricial young; litter sizes range from one to six. Claws are noticeable on the young by the seventh day. Fathers assist in rearing their young by bringing them insects. In this sense, they are similar to canids in which the male brings meat to the den for his pups. In fact, paternal care is common in monogamous species, regardless of the group. In northern grasshopper mice, even though males assist their mates, the pair bond does not necessarily last for more than one mating. The young, themselves, also act much like those of coyotes or wolves, fighting and mounting one another. In about three weeks, these feisty young are weaned; they can breed during their first year.

## SOUTHERN GRASSHOPPER MOUSE (*Onychomys torridus*)

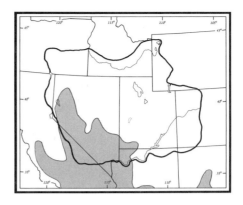

DISTRIBUTION OF SOUTHERN GRASSHOPPER MOUSE.

Total length: 4 3/4 to 6 1/2 inches; tail length: 1 1/4 to 2 5/8 inches.

In appearance, southern grasshopper mice are similar to their northern relative. They, too, are stocky and have a relatively short, thick tail. In their case, however, the tail is longer; its length is equal to or greater than half that of the body. Above, they vary from grayish to light pinkish cinnamon marked with a blackish shade high on the back. The belly is white. The tail is correspondingly bicolored and has a white tip. Considerable variation exists in the upper body color; each particular shade probably affords protection by matching an animal to its local environment. Upper fur color also shifts with age. Juveniles are gray, whereas adults are browner. Southern grasshopper mice are not as widespread as the northern species, either regionally or continentally. They are restricted to the southwestern United States and northern Mexico. In the Intermountain West, they occur throughout southern Nevada and Utah's far southwestern corner.

These mice are found in hot, low-lying deserts and valleys that support scrub and semiscrub plants, such as creosote bush, mesquite, and yucca. They are insectivorous; principal foods include scorpions, grasshoppers, spiders, and insect cocoons. To kill a scorpion, they first immobilize its dangerous tail by biting it repeatedly before finally attacking the head. They are adept at "disarming" beetles that secrete defensive chemicals from the tips of their abdomens. After grabbing a beetle with their forepaws, they hold it at a distance. Then, they shove its abdomen into the ground, thus avoiding the unpleasant secretion. They are strongly nocturnal and active in every season. Nesting occurs in burrows, often in those abandoned by other animals. Their living arrangements are not as well known as those of the northern grasshopper mouse. Males are highly territorial. Caged individuals will get up on their hind legs, boxing, wrestling, and eating one another.

Gestation lasts from 27 to 32 days. After birth, mothers eat the placenta and the amnion, the fluid-filled sac that surrounds the embryo. Litter sizes range from two to seven young, with a mean of about two and a half. Females commonly produce two or three litters in one breeding season, with a peak in deliveries between May and July. The altricial young open their eyes after about two weeks, begin to fight with littermates several days later, and are weaned after three weeks. Males and females breed within several weeks of weaning. After the first year, there is a drastic decline in reproductive ability, with only a small proportion having young as two-year-olds. Males take an active role in parenting, grooming the young, providing warmth by huddling over them, likely supplying them with food and attacking intruders. Due to their reproductive biology and perhaps low food availability, population sizes are generally small. They actively maintain large territories. In one study, an average home range, the total area utilized, was about seven acres.

If one is interested in making a small fortune by promoting a natural insect control, one might consider using one's entrepreneurial skills with the grasshopper mouse. Within just one month, a cageful of these rodents cured a house of its kitchen cockroach infestation. The door to their cage was left open at night, allowing them to go on search and devour missions. After their "assignment," the mice freely returned to their cage. The lucky housekeeper was left only with the minor task of cleaning up the uneaten legs of the adult cockroaches; juveniles were entirely eaten.

## WHITE-THROATED WOODRAT
### (*Neotoma albigula*)

Total length: 11 1/8 to 15 3/4 inches; tail length: 3 to 7 3/4 inches.

The woodrats, also known as "packrats," are about the same size as the all-too-familiar Norway and black rats, vermin native to Europe. Woodrats, however, are indigenous to our continent and six species are found in the Intermountain West.

They are easily distinguished from the Old World rats by their hairy rather than scaly tails. Also, they have much larger ears, white feet and bellies, and a fine, soft fur. Woodrats live in wild areas and are relatively harmless. They occasionally damage cabins and vacation homes.

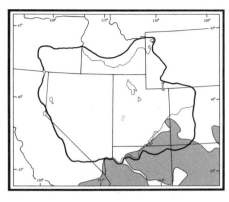

DISTRIBUTION OF WHITE-THROATED WOODRAT.

White-throated woodrats are medium-sized, brownish gray above and either white or grayish below, including the feet. The hairy tail is similarly but not sharply bicolored. As expected, their most distinguishing trait is the color of the throat, which is white to the base. Over the rest of the body, their hair is gray at the base. To the contrary, the throat hairs of similar regional species, the desert, Mexican, and Stephens' woodrats, are gray at the base. Stephens' woodrat, which occurs in this region only around south-central Utah, also differs by having longer hairs at the tip of its tail. Dusky-footed woodrats have dark hind ankles and a tail that is blackish above. But they barely enter the Intermountain West in northeastern California. The white-throated woodrat is a Southwestern species. The northern limit of its distribution is in the Four Corners region, where it joins the Intermountain fauna. Here, the Colorado River appears to have served as a barrier preventing its westward expansion.

Prime habitats of this woodrat are the brushlands of arid plains and deserts. Rocky cliffs with shallow caves are also potential living quarters. Habitat selection differs among the sympatric species in the region. For example, in southwestern Colorado, white-throated woodrats occupy the lowest, driest sites; Mexican woodrats inhabit the foothills and lower mountains, living in horizontal rock shelters; and bushy-tailed woodrats occur at higher elevations, where they live daringly in rock fissures and caves. White-throated woodrats consume large helpings of cactus, mesquite beans, juniper branches and berries, and leafy vegetation. Neither grasses nor animal material are prominent in their diet. Drinking water is unnecessary since they obtain what they need from the moisture in their food. They are preyed upon by owls, ringtails, coyotes, badgers, and snakes. Like other woodrats, they construct individual homes. They are built from sticks, cactus pads, and a grab bag of items, including bottles, mule droppings, and mousetraps. They are excellent contractors, even compared to other woodrats, erecting homes that are two to four feet high, often under a prickly pear or cholla cactus. Good climbers, they scale hazardous cacti, removing sharp spines to use in covering their homes. Indeed, spines scattered around their dens are a telltale sign of their presence. Usually, only one adult resides in a den, although several dens may be located close by. Nest chambers are lined with juniper bark, grass, fur, and yucca fibers. This rat is basically diurnal and active year-round.

White-throated woodrats breed from January to August, probably producing more than one litter a year. Litter sizes range only from one to three, with an average of two altricial young born after a one-month pregnancy. Most young disperse to a new area when they are two or three months old. Usually, they do not breed until they are yearlings. They are promiscuous, randomly choosing partners.

## DESERT WOODRAT
(*Neotoma lepida*)

Total length: 8 3/4 to 15 1/8 inches; tail length: 3 3/4 to 7 3/8 inches.

If you are ever hiking through the desert and happen to hear an ominous, rattlelike sound, try not to become alarmed. It might only be a desert woodrat, exhibiting a

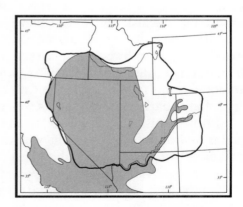

DISTRIBUTION OF DESERT WOODRAT.

common behavior, vibrating its tail against some dried plants. But be sure to look before deciding it is not a rattlesnake. These small- to medium-sized woodrats are yellowish brown to grayish brown streaked with black on top. Some have a small white patch on the throat and breast area. Below they are grayish, often washed with buff. The tail is correspondingly bicolored and the hind feet are white. Similar regional species are differentiated as follows: the hairs on the larger throat patch of the white-throated woodrat are white to the base; Stephens' woodrat has a slightly bushy tail; the tail of the Mexican woodrat is white below; and the upper hind feet of the larger dusky-footed woodrat are dark. In the desert woodrat, we have a "bonafide" Intermountain mammal. Most of its distribution falls within the Great Basin and adjacent deserts, extending south into Baja California.

Desert woodrats inhabit desert floors or rocky slopes with shrubby vegetation and pinyon-junipers. In a western Nevada study, they were typically captured in areas near rock islands with little shrub cover. In southern Idaho, they occur in isolated colonies on basaltic rock outcrops. Along the North Rim of the Grand Canyon, they live under rocks, whereas bushy-tailed woodrats reside within the rock's deep cracks. They eat spiny cacti, yucca pods, bark, pinyon nuts and other seeds, and virtually any green plant. Extra food is stored in their homes, which are often in abandoned burrows of kangaroo rats or ground squirrels. Compulsive remodelers, they fortify the entrance to a new home with sticks and cactus spines. The nest is positioned deep within a cooler part of the burrow. Although they construct accommodations from scratch, their building instinct may not be too strong. Occasionally, they use rock dens and may even nest in trees. Like many of their relatives, they have excellent climbing skills.

An average of two altricial young are born after a 30-to-36-day pregnancy. Litter sizes range from one to three, with up to four litters produced a year. After two months, the young can reproduce.

## STEPHENS' WOODRAT (*Neotoma stephensi*)

Total length: 10 1/5 to 14 inches; tail length: 4 1/5 to 5 3/5 inches.

Stephens' woodrat is of minor importance in the Intermountain West, occurring here only in the Navajo Mountain region of south-central Utah. It is yellowish to grayish buff, darker high on the back. The belly is white to creamy, often washed with a pinkish buff. The tail is correspondingly bicolored; it is slightly bushy. A dis-

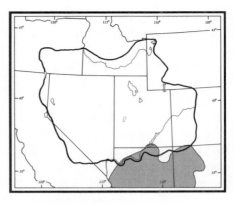

DISTRIBUTION OF STEPHENS' WOODRAT.

tinguishing trait is the dusky, wedge-shaped pattern on the hind feet, extending from a quarter to a third of the distance below the ankle. The desert, white-throated, and Mexican woodrats all have hind feet that are white up to the ankle and tails that are not even slightly bushy. However, the ranges of the desert and Stephens' woodrats barely overlap in our region. Bushy-tailed woodrats can be recognized by their squirrel-like tails. Stephens' woodrats have a small distribution; essentially, they are found only in northern Arizona and western New Mexico.

Along the Grand Canyon's South Rim, they live in rocky places among or near pinyon-juniper stands. This is in contrast to white-throated woodrats, which are typically found in the sagebrush-yucca-cholla associations there. For food, they concentrate heavily on juniper foliage, although they also eat its cones, as well as leaves, seeds, and bark of other species. It may be difficult to notice their stick houses since they are often far back in the rock piles.

Ordinarily, they have but a single young, which grows relatively slowly and is weaned later than those of comparably sized woodrats. Births typically occur between March and May. Females do not become sexually mature until they are about 10 months old, which is rather late for a woodrat. While nursing, mothers lose a proportionately large amount of weight, a loss they recover slowly from. Few produce more than one litter in their lifetime. These unusual reproductive habits are suspected to be a result of their specialized feeding on juniper leaves. The leaves contain various compounds which reduce their digestibility. The woodrats may not be able to put much energy into reproduction because their food is "energy-poor."

## MEXICAN WOODRAT
(*Neotoma mexicana*)

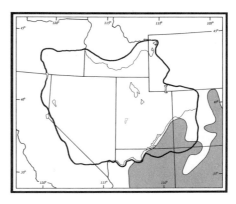

Total length: 11 3/8 to 16 5/8 inches; tail length: 4 1/8 to 8 1/8 inches.

Mexican woodrats are a medium-sized species, usually grayish to brownish above, darkened on top with blackish hairs, and white to yellowish below. Some

DISTRIBUTION OF MEXICAN WOODRAT.

populations consist of reddish- or rust-colored individuals and there are blackish ones on lava flows. Their hairy tails are distinctly bicolored, dusky to black above and gray, whitish, or yellowish below. A narrow fringe of dark hairs surrounds the mouth. Some have a brown spot on the chest. They are easily differentiated from white-throated woodrats by their throat color. It is considerably more difficult to separate them from desert woodrats, although these are usually more grayish below and have a less sharply bicolored tail. Fortunately, the two barely occur together in our region. As the name indicates, Mexican woodrats are widely distributed in Mexico. They are also found through Guatemala and western Honduras. Their occurrence in the Intermountain West is centered around the Four Corners area, which forms the northwest boundary of their distribution.

They are largely restricted to the rocky areas of mountains, such as outcroppings and cliffs. Open conifer woodlands and shrublands are typical plant communities in their habitats. In Colorado, most occur in pinyon-juniper stands, but they are also common among scrub oaks and ponderosa pines. The exact combination of plants differs widely over their vast range; in Mexico, they are found in areas as diverse as tropical thorn forests and fig tree stands. In this region, they often coexist with rock squirrels. Where sympatric with other woodrats, they inhabit separate zones. For example, bushy-tailed woodrats use the crevices of higher cliffs, whereas Mexican woodrats stay on the lower ledges and talus slopes. But where bushy-tailed woodrats are not present, the Mexican woodrats will occupy the higher cliffs. In the Dolores Canyon of southwestern Colorado, Mexican woodrats live on steep canyon walls and cliffs, whereas white-throated woodrats occupy the valley floors. In our area, Mexican woodrats eat acorns, pinyon nuts, and juniper berries, but generally subsist more on foliage than on fruit, flowers, or woody parts. They store great quantities of food, mostly in late summer and early fall. They usually do not build the large stick houses typical of the other species. Instead, they construct nest chambers, mainly of shredded juniper bark, in well-protected rock crevices, tree cavities, or vacant buildings. They are not above setting up quarters in the abandoned homes of their more industrious cousins. Predators include rattlesnakes and, undoubtedly, a host of avian and mammalian meat lovers.

In north-central Colorado, they breed from March through May, producing two litters. This is probably the pattern in the Intermountain West as well, although the breeding period is extended in their southern range. Gestation lasts for about 33 days, usually resulting in two altricial young. Litter sizes range from one to four. Females normally reproduce in the year they are born, although not as successfully if they are from late litters. Males do not breed until they are yearlings. As a male approaches a female in heat, he may emit a low-pitched gasp that becomes louder as the two get closer. Perhaps the female rats find husky-voiced males irresistible. Maybe the males simply cannot help themselves.

## DUSKY-FOOTED WOODRAT (*Neotoma fuscipes*)

Total length: 13 1/4 to 18 3/4 inches; tail length: 6 1/4 to 12 3/4 inches.

The large, dusky-footed woodrat is an interesting species with unusual nesting and mating habits. It is buff to grayish brown above, grayer on the face, and grayish to whitish occasionally washed with tan below. The name gives away its telltale trait: the tops of the hind feet and ankles are sprinkled with dusky hairs, giving the effect of long dark spats over the white toes. Although the tail is brown above and lighter below, it is indistinctly bicolored. In our

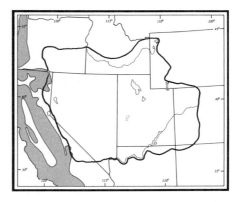

DISTRIBUTION OF DUSKY-FOOTED WOODRAT.

region, these dapper animals overlap with desert and bushy-tailed woodrats. The former is distinguished by its white hind feet, the latter by its flat bushy tail. Dusky-footed woodrats barely place their dark feet in our region, occurring here only in far northeastern California. They are a West Coast species whose range extends from northern Baja California to northwestern Oregon. They are common in the western Sierra Nevadas.

Major habitats are conifer and hardwood forests, heavy chaparral, and streamside thickets. They subsist on green vegetation but supplement their diet with fruit, nuts, and seeds. Predators include coyotes, skunks, and owls. Predation rates could be high since they often build their houses in exposed areas. But where they live in forests, they construct their homes up to 50 feet high in the trees. And these houses can be enormous, up to eight feet in diameter. They have several compartments, which often serve as living quarters for other small mammals, frogs, and invertebrates.

These woodrats are semicolonial, with several living in the same area; males and females pair for the breeding season. Thus, compared to most other woodrats, they are remarkably tolerant of each other and even social. Between one to four altricial young, with an average of two to three, are usually born in May and June.

216

## BUSHY-TAILED WOODRAT (*Neotoma cinerea*)

Total length: 11 1/2 to 18 1/2 inches; tail length: 4 3/4 to 9 1/4 inches.

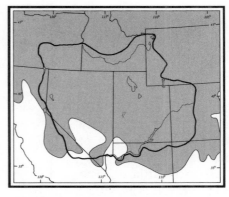

DISTRIBUTION OF BUSHY-TAILED WOODRAT.

The large, bushy-tailed woodrat is the one for which the name "pack rat" was originally used. A tendency to collect shiny objects, such as coins, is most pronounced in this species; it is surely a most odd and inexplicable habit. These woodrats are also called "trade rats," in reference to their practice of dropping one item to exchange it for another. They are pale grayish washed with buff to blackish above or brownish sprinkled with black. Below, they are whitish, pinkish, or buff. Their whiskers are relatively long. Most distinctive of all is the flattened, bushy, squirrel-like tail; it is most evident in males. Because the tail is used for balance in climbing and jumping, one would suspect males of being more adept at these skills. These rats are excellent climbers, and jump from limb to limb in trees. All other woodrats have rounded, short-haired tails. Bushy-tails are widespread, occurring across the western United States and northwestern Canada up into the Yukon. Except for part of southern Nevada, they occupy almost all of the Intermountain West.

They commonly occur in rocky areas, usually in the mountains. Prime habitats include rimrock, rockslides, and conifer forests. As with the dusky-footed woodrat, they build houses high up in trees. These are not necessarily homes, but serve as storage sheds for vegetation collected for the upcoming winter. In much of the West, they live in rocky crevices behind a shield of sticks or in a stick house. Highly territorial, they try to prevent other individuals from entering their turf and mark their territories with an unpleasant musky scent. They prefer the green parts of shrubs and forbs, but also eat twigs, nuts, and seeds. However, they are not especially choosy; one study in

BUSHY-TAILED WOODRAT

Colorado revealed a use of 75 percent of the available plants. Major predators include spotted owls, bobcats, coyotes, and long-tailed weasels. They are nocturnal and not easily seen by their enemies. But they may be detected by their excrement which accumulates due to their depositing it in one area. It consists of piles of black tarlike material. The encrusted, white calcareous remains from their urine on cliff faces is often mistaken for minerals.

Between May and September, they usually have three or four altricial young, with litter sizes ranging from one to five. The gestation period is approximately 35 days. Up to two litters are produced per year. Usually, a single family will live in one rockslide area. Families are often harems, composed of a dominant, larger male and several females. When it is time for the young males to disperse, they may have to be driven out of the area by their father.

SOUTHERN or BOREAL
RED-BACKED VOLE (*Clethrionomys gapperi*)

Total length: 4 3/4 to 6 1/4 inches; tail length: 1 1/4 to 2 inches.

Voles are thickset, short-tailed, short-eared mice which comprise almost all of the microtine rodents. In the Intermountain West, there are four different major groupings: red-backed, heather, meadow, and sagebrush voles. Here, only one of these groups, the meadow voles, contains more than a single species.

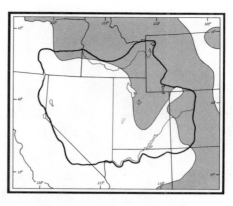

DISTRIBUTION OF SOUTHERN OR BOREAL RED-BACKED VOLE.

The southern red-backed vole is easily recognized by a broad, colorful band of hairs on its back, which extends from the forehead to the base of the tail. Usually, this band is a reddish rust, but varies from bright chestnut to yellowish brown. Due to this distinctive trait, there is no other animal in our region which could be mistaken for it. On the nose and sides, it is grayish mixed with buffy, and is buff-white to silvery gray below. The short tail is slightly bicolored. Compared to other voles, it has a large head with big ears. It is usually darker in summer than in winter. These voles have an enormous distribution that encompasses all of the southern Canadian provinces and the northern United States. It extends down through the Rocky Mountains, where they find a home in the higher elevations of this region.

They are usually found in cool, moist forests with an ample supply of fallen timber and exposed roots. These provide cover for nest sites as well as surfaces for the growth of foods, such as fungi. Their runways and burrows go right under this debris. Coniferous, deciduous, and mixed forests are all home to red-backed voles. In the West, they occur in ponderosa pine, red and white cedar, hemlock, and spruce-fir forests. Yet they are not restricted to forests, occasionally inhabiting grassy meadows, chaparral, willow-grass-sedge communities, and even rockslides. But wherever they occur, available drinking water is required. One of these thirsty animals drinks roughly 10 times as much

SOUTHERN or BOREAL RED-BACKED VOLE

water as a deer mouse. As omnivores, they feed on a variety of items, such as green plant parts, berries, mosses, lichens, ferns, and insects. In summer and fall, the fungus *Endogone* becomes an important food. Bulbs and stems are stored for winter use and conifer seeds are stolen from red squirrel middens. In a Colorado study, individuals weighed less and had lower metabolic rates in the winter than in the summer. This might reduce food requirements during a period of low food availability. They may be valuable to certain predators; in Minnesota, they are heavily utilized by short-tailed weasels; in central Alberta, they are important to broad-winged hawks.

Litter sizes range from two to eight young, with an average of four to six. Populations at higher latitudes and elevations tend to have larger litters, a pattern which may be common to many species. N. P. Ashmole suggested the following explanation for birds which should also apply to mammals. At higher latitudes, there is usually greater climatic seasonality. During the extreme winters in such places, there typically is an increase in mortality which leads to a decline in population density. With fewer individuals around in the following spring, breeders would have a relatively high level of resources available to them. They could then put this extra energy into the production of larger litters.

Breeding takes place from late winter to late fall. They are not deterred from mating when heavy snow is still on the ground. Gestation only lasts for 17 to 19 days and several litters are produced a year. The altricial young first open their eyes after about 12 days and are weaned shortly thereafter. Sexual maturity is attained at two to four months. Although promiscuous, they may form small colonies during the winter. Males do not engage in parental care, but are still tolerated by the mother and her young. The nests, which are about eight inches across and lined with plant matter, are built in the abandoned homes of other mammals.

## HEATHER VOLE
(*Phenacomys intermedius*)

Total length: 5 1/8 to 6 inches; tail length: 1 to 1 3/4 inches.

The heather vole is one rodent that most of us have little chance of encountering. Although widespread, it is generally rare. Furthermore, in our region it usually

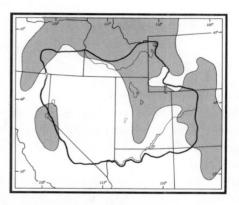

DISTRIBUTION OF HEATHER VOLE.

lives high on the tops of mountains. But those who take the opportunity to find these creatures may be richly rewarded by their attractiveness and a hike in the rugged terrain they inhabit. The long, soft upper fur is typically gray, washed with brown to dark brown, giving them a grizzled appearance. Some individuals have yellowish faces or noses. The silvery belly is sometimes highlighted with buff, and the feet are white. An important distinguishing trait is the proportionately short, bicolored tail. Yet it is still difficult to tell them apart from the montane vole, even with its relatively longer tail. And the tail of the long-tailed vole is considerably lengthier, usually over two inches. Their distribution pattern is similar to that of the southern red-backed vole; they range across southern Canada and through the Rocky Mountains. In our region, there is also an isolated group along the central Nevada-California border.

These voles inhabit the grassy areas and blueberry patches along mountaintops and the open areas in conifer forests. Other habitats include rocky slopes, brushy areas along forest streams, and even tundra. In Idaho, they usually occur in conifer forests and above timberline in alpine heather meadows. Similarly, in Colorado, they occur at high elevations from about 7,000 to 12,000 feet. They are found in wet or dry environments and seem adaptable to a greater variety of habitats than do many other voles. Most active at dusk and during the night, they feed on birch and willow bark, berries, seeds, and other plant parts. In summer, they nest below the surface, in trees, and under rocks or tree stumps. During the winter, their soft shredded-grass nests are above the surface but covered with snow.

Their breeding season lasts from June through September. Gestation estimates range from 21 to 30 days. An average of five, with a range of one to eight, young are born. Several litters are produced in a single breeding season. The altricial young become mature during their second month, with those from early litters breeding in their first year. Heather voles may be found in small colonies.

## MEADOW VOLE
(*Microtus pennsylvanicus*)

Total length: 5 1/2 to 7 3/4 inches; tail length: 1 1/4 to 2 1/2 inches.

Members of the genus *Microtus* are the most well-represented voles, both regionally and on the continent. The genus name stems from two words mean-

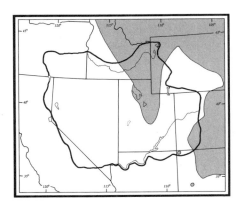

DISTRIBUTION OF MEADOW VOLE.

MEADOW VOLE

ing "small ear." Of the six species in this region, it is the meadow vole about which the most is known. It is the subject of extensive research, has the greatest distribution of any *Microtus* species, and exists in large numbers throughout its range. Above, its color is highly variable, ranging from yellowish or reddish brown, sprinkled with black, to blackish brown. Subspecies in the West are at the light end of the spectrum. Below, the gray hair terminates in characteristic silver tips. Another feature useful in distinguishing meadow voles is their comparatively long, bicolored tail which is usually at least twice the length of the hind foot. Nevertheless, it is difficult to tell them apart from montane voles. Other than skeletal or genetic attributes, habitat is often used to separate the two. Simply put, montane voles are likelier to occur in mountains. Where meadow voles occur with montane voles, the former are usually limited to wetter areas. A common sign of the meadow vole is the piles of grass cuttings that it leaves in its runways, located within dense vegetation. These voles occupy almost all of the northern continent except for portions of western and northern Alaska. In the Intermountain West, they extend down through central Utah.

They also occur in the Four Corners region in a separate "block" of their range in the central Rockies.

Their common habitat is moist to wet grasslands and meadows. A strong association with grasslands is emphasized by their apparent ability to exclude southern red-backed voles and deer mice from such environments. Although they often inhabit woodlands, such populations have lower reproductive success and adult survival than those in grasslands. In Utah, most occur in northern valleys or along the western flank of the Wasatch Range. Almost any grasses, sedges, or herbaceous plants are eaten; one study revealed over 70 species in their diet. At high densities, they can be a serious pest in fruit orchards, killing trees by "girdling" them, removing the bark in a circle at the base. They are active at any time but more so during the day if protected by dense vegetative cover. Predators include hawks, owls, carnivorous mammals, and snakes.

They exhibit periodic population cycles of two to five years. Many factors have been implicated in the regulation of these cycles, including food quality, predation, dispersal opportunities, genetics, and climate. John Christian suggested that stress suffered by individuals at high densities regulates their population growth. The body responds to this stress by secreting higher levels of adrenal gland hormones, which ultimately can cause a decline in reproductive functions. Furthermore, stress results in mortality, which together with an inhibition of reproduction fosters a decrease in the population's growth rate. If suitable habitat for dispersal is unavailable, the number of voles in an area could build to a point where stress becomes a regulatory factor. Working with Professor Christian, I have found that human populations exhibit some of the same dynamics at increasing densities as do small mammals.

Meadow voles are a premier example of an organism that puts a large portion of its energy into high, rapid, and early reproduction rather than growth or longevity. After a 21-day pregnancy, the female produces an average of 4 to 6 altricial offspring. Litters range in size from 1 up to 11. Because several litters are produced per season, meadow voles are prodigious in leaving descendants. But survival of the young is far from guaranteed; the production of so many young certainly seems related to this. In the first month after birth, close to 90 percent of the young perish. At most, they live just over a year. Those born in the spring reach adult size within three months, those born later do so after the winter. Unlike some other voles, these appear to be promiscuous rather than monogamous.

## MONTANE VOLE
### (*Microtus montanus*)

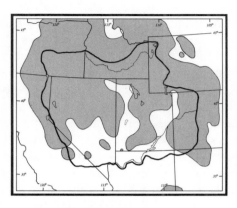

DISTRIBUTION OF MONTANE VOLE.

Total length: 5 1/2 to 7 1/2 inches; tail length: 1 1/4 to 2 3/4 inches.

As its name reveals, the montane vole is usually a mammal of the mountains. On top, it is a brown shade mixed with black or reddish, often washed with buffy or gray, creating a grizzled look. The sides are paler and more buffy and the belly varies from white to gray, also sometimes washed with buffy. The bicolored tail is blackish brown or black above and grayish below; it is moderately long, close to two and a half times the size of the hind foot. The feet are either dusky or silvery-gray. Unfortunately, montane voles are difficult to tell apart from their more widely distributed cousin, the meadow vole, which is usually browner, has darker feet, and is uncommon in the mountains. It is also hard to distinguish them from the long-tailed vole despite its longer tail. California voles, which barely occur in our region, inhabit the lowlands; they have pale feet. A characteristic Rocky Mountain species, montane voles are widely distributed across most of the Intermountain West. They are absent from southern Nevada and much of eastern and western Utah.

Their common habitats are moist, high mountain meadows and grassy valleys. Where they occur with meadow voles, they usually inhabit drier spots. At Timpie Springs, south of the Great Salt Lake, and elsewhere, they occur in marshes, an atypical place for them. Like other *Microtus* voles, they live in runways and burrows under the cover of high grasses. Their diet consists mostly of grasses, sedges, rushes, and an occasional fungus. At high densities, they can be devastating to hay and other crops. Predators include coyotes, hawks, and owls.

Throughout their mountainous habitats, montane voles exhibit population cycles. Cycle lengths, measured from one peak to the next, are three or four years. The marsh population at Timpie Springs, however, has not shown such fluctuations, remaining instead at a high density for at least eight years. Norman Negus and his colleagues attribute this to the relative predictability of the environment there; salt grass, largely their sole food source, sprouts at the same time each year. The voles produce their first litter shortly thereafter; the three other litters also arrive at roughly the same times each year. The young from the third litter form the breeding nucleus of the population the following spring, beginning the process once again. Alternately, food availability in the mountains can fluctuate dramatically from one year to the next, due to differences in winter precipitation levels and timing of the spring snowmelt. This prevents vole populations from attaining a comparable stability at high densities. Reports suggesting that montane voles are always cyclic are thus incorrect.

As indicated above, they are prolific breeders. Reproduction takes places from March until November. Their gestation period and the number of litters are similar to those of the meadow vole. Similarly, there is little if any male parental care in this species. Average litter size is about five young, yet in cyclic populations the litter size varies with the phase of the cycle. Negus and his group have also established that montane vole reproduction is stimulated by a specific chemical factor which appears in their food in the early spring. This finding has implications for the control of the onset of breeding in herbivores utilizing similar food sources.

CALIFORNIA VOLE (*Microtus californicus*)

Total length: 6 1/4 to 8 3/8 inches; tail length: 1 1/2 to 2 3/4 inches.

The California vole is similar to the meadow and montane voles. It is grizzled grayish brown with long, dark hairs sprinkled across the top. Individuals in desert habitats tend to be redder. The typically gray-ish belly is often highlighted by white-tipped hairs. California voles are differentiated from long-tailed voles by a shorter tail, which is less than a third of their total length. Another distinguishing trait is their pale feet, which contrast with their back color. But in the Intermountain West, you

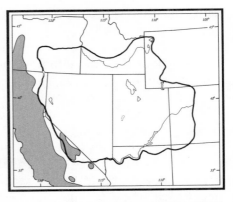

DISTRIBUTION OF CALIFORNIA VOLE.

probably will not have the chance to get close to its feet. This is because they marginally occur here along a few areas west of the Nevada-California border. Their distribution is from southwestern Oregon across most of California, terminating in Baja California.

They inhabit grassy meadows over a large range of elevations, from sea level to up in the mountains. They are found in salt and fresh water marshes, in wet meadows, and on dry, grassy slopes. Mostly feeding on grasses and their seeds, they will eat other available vegetation. During the winter, they supplement their diet with roots, tubers, and other subterranean plant parts. They can be a serious pest in orchards and vineyards, although a preference for wine has not been determined. Predators include common vole enemies, such as owls, hawks, snakes, and weasels. Their populations exhibit a three-to-four-year cycle. Peak densities can harbor 200 individuals per acre. In the San Francisco Bay area, it was found that their declines are attributable to predation. But it remains to be seen whether this is the case throughout their range, particularly in our region where they encounter different ecological conditions.

Breeding takes place throughout the year, with most litters produced between March and September. Following a 21-day pregnancy, from one to nine altricial young are born; an average litter has five offspring. Most females have between two to five litters in a year. The young are weaned after just two weeks. A recent study by R. S. Ostfeld strongly suggests that these voles are polygynous. Adult males are territorial, whereas several females might inhabit the same area and even share a nest.

## LONG-TAILED VOLE
(*Microtus longicaudus*)

Total length: 6 1/4 to 10 3/8 inches; tail length: 2 to 4 1/2 inches.

The long-tailed vole is a large species with a long, bicolored tail. It is close to half the body length, the longest of any of the voles in this region. However, shorter-tailed individuals

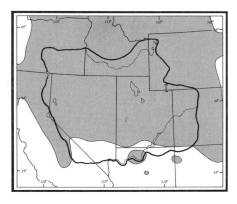

DISTRIBUTION OF LONG-TAILED VOLE.

are difficult to distinguish from meadow, California, and montane voles. Above, the voles range from a dull grayish to reddish or dark brown, streaked with black-tipped hairs. The belly is grayish with a white to dull buffy wash. Because the sides are paler than the back, the top stands out as a darker band. The feet are a dusky or soiled whitish color and the ears and eyes are large. Long-tailed voles occur throughout the western United States and northwestern Canada up into eastern Alaska. They are distributed across almost the entire Intermountain West except for small areas in southern Nevada and Utah.

They are found in a variety of environments from sea level up to at least 12,000 feet. Habitats include dry grassy areas, streambanks, mountain meadows, willow-sedge communities, dense conifer forests, and arctic tundra. They are not as dependent on moist areas as are meadow or montane voles. Grass is preferred, particularly in summer. When it is scarce, they eat underground plant parts and the inner bark of shrubs and small trees. Predators include owls, prairie falcons, weasels, and pine marten. In California, long-tailed voles commonly live above agricultural zones and thus are not as much of a pest as the California vole. Similarly, in Colorado, most live above 7,000 feet. Unlike other voles, they rarely make runway systems; those that are constructed are relatively undefined. In summer, they nest in burrows or under fallen logs or stumps, but in winter, they do so aboveground, under the snow or seek out brushy areas.

Litters of 1 to 10, averaging 5 or 6, altricial young are born from May to October. The peak of the breeding season is during June and July. They rarely live longer than a year, and females seldom produce more than two litters during their lives. After about three weeks, the young are sexually mature; those from early litters are likely to breed the same year. They seem to be more solitary than most other voles.

## MEXICAN VOLE
### (*Microtus mexicanus*)

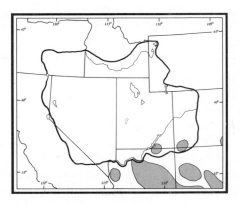

DISTRIBUTION OF MEXICAN VOLE.

Total length: 4 3/4 to 6 inches; tail length: 7/8 to 1 3/8 inches.

Mexican voles are the only primarily Southwestern vole in this region. Here, they are grizzled buffy gray above, but vary throughout their range from cinnamon-buff to dark cinnamon-brown. The sides are paler than the back, and they are buff to cinnamon below and have dusky feet. Even for such a small animal, the slightly bicolored tail is very short. Mexican voles are distinguished from similar species on the basis of belly color; the montane vole's is white to gray. Meadow voles are similarly differentiated, although they, too, are occasionally buff-colored below. Mexican voles are also sympatric with long-tailed voles, but there is no comparison in their tail lengths. Only the most northern segment of their range crosses into the Intermountain West in the Four Corners region. In Colorado, they occur in Mesa Verde National Park.

Habitats include unusual areas for voles, such as clearings in yellow pine forests, and dry, sparsely vegetated grasslands. They also reside in more typical vole habitats like mountain meadows and wet or boggy areas. Some of their predators are gray foxes, badgers, and skunks.

Nesting occurs either in runways or aboveground, protected by plants or debris. Litter sizes range from two to five, although three or four altricial young are usually born.

## WATER VOLE
### (*Microtus richardsonii*)

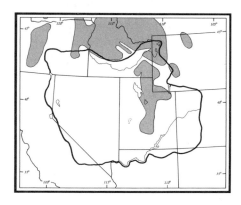

DISTRIBUTION OF WATER VOLE.

Total length: 7 3/4 to 10 1/4 inches; tail length: 2 3/4 to 3 5/8 inches.

The water vole is a unique member of our fauna for several reasons. It is the largest vole, it rarely occurs away from high mountain streams, and it is semiaquatic. Water voles only exist in small numbers, but are easy to recognize. The long fur is grayish brown to dark reddish brown above, and often appears darker due to the black-tipped hairs. Below, the fur is grayish, washed with white or silver. The bicolored tail is relatively long. Other identifying traits include long hind feet and flank glands which enlarge and make the hair greasy during the breeding season. Water voles are distributed in two separate bands in the Northwest: a narrow area from south-central Oregon up through southern British Columbia and a broader one from central Utah that widens across Idaho and eventually terminates along the Alberta-British Columbia border. They occur primarily in the eastern and northern mountain ranges of the Intermountain West.

They are found close to water in alpine or subalpine meadows. Not just any water is suitable; it is almost always a fast-moving, clear, spring-fed or glacial stream with a gravel bottom. Occasionally, they occur alongside high altitude ponds and in marshes or bogs. Major foods are the leaves and, to a lesser extent, stems of forbs. Others include grasses, sedges, roots, bulbs, and seeds. Although they are not particularly important to any predator, they are taken by short-tailed weasels, marten, and possibly hawks. Their runway systems are different from

230

those of other voles, weaving over the soil and below it in wide burrows and crossing through springs and streams. They are capable swimmers and divers. In summer, nesting is in burrows below the surface and under stumps, logs, or exposed roots. They remain beneath the snow for over half the year, where they probably are in aboveground nests.

The breeding season of water voles is shorter than that of most of their relatives, occurring from late May through August. Young usually do not appear until July. Pregnancy lasts for about three weeks, resulting in 2 to 10 naked and blind young; an average litter has 5 or 6 young. Even though they are sexually mature within two months, only some 25 percent breed the first year. At high densities, one male usually inhabits an area occupied by several females, suggesting that they are polygynous. Territories are marked with feces and flank gland deposits.

## SAGEBRUSH VOLE
## (*Lemmiscus curtatus*)

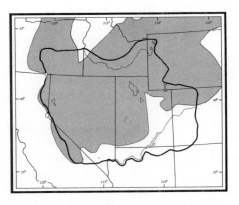

DISTRIBUTION OF SAGEBRUSH VOLE.

Total length: 4 1/4 to 5 5/8 inches; tail length: 5/8 to 1 1/8 inches.

If ever an animal was aptly named, it is the sagebrush vole. It lives under this plant, constructs nests from its shredded bark, and eats its leaves, bark, twigs, and roots. Sagebrush voles are easily distinguished from other voles, not only by their appearance but also because they usually are the only vole in their habitat. The dense fur is long, pale gray above, with paler sides, and is whitish, silvery, or buffy below. Occasionally, the ears and nose are tinged with buff. The slightly bicolored tail is furry and short. Sagebrush voles range throughout the western United States and adjacent southern Canada. They occur in most of the Intermountain West except for much of eastern Utah.

They occupy such environments as semiarid prairies, rolling hills, and brushy canyons. But almost everywhere, their homes are dominated by sagebrush and bunchgrasses, such as crested wheatgrass and rabbitbrush. Despite this habitat restriction, they are not particularly limited in their food choices; almost anything green, especially grass, is eaten. In southeastern Idaho, the castellaja plant is favored in the early summer; lupine composes most of their diet in late summer. In spring, they travel in groups to places where plant growth is most advanced, such as on south-facing slopes. Their most significant predators are owls; they are particularly important to short-eared and burrowing owls. Shrikes, bobcats, and long-tailed weasels also enjoy them. Burrows are arranged in clusters, usually near sagebrush, each having up to 30 entrances. An identifying sign is their oblong, green fecal pellets which they deposit around burrow entrances. In addition to sage bark, nests are fabricated from leaves, stems, and grass seed-heads. They are active at any time, especially from just before sunset until several hours after dark, and in the early morning. In certain respects, they are extremely clean, defecating and urinating far from the nest. However, their habit of hollowing out "cow chips," dried cow dung, for shelter from predators and harsh weather, counters this squeaky clean image.

Sagebrush voles reproduce throughout the year; even in their northern range they breed from March through December. Most pregnancies occur from March to May and again from October through December. Females typically have up to three litters per year. After a 25-day pregnancy, usually 5 to 6 altricial young are born. From 1 to 13 young may be in a litter. After three weeks of rapid growth, they are weaned. They become sexually mature at one to two months. It seems that they are more social than most voles, often living in colonies and traveling en masse to new feeding areas. They are also unlike other voles in the apparent lack of cycles in their population densities.


MUSKRAT (*Ondatra zibethicus*)

Total length: 16 1/8 to 24 3/8 inches; tail length: 7 1/8 to 12 1/8 inches.

The largest and most aquatic of the microtines, muskrats are familiar to even the most casual observer of natural history. This awareness might only involve stroking a garment made from their lustrous fur. Indeed, they are the most valuable semiaquatic furbearer on the continent, responsible for a multi-

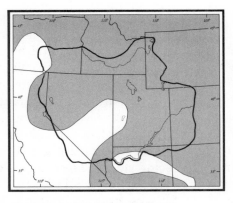

DISTRIBUTION OF MUSKRAT.

million-dollar industry. Their name is derived from the distinctive odor of their musk gland secretions, a pair of which are beneath the skin at the base of the tail. Like their relatives, the voles, muskrats have a relatively large blunt head, small eyes, and short, rounded ears. They are highly modified for their semiaquatic existence: the partial webbing of the large hind feet provides propulsion for swimming and the laterally flattened, long tail serves as a rudder. Furthermore, the underfur is waterproof and traps air bubbles, enhancing buoyancy and insulation. They are usually dark brown above with a darker tail and hind feet. Color varies, though, from white in albinos to black. Below, they are silvery gray. They occur throughout most of North America except for some of the southern United States. In the Intermountain West, they are prevalent except in southern Nevada and adjacent western Utah due to the scarcity of water in these areas.

Muskrats live in almost any aquatic environment. In the West, they are often found in ponds that beavers create from mountain streams. They are largely herbivorous, feeding on aquatic plants. A preference for cattails is often noted. At high densities, they can severely reduce an area's vegetaion in what is called an "eat-out." These are typically followed by a sharp decline in their numbers. Little realized is their occasional foraging on such animals as clams, crayfish, turtles, and fish. Overall, humans are the most important cause of their mortality, but raccoons and especially mink also take a fair share. Interest-

MUSKRAT

ingly, they are also preyed upon by raptors: bald eagles, great horned owls, and several hawks.

These rodents build either small, cone-shaped lodges or live in burrows dug upward into banks. In winter, they also make "push-ups," masses of vegetation for feeding that they shove up through cracks in the ice. Lodges, which are built on the marsh soil from aquatic plants, rise above the water level. Several underwater tunnels lead into each lodge. Two different types of lodges are constructed: larger dwelling units or "nest houses," as much as 20 feet in circumference, and feeding houses. Their homes are not as substantial as beaver lodges, usually remaining intact for but several months. Nevertheless, they have an important protective function and enable them to remain warmer in the winter. Muskrat burrowing may cause extensive damage to river banks and farm irrigation dikes. They have thus been the subject of intensive control programs. Yet, due to their high commercial value, they are also managed to increase their numbers in many areas. Their populations are cyclical: the cycle length varies geographically but is usually about 10 years.

234

After a 25-to-31-day pregnancy, an average of six or seven altricial young are born. Larger litters seem to be more common in northern locales. Two or three litters are commonly raised each year. After only two weeks, the young can swim; they are weaned two weeks later. A few muskrats breed in their first year, but the large majority wait until the following spring. Pairs form temporary bonds; they have been described as "loosely monogamous." In summer, the family lives in a nest house, defending a small surrounding territory.

## JUMPING MICE—FAMILY ZAPODIDAE

The jumping mice comprise a small family of but four species, all of which occur in the colder areas of North America and Eurasia. They are distinguished by striking colors and remarkable leaping abilities. Although they resemble kangaroo rats and pocket mice, they are not closely related to them. Jumping mice lack fur-lined cheek pouches and prefer moist, forested habitats. They have a stronger affinity with the jerboas of the Old World deserts and steppes. One species, the western jumping mouse, occurs in this region.

WESTERN JUMPING
MOUSE (*Zapus
princeps*)

Total length: 8 1/2 to 10 1/4 inches; tail length: 5 to 6 1/4 inches.

Although difficult to detect, the western jumping mouse cannot be confused with any other animal. It has yellow sides and a dark, broad band down the

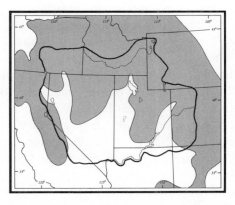

DISTRIBUTION OF WESTERN JUMPING MOUSE.

middle of the back that varies from yellowish gray to salmon-brown. The belly is white, occasionally with a yellowish tinge. It possesses an exceptionally long tail which functions as a balance organ in its leaps of three to five feet. The hind legs and feet are large, providing the propulsive power behind these jumps. Such jumping ability is curious in a species which often inhabits woodlands. Most small mammals displaying this type of loco-motion occur in open areas where erratic leaping enables them to evade predators. Western jumping mice occupy the western United States and southwestern Canada, occurring largely throughout the northern half of the Intermountain region.

They are found in several different habitats, most commonly in moist fields close to water, where low-lying grasses and herbs are lush and tall. In addition, they occur in thickets and wood-lands near watercourses. They either dig their own burrows or use those abandoned by other mammals. Primarily nocturnal, they largely feed on the seeds of grasses, docks, other green plants, and fungi. Insects and other invertebrates become more important in their diets in the spring. Predators which exact the greatest toll on them are birds of prey, bobcats, weasels, and garter snakes. Because they spend so much time hibernating underground, they may suffer less from predation than most other small rodents. Between August and October, they put on a large amount of fat to prepare for hibernation. Just prior to it, up to two-thirds of their weight consists of this stored fat. This enables them to stay asleep most of the year; hibernation lasts from September or October until April or May. In Utah, they are active for an average of only 87 days a year. They thus have an extremely short time to accomplish such vital tasks as breed-ing and fat accumulation. If they are even slightly inefficient in these activities, they might not leave descendants or even survive the winter. Indeed, roughly one-quarter of all adults and more than two-thirds of the juveniles die during the winter.

Soon after arousal from hibernation, the survivors mate. The altricial young are usually born in June or July after an 18-day gestation. From two to eight are produced; an average litter size is five or six. Most females have but one litter a year. They are raised in a round nest of interwoven grasses or moss located in a depression in the ground. Development is slow com-pared to most small rodents. The young nurse for about a month and continue even after they begin to eat solids. Adults are essentially solitary but are tolerant of others that enter their home range.

## NEW WORLD PORCUPINES – FAMILY
## ERETHIZONTIDAE

This is a small family consisting of only eight species, all of which occur in the Western Hemisphere. Each is arboreal or inhabits trees. Porcupines have broad feet, the soles of which are covered with little bumps called tubercles which increase traction. They are relatively large and have quills which are used to deter predators.

### PORCUPINE
(*Erethizon dorsatum*)

Total length: 25 1/2 to 36 1/2 inches; tail length: 5 3/4 to 11 3/4 inches.

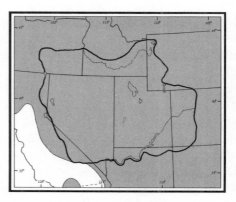

DISTRIBUTION OF PORCUPINE.

Unlike most rodents, which require elaborate descriptions for recognition, the porcupine needs no such introduction. The only member of this family north of Mexico, it is the continent's second largest rodent, bigger than any except the beaver. Above, it is covered with up to 30,000 quills; the longest are close to five inches. Quills are actually modified hairs, the longest ones are on the rump and the shortest on the cheeks. They are yellowish white with brown or black tips. Beneath them lies a thick underfur of typical mammalian hair; there are also long guard hairs among the quills. There are no quills on the undersurface. Porcupines have short legs and long, curved claws for climbing. They occur in almost all of northern North America down into northern Mexico. Except for a small area in southeastern California, porcupines are found throughout the Intermountain West.

Their habitats are varied and include forests, rangelands, open tundra, and even deserts. In the West, they occur in yellow pine forests, often close to vegetated riparian zones. In more

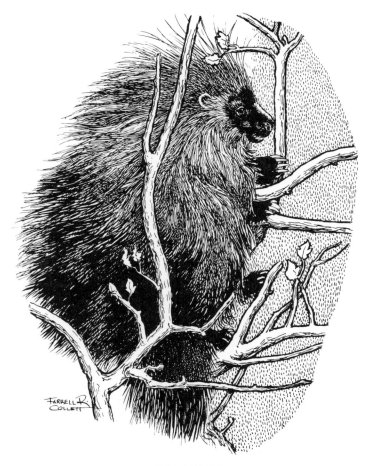

PORCUPINE

open areas, they inhabit brushy stream bottomlands. Because
their vision is not keen, they rely on an excellent sense of smell
to locate food. During the summer, their diet consists of a multitude of items. Virtually all parts of many plants are consumed.
In winter, however, they are usually restricted to inner tree bark
and evergreen needles; in some parts of the region, they prefer
Gambel's oak at this time. Often, one returns to feed on the
same tree, damaging it in the process. As a result, porcupines
have earned the reputation of being a forest pest. But because
the same one is used, few trees are likely to be affected. Their

signs include large patches of stripped bark and neatly sawed-off tree limbs.

Other than humans, their major predator is the fisher, which is adept at flipping a porcupine onto its back to avoid the quills. They are also victimized by other carnivorous mammals and several predatory birds. Although quills are not necessarily lethal, they may become so if lodged in a vital area. Contrary to a widely held belief, porcupines do not shoot their quills. Rather, when they strike out, usually with the tail, the loosely rooted quills detach after being driven into an adversary. Many quills are barbed at the end and are thus hard to remove. With time, they can move further into the victim's body. They are reportedly easier to extricate after cutting them, as this relieves pressure. This should be followed by a slight twisting and pulling with pliers.

Typical den sites include caves and hollow logs or trees. Little aggression is shown between individuals; they do not defend an area except for the tree on which they are feeding. Several might use the same den on an alternating basis. In winter, these ordinarily solitary beasts have even been known to share a den. They do not hibernate.

Contrary to most rodents, porcupines mate in the fall and early winter. They are quite vocal during their courtship. This is not due to any pain endured while mating with a quilled partner. The female flattens her quills and twists her tail so that the male can mount her in a "normal" fashion. Pregnancy is longer than that of any rodent in the region, 205 to 217 days. Such a long gestation results in the birth of usually one precocial (relatively mature) young in May or June. At birth, the young's eyes are already open. The quills are relatively soft, preventing a painful delivery, but harden within an hour. Nevertheless, they are still sharp and stiff enough to inflict hurt at this time. They can climb shortly after birth and assume a defensive posture a short time later. Such abilities ensure a high rate of survival for the newborn despite a small amount of parental care. Porcupines make a characteristic whining or crying sound that bears a close resemblance to a small child's. While visiting us in Jackson Hole one summer, my parents were amazed to learn that the noise outside their cabin emanated from this most unusual of mammals.

# REFERENCES

Alcorn, J. R. 1940. Life history notes on the Paiute ground squirrel. *Journal of Mammalogy* 21: 160–170.

Andersen, D. C., and J. A. MacMahon. 1981. Population dynamics and bioenergetics of a fossorial herbivore, *Thomomys talpoides* (Rodentia: Geomyidae) in a spruce-fir sere. *Ecological Monographs* 51: 179–202.

Anderson, P. K. 1980. Evolutionary implications of microtine behavioral systems on the ecological stage. *Biologist* 62: 70–88.

Armitage, K. B. 1981. Sociality as a life-history tactic of ground squirrels. *Oecologia* 48: 36–49.

Ashmole, N. P. 1961. The biology of certain terns. Ph.D. diss., Oxford University, England.

Balph, D. F. 1984. "Spatial & social behavior in a population of Uinta ground squirrels: Interrelations with climate and annual cycle." *In* J. O. Murie and G. R. Michener, eds. *The Biology of Ground-Dwelling Sciurids*, pp. 336–352. Lincoln: University of Nebraska Press.

Bandoli, J. H. 1981. Factors influencing seasonal burrowing activity in the pocket gopher, *Thomomys bottae. Journal of Mammalogy* 62: 293–303.

Bartholomew, G. A., and T. J. Cade. 1957. Temperature regulation, hibernation, and aestivation in the little pocket mouse, *Perognathus longimembris. Journal of Mammalogy* 38: 60–72.

Batzli, G. O. 1986. Nutritional ecology of the California vole: Effects of food quality on reproduction. *Ecology* 67: 406–412.

Boyce, M. S. 1981. Beaver life-history responses to exploitation. *Journal of Applied Ecology* 18: 749–753.

Brown, J. H. 1971. Mechanisms of competitive exclusion between two species of chipmunks. *Ecology* 52: 305–311.

Bushberg, D. M., and W. G. Holmes. 1985. Sexual maturation in male Belding's ground squirrels: Influence of body weight. *Biology of Reproduction* 33: 302–308.

Busher, P. E., and S. H. Jenkins. 1985. Behavioral patterns of a beaver family in California. *Biology of Behaviour* 10: 41–54.

Busher, P. E., R. J. Warner, and S. H. Jenkins. 1983. Population density, colony composition, and local movements in two Sierra Nevadan beaver populations. *Journal of Mammalogy* 64: 314–318.

Carleton, M. D., and G. G. Musser. 1984. "Muroid rodents." *In* S. Anderson and J. K. Jones, Jr., eds. *Orders and Families of Recent Mammals of the World*, pp. 289–379. New York: John Wiley and Sons, Inc.

Carroll, L. E., and H. H. Genoways. 1980. *Lagurus curtatus*. Mammalian Species no. 124. American Society of Mammalogists.

Christian, J. J. 1971. Population density and reproduction efficiency. *Biology of Reproduction* 4: 248–249.

Clark, T. W., R. S. Hoffman, and C. F. Nadler. 1971. *Cynomys leucurus*. Mammalian Species no. 7. American Society of Mammalogists.

Collier, G. D., and J. J. Spillett. 1973. The Utah prairie dog — decline of a legend. *Utah Science* 34: 83–87.

Cornely, J. E., and R. J. Baker. 1986. *Neotoma mexicana*. Mammalian Species no. 262. American Society of Mammalogists.

Daly, J. C., and J. L. Patton. 1986. Growth, reproduction, and sexual dimorphism in *Thomomys bottae* pocket gophers. *Journal of Mammalogy* 67: 256–265.

Daly, M., M. I. Wilson, and P. Behrends. 1984. Breeding of captive kangaroo rats, *Dipodomys merriami* and *D. microps*. *Journal of Mammalogy* 65: 338–341.

Davis, W. B. 1937. Variations in Townsend pocket gophers. *Journal of Mammalogy* 18: 145–158.

Dobson, F. S. 1979. An experimental study of dispersal in the California ground squirrel. *Ecology* 60: 1103–1109.

————— . 1982. Competition for mates and predominant juvenile male dispersal in mammals. *Animal Behaviour* 30: 1183–1192.

Downhower, J. F., and K. B. Armitage. 1971. The yellow-bellied marmot and the evolution of polygamy. *American Naturalist* 105: 355–370.

Egoscue, H. J. 1981. Additional records of the dark kangaroo mouse (*Microdipodops megacephalus nasutus*), with a new maximum altitude. *Great Basin Naturalist* 41: 333–334.

Ernest, K. A., and M. A. Mares. 1987. *Spermophilus tereticaudus*. Mammalian Species no. 274. American Society of Mammalogists.

Finley, R. B., Jr., J. R. Choate, and D. F. Hoffmeister. 1986. Distributions and habitats of voles in southeastern Colorado and northeastern New Mexico. *Southwestern Naturalist* 31: 263–266.

Frase, B. A., and R. S. Hoffman. 1980. *Marmota flaviventris*. Mammalian Species no. 135. American Society of Mammalogists.

Garrott, R. A., and D. A. Jenni. 1978. Arboreal behavior of yellow-bellied marmots. *Journal of Mammalogy* 59: 433–434.

Gittleman, J. L. 1985. "Functions of communal care in mammals." *In* P. J. Greenwood, P. H. Harvey, and M. Slatkin, eds. *Evolution — Essays in Honour of John Maynard Smith*, pp. 187–205. Cambridge: Cambridge University Press, England.

Hansen, R. M. 1962. Movements and survival of *Thomomys talpoides* in a mima-mound habitat. *Ecology* 43: 151–154.

Hasler, J. F. 1975. A review of reproduction and sexual maturation in the microtine rodents. *Biologist* 57: 52–86.

Hoffmann, R. S., and J. W. Koeppl. 1985. "Zoogeography." *In* R. H. Tamarin, ed. *Biology of New World Microtus*, pp. 84–115. American Society of Mammalogists Special Publication no. 8.

Hoffmeister, D. F. 1981. *Peromyscus truei*. Mammalian Species no. 161. American Society of Mammalogists.

Hoogland, J. L. 1981. The evolution of coloniality in white-tailed and black-tailed prairie dogs (Sciuridae: *Cynomys leucurus* and *C. ludovicianus*). *Ecology* 62: 252–272.

———. 1982. Reply to a comment by Powell. *Ecology* 63: 1968–1969.

Jenkins, S. H., and P. E. Busher. 1979. *Castor canadensis*. Mammalian Species no. 120. American Society of Mammalogists.

Jenkins, S. H., and B. D. Eshelman. 1984. *Spermophilus beldingi*. Mammalian Species no. 221. American Society of Mammalogists.

Johnson, D. W., and D. M. Armstrong. 1987. *Peromyscus crinitus*. Mammalian Species No. 287. American Society of Mammalogists.

Johnson, K. 1981. Social organization in a colony of rock squirrels (*Spermophilus variegatus*, Sciuridae). *Southwestern Naturalist* 26: 237–242.

Jones, W. T. 1985. Body size and life-history variables in heteromyids. *Journal of Mammalogy* 66: 128–132.

Knopf, F. L., and D. F. Balph. 1977. Annual periodicity of Uinta ground squirrels. *Southwestern Naturalist* 22: 213–224.

Koford, R. R. 1982. Mating system of a territorial tree squirrel (*Tamiasciurus douglasii*) in California. *Journal of Mammalogy* 63: 274–283.

Lair, H. 1985. Length of gestation in the red squirrel, *Tamiasciurus hudsonicus*. *Journal of Mammalogy* 66: 809–810.

Lancia, R. A., and H. E. Hodgdon. 1983. Observations on the ontogeny of behavior of hand-reared beavers (*Castor canadensis*). *Acta Zoologica Fennica* 174: 117–119.

Linsdale, J. M. 1946. *The California Ground Squirrel*. Berkeley: University of California Press.

Llewellyn, J. B. 1981. Habitat selection by the desert woodrat (*Neotoma lepida*) inhabiting a pinyon-juniper woodland in western Nevada. *Southwestern Naturalist* 26: 76–78.

Ludwig, D. R. 1984. *Microtus richardsoni*. Mammalian Species no. 223. American Society of Mammalogists.

McCarty, R. 1975. *Onychomys torridus*. Mammalian Species no. 59. American Society of Mammalogists.

————. 1978. *Onychomys leucogaster*. Mammalian Species no. 87. American Society of Mammalogists.

McGuire, B., and M. Novak. 1986. Parental care and its relationship to social organization in the montane vole (*Microtus montanus*). *Journal of Mammalogy* 67: 305–311.

Merritt, J. F. 1981. *Clethrionomys gapperi*. Mammalian Species no. 146. American Society of Mammalogists.

Michener, G. R., and J. W. Koeppl. 1985. *Spermophilus richardsonii*. Mammalian Species no. 243. American Society of Mammalogists.

Modi, W. S. 1984. Reproductive tactics among deer mice of the genus *Peromyscus*. *Canadian Journal of Zoology* 62: 2576–2581.

Morgart, J. R. 1985. Carnivorous behavior by a white-tailed antelope ground squirrel, *Ammospermophilus leucurus*. *Southwestern Naturalist* 30: 304–305.

Mullican, T. R., and B. L. Keller. 1986. Ecology of the sagebrush vole (*Lemmiscus curtatus*) in southeastern Idaho. *Canadian Journal of Zoology* 64: 1218–1223.

Nash, D. J., and R. N. Seaman. 1977. *Sciurus aberti*. Mammalian Species no. 80. American Society of Mammalogists.

Negus, N. C. 1950. Habitat adaptability of *Phenacomys* in Wyoming. *Journal of Mammalogy* 31: 351.

Negus, N. C., P. J. Berger, and B. W. Brown. 1986. Microtine population dynamics in a predictable environment. *Canadian Journal of Zoology* 64: 785–792.

Oaks, E. C., P. J. Young, G. L. Kirkland, Jr., and D. F. Schmidt. 1987. *Spermophilus variegatus*. Mammalian Species no. 272. American Society of Mammalogists.

O'Farrell, M. J., and A. R. Blaustein. 1974. *Microdipodops megacephalus*. Mammalian Species no. 46. American Society of Mammalogists.

———. 1974. *Microdipodops pallidus*. Mammalian Species no. 47. American Society of Mammalogists.

O'Farrell, M. J., and W. A. Clark. 1986. Small mammal community structure in northeastern Nevada. *Southwestern Naturalist* 31: 23–32.

Ostfeld, R. S. 1986. Territoriality and mating system of California voles. *Journal of Animal Ecology* 55: 691–706.

Oveson, M. C. 1983. Behavioral and metabolic adaptations of porcupines (*Erethizon dorsatum*) to winter stress. M.S. thesis, Brigham Young University, Provo, Utah.

Patterson, B. D. 1984. Geographic variation and taxonomy of Colorado and Hopi chipmunks (genus *Eutamias*). *Journal of Mammalogy* 65: 442–456.

Pinter, A. J. 1986. Population dynamics and litter size of the montane vole, *Microtus montanus*. *Canadian Journal of Zoology* 64: 1487–1490.

Pizzimenti, J. J., and G. D. Collier. 1975. *Cynomys parvidens.* Mammalian Species no. 52. American Society of Mammalogists.

Pizzimenti, J. J., and R. S. Hoffmann. 1973. *Cynomys gunnisoni.* Mammalian Species no. 25. American Society of Mammalogists.

Powell, R. A. 1982. Prairie dog coloniality and black-footed ferrets. *Ecology* 63: 1967–1968.

Price, M. V., and J. H. Brown. 1983. *Patterns of morphology and resource use in North American desert rodent communities.* Great Basin Naturalist Memoirs no. 7: 117–134. Provo: Brigham Young University.

Reich, L. M. 1981. *Microtus pennsylvanicus.* Mammalian Species no. 159. American Society of Mammalogists.

Reichman, O. J., D. T. Wicklow, and C. Rebar. 1985. Ecological and mycological characteristics of caches in the mounds of *Dipodomys spectabilis. Journal of Mammalogy* 66: 643–651.

Rickart, E. A. 1987. *Spermophilus townsendii.* Mammalian Species no. 268. American Society of Mammalogists.

Sharples, F. E. 1983. Habitat use by sympatric species of *Eutamias. Journal of Mammalogy* 64: 572–579.

Sherman, P. W., and M. L. Morton. 1979. Four months of the ground squirrel. *Natural History* 88(6): 50–57.

Skinner, T. H., and J. O. Klemmedson. 1978. *Abert squirrels influence nutrient transfer through litterfall in a ponderosa pine forest.* U.S. Department of Agriculture Research Note RM-353. Washington, D.C.: U.S. Government Printing Office.

Slade, N. A., and D. F. Balph. 1974. Population ecology of Uinta ground squirrels. *Ecology* 55: 989–1003.

Smith, C. C. 1968. The adaptive nature of social organization in the genus of tree squirrels *Tamiasciurus. Ecological Monographs* 38: 31–63.

———. 1970. The coevolution of pine squirrels (*Tamiasciurus*) and conifers. *Ecological Monographs* 40: 349–371.

Smolen, M. J., and B. L. Keller. 1987. *Microtus longicaudus.* Mammalian Species no. 271. American Society of Mammalogists.

Streubel, D. P., and J. P. Fitzgerald. 1978. *Spermophilus spilosoma*. Mammalian Species no. 101. American Society of Mammalogists.

———. 1978. *Spermophilus tridecemlineatus*. Mammalian Species no. 103. American Society of Mammalogists.

Thaeler, C. S., Jr. 1972. Taxonomic status of the pocket gophers, *Thomomys idahoensis* and *Thomomys pygmaeus* (Rodentia, Geomyidae). *Journal of Mammalogy* 53: 417–428.

Thaeler, C. S., Jr., and L. L. Hinesley. 1979. *Thomomys clusius*, a rediscovered species of pocket gopher. *Journal of Mammalogy* 60: 480–488.

Vaughan, T. A., and N. J. Czaplewski. 1985. Reproduction in Stephens' woodrat: The wages of folivory. *Journal of Mammalogy* 66: 429–443.

Veal, R., and W. Caire. 1979. *Peromyscus eremicus*. Mammalian Species no. 118. American Society of Mammalogists.

Webster, W. D., and J. K. Jones, Jr. 1982. *Reithrodontomys megalotis*. Mammalian Species no. 167. American Society of Mammalogists.

Wells-Gosling, N., and L. R. Heaney. 1984. *Glaucomys sabrinus*. Mammalian Species no. 229. American Society of Mammalogists.

Williams, S. L. 1976. Effects of floods on *Thomomys bottae* in Texas. *Southwestern Naturalist* 21: 169–175.

Willner, G. R., G. A. Feldhammer, E. E. Zucker, and J. A. Chapman. 1980. *Ondatra zibethicus*. Mammalian Species no. 141. American Society of Mammalogists.

Woods, C. A. 1973. *Erethizon dorsatum*. Mammalian Species no. 29. American Society of Mammalogists.

Zegers, D. A. 1984. *Spermophilus elegans*. Mammalian Species no. 214. American Society of Mammalogists.

# The Carnivores — Order Carnivora

The term "carnivore" has a tendency to be misunderstood.
Because it refers to an organism that eats meat, any one doing
so is, in effect, a carnivore. But in regards to mammalian classification, a carnivore is a species which belongs to the Order
Carnivora. Therein lies another problem since there are several
mammals in this order which do not eat meat. Some, like the
giant panda, *Ailuropoda melanoleuca*, are herbivores; others,
such as bears and raccoons, are best described as omnivores;
that is, they eat a variety of foods. Nevertheless, as is true for
species in all orders, the Carnivora share a common ancestry,
even if the food habits of some have become modified from the
original type. The great success of the order is probably due, in
large part, to opportunistic feeding habits. Carnivores have a
nearly worldwide distribution. Originally, they were absent from
Australia, but the dingo, a wild dog, has now been successfully
introduced there.

Most of the species are indeed carnivorous predators. Their
canine teeth are usually enlarged and sharp. The majority have
a superb sense of smell and a comparatively large brain case,
indicating a keen intelligence. Undoubtedly, this combination of
traits has enabled them to become superb killers. Most have a
plantigrade posture: when walking, they place the entire sole of
the foot on the ground. However, the cursorial groups, those
disposed toward running, exhibit digitigrade locomotion: they
walk or run on their digits. These include the canids and felids.
With few exceptions, carnivores bear altricial young and exhibit
extended maternal and, frequently, paternal care. There are
about 40 species of carnivores worldwide with 23 in the
Intermountain West. In addition to the other measurements,
shoulder heights are usually provided to assist in identification.

## COYOTE, WOLVES, AND FOXES—FAMILY CANIDAE

For many, it is the canids more so than any other group that command intense interest and admiration. This is borne out by the universal popularity of dogs and the appeal of wild species, like the wolf. The members of this family are the most cursorial carnivores, a trait reflected in the lithe bodies and long limbs which enable them to pursue prey over great distances. Canids strongly rely on a terrific sense of smell for both prey location and communication, although hearing and vision are also well developed. Most are diurnal in their habits.

Within this family, more strictly carnivorous species, such as coyotes and wolves, give birth to relatively lighter offspring than more omnivorous forms, such as the gray fox. Reproduction should be less energetically demanding for omnivores, given the greater variety of foods they rely on. As a result, they can afford to put more energy into the production of an offspring. More carnivorous canids might produce comparatively lighter young to reduce the risks associated with fluctuating prey availability. Some type of male parental care probably occurs in every species in this family. In the Intermountain West, there are five canid species, including the gray wolf, whose status here is questionable.

### COYOTE (*Canis latrans*)

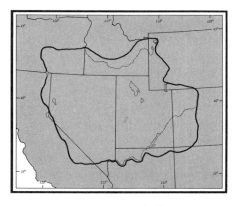

DISTRIBUTION OF COYOTE.

Total length: 41 3/8 to 52 inches; tail length: 11 3/4 to 15 1/2 inches; shoulder height: 23 to 26 inches.

The coyote is one of the enduring symbols of the American West. Indians, ranchers, hikers, and cowboy-movie audiences alike, have all shared a moonlit evening with the high-pitched howls and yips of this mammal. Yet, it is its barking that the name "coyote" is derived from, a Spanish

word based on an Aztec term for barking dog, *coyotl*. It is
the fastest North American canid, cruising at 25 to 30 miles
per hour and capable of bursts of 40 miles per hour. About the
size of a small shepherd dog, coyotes are a grizzled grayish
buff to brownish gray above. In winter, the coat is longer,
softer, and paler. Underneath they are whitish or buff. Their
ears are relatively long, particularly compared with a wolf's,
and are buffy to reddish on the back. The bushy tail has a
black tip.

Coyotes are confused with wolves and dogs, both of which
they can reproduce with. Interbreeding between domestic dogs
and coyotes has resulted in many wild "coydogs," which may be
hard to distinguish from the real item. Such interbreeding is difficult to reconcile with the notion that species are reproductively
isolated entities. In many other ways, however, especially in the
ecological and behavioral differences that normally prevent mixing, these canids are distinct. Wolves are larger and have a nose
pad greater than an inch wide. Further, they hold the tail horizontally while running, rather than almost between the legs as
does the coyote. Dogs, too, do not hold their tail so low while
running, and lack the coyote's characteristic dark vertical line on
the lower foreleg. Coyotes occur throughout most of the continent and the entire Intermountain West.

Originally, coyotes were denizens of open country and grasslands, and probably are still most numerous there. However,
they are highly adaptable and are now found in a wide diversity
of habitats. This is due to both their opportunistic habits and
their being transplanted to many new locations. Their diet is
similarly varied, consisting of various rodents, rabbits, deer,
sheep, ground-nesting birds, other vertebrates, invertebrates, and
many plants. Their great speed is evidenced by an ability to
catch jackrabbits. In winter, they rely on the carrion of large
mammals, such as deer and elk. During this time, it is a safe bet
that you can observe them on the National Elk Refuge in Jackson, Wyoming, where they are almost guaranteed an elk carcass
to dine upon. Small mammals are killed by a stalk-and-pounce
strategy; larger ones are taken by attacks to the head and belly,
often by several coyotes. Although there is considerable doubt
about the amount of damage they inflict, coyotes have earned
the enmity of many ranchers for their attacks on sheep. As a

result, they have been subject to intensive eradication programs, few of which have been effective. More research is needed if there is ever to be a resolution to this emotional topic. They, too, may become the victims of predators. Other than humans, who shoot them for pelts and to protect livestock, young ones are preyed on by cougars.

They usually breed between January and March. Females have just one heat, which lasts from two to five days. Following a 63-day pregnancy, an average of six altricial pups are born. In areas with great numbers of rodents, litter sizes tend to be higher. Pups are raised in den sites on brush-covered slopes, riverbanks, and rock ledges. Often, the same site is used for several years. The father assists in rearing the pups by bringing food to them and their nursing mother. Coyotes are monogamous and may remain mated to the same individual for several years, perhaps even for life. Some males, however, have more than one mate. After about six weeks, the young are weaned, dispersing from the den at six to nine months. They are thus with parents and littermates for an extended period, a time in which much learning and socialization takes place. A delay of independence and dispersal is associated with a high degree of sociality throughout the canids. Although yearlings can breed, they ordinarily do not. Coyotes are not as sociable as wolves but large packs do occur.

## GRAY or TIMBER WOLF (*Canis lupus*)

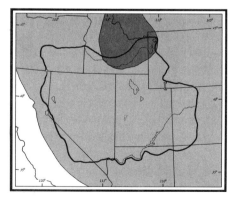

Total length: 39 1/2 to 80 5/8 inches; tail length: 14 to 19 3/4 inches; shoulder height: 26 to 38 inches.

The wolf is one of those rare animals which has thoroughly captured our imagination. Unfortunately, it is all too rare nowadays due to a long history of systematic

DISTRIBUTION OF GRAY OR TIMBER WOLF; HISTORICAL RANGE (DARK) AND AREA OF POSSIBLE PRESENT OCCURRENCE (LIGHT).

extermination, one that is still ongoing in much of the world. As the largest wild canid, its natural history has been a subject of intense interest. Hopefully, what we have learned will stimulate and enable us to stop persecuting this magnificent animal and restore it to the remnants of its former range.

Wolves are easy to recognize. Compared to the coyote, the other large western canid, it is larger, has a nose pad at least an inch wide, a broader snout, proportionately smaller ears, and holds its bushy tail horizontally while running. Males range from 45 to 175 pounds, females from 40 to 120 pounds. The long fur is usually grizzled gray but varies from white to black. It is highly unlikely that even the most ardent sleuth will observe one of these storied animals in the western United States. Wolves formerly occupied most of the continent, but were essentially exterminated from the lower 48 states by the beginning of this century. Populations currently exist in Canada, Alaska, Isle Royale National Park in Michigan, Superior National Forest in Minnesota, and in small numbers in other parts of Michigan and Wisconsin. Reports have surfaced indicating that there are some in several national forests in Idaho. As late as 1978, an adult male was shot in the Boise National Forest, which was followed by the sighting of a female and four young in that area. Some investigators believe that wolves also occur in Yellowstone National Park and its surrounding areas, but this is unproven. There is intense interest in releasing them in the park, with the hope of restoring a viable population. This is a controversial proposal, with many residents along the park's boundaries concerned about the livestock losses that might result from a reintroduction.

Originally, wolves inhabited most North American environments, except for deserts and high mountaintops. Primary foods are large mammals: deer, elk, moose, caribou, and bison. Because they are most successful at taking down young, old, and infirm animals, it is assumed that they "improve" a prey population by removing its least fit members from the breeding pool. The degree to which this occurs is debatable since high-quality young could also be eliminated before they breed. The smallest animal they prey on with regularity is the beaver. Yet they will eat almost any creature, including livestock, which is largely the reason for their persecution. Another rationale for getting rid of them is their supposed tendency to attack people. In actuality, Little Red Riding Hood cried "wolf": attacks on humans are extremely rare.

Wolves hunt in packs, typically of 4 to 8 individuals, although groups of up to 36 have been observed. Aided by great endurance, they chase prey over considerable distances. Especially large animals are initially attacked on the rump, but deer may first be bitten on the head, shoulders, flank, or rump. Wolves can suffer injuries, sometimes fatal ones, while trying to kill the bigger animals. Except for some hide and the largest bones, they consume everything. If anything is left, a scavenger might find a meal. The only nonhuman predator wolves have to deal with is the grizzly bear, which could stumble upon a den and take the pups.

Wolves are highly social animals whose packs actually are family groups. Pack cohesion is maintained by affectionate bonds that develop early in life. A "dominance hierarchy" exists with an adult "alpha" male dominant over a female who, in turn, is dominant over the pups. In larger packs, an extended order develops with one alpha male ascendant over the others, and a female similarly reigning over those of her sex. They travel together over great distances; a pack's territory can encompass over 250 square miles. Their familiar, haunting howl has several functions: it assembles the pack by enabling individuals to locate one another, and it appears to advertise the territory. Scent-marking by defecation and urination are probably also used for the latter purpose.

Breeding occurs once a year between January and April, toward the end of this period at higher latitudes. After courtship, females are pregnant for about 63 days. An average litter consists of 6 or 7 altricial pups; the range is 1 to 14. The den, located within a secure place, such as a rock-shelter, may be used for several years. Females remain with the young for about two months, during which time the male and the rest of the pack bring them food. After this period, the young play in an open, grassy area called a "rendezvous site." If strong enough, pups will join the pack that fall. Wolves typically do not breed until they are three years old. Although they can live for up to 16 years in the wild, a 10-year-old is already getting on in years.

RED FOX (*Vulpes vulpes*)

Total length: 35 3/8 to 40 3/8 inches; tail length: 13 3/4 to 17 inches; shoulder height: 15 to 16 inches.

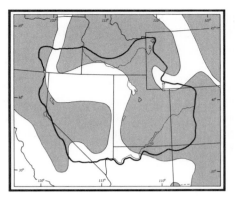

DISTRIBUTION OF RED FOX.

For one who finds excitement in the natural world, little compares with the thrill of seeing a red fox in the wild. I doubt if I will ever forget the time, after an evening of fishing in eastern Wyoming, when a red fox casually strolled across the dirt road in front of my car. It would be hard to describe the thick, rusty reddish to reddish yellow coat as anything other than beautiful. Below, the fur is paler, ranging from white to grayish. Highlighting this animal's appearance is the large bushy tail, tipped with white, and the black on the nose, lower legs, and backs of the ears. Some melanistic, or black, individuals have white-tipped guard hairs on the back, giving them a silvery appearance; these are known as "silver foxes." Another variation involves a cross of brown hairs over the shoulders and down the middle of the back; these animals are "cross foxes." Fortunately, such prized individuals are relatively common in the mountains of the West. Red foxes are found in almost all of North America. They are present in most of the Intermountain West except for a zone encompassing northern Nevada, western Utah, and adjacent areas.

They occur in many different habitats. Characteristic ones include "edges" where the forest meets an area with shorter vegetation, riparian zones in semidesert scrub communities, and brushlands. Such places often support high numbers of small mammals and are thus likeliest to contain the most foxes. The majority of their diet consists of other animals. Rabbits and hares account for about a third of their intake, another third is rodents, with the rest composed of other mammals, birds, invertebrates, and vegetation. People with farm backgrounds know all too well of their taste for poultry and pork. Usually, they hunt by moving along with their sensitive nose to the ground, trying to pick up an animal's scent. When they find their prey, it is quickly killed by snapping it up with the jaws a la the gingerbread man or by pouncing on it. Running after prey, typical of the larger canids, is rarely employed. Their reputation as sly and clever creatures is due to their cooperative hunting endeavors. Individuals may work together in pairs, circling brush piles to drive a victim to the partner. They have been known to crawl through culverts, ostensibly forcing prey to a colleague waiting on the other end. It is unclear, though, how important cooperation is as a hunting strategy. They occasionally cache food for use at a later date. As with many other predators, humans are the major cause of their mortality, with trapping, hunting, and automobiles all taking a toll. Young foxes occasionally fall victim to coyotes or birds of prey.

In the middle of winter, a male teams up with a female to form a hunting pair. They mate in January or February. After a 53-day pregnancy, from 1 to 12 grayish black altricial kits are born. The mean litter size is about 4 or 5. The father is involved in parental care in the manner of most canids, bringing food to the den for the vixen and young. Dens are typically in an area with a commanding view, such as high on a riverbank. Occasionally, the foxes excavate a den; usually, they appropriate one formerly belonging to another mammal. After five weeks, the young emerge from the den. Their parents then begin to bring them live prey so they can practice the art of killing. This will make them useful when they join their parents several weeks later on hunting forays. Families break up in the early fall. Young may breed in their first year several miles from the natal area, although some disperse over a hundred miles away. Dens are abandoned in winter. The foxes may not even seek shelter in snowstorms. Instead, they stay warm by wrapping themselves with their luxurious tails.

## KIT FOX
(*Vulpes macrotis*)

Total length: 28 3/4 to 33 inches; tail length: 10 1/4 to 12 5/8 inches; shoulder height: 12 inches.

With its oversized ears and tail, the kit fox looks like it left the stockroom with the wrong parts. Its ears are proportionately the longest of any North American canid and the tail accounts for about 40 percent of its total length. Other unusual features include well-haired soles, which could be an adaptation

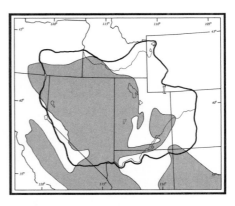

DISTRIBUTION OF KIT FOX.

for traction on sand, and a thick fringe of whitish hairs along the inner borders of the ears. On top, it is light grizzled to yellowish gray, dark brown to blackish on the lips and sides of the muzzle, buffy to orange along the shoulders and sides, and white below. Kit foxes are the smallest canids in the region, 25 percent less than red foxes in most measurements. They are further differentiated from red foxes by their feet and legs, which are either whitish or the same color as the body; those of the red fox are blackish. Kit foxes have a black-tipped tail, whereas the red fox's is white-tipped. Gray foxes are distinguished by their "mane" of coarse black hairs and a tail that appears triangular rather than round in cross section.

The swift fox (*Vulpes velox*) so closely resembles the kit fox that they are considered to be a single species by some. They are most likely distinct, however, and are treated as such herein. Recently, there have been some unconfirmed sightings of swift foxes in western Wyoming, so it is possible that they also occur in this region. Primarily a Southwestern mammal, kit foxes are found in most of Nevada, throughout western and much of eastern Utah, and nearby areas in the Intermountain West.

Inhabitants of desert and semiarid regions, they are generally found in flat shrub or shrub-grass communities with little ground cover on light desert soils. In some areas, they hunt in dunes with greater vegetative cover. Where they occur in the Great Basin, shadscale, greasewood, and sagebrush are common. Their major prey are the rodents or lagomorphs which are

KIT FOX

common in an area. Kangaroo rats and black-tailed jackrabbits are especially important; other victims include ground-nesting birds, reptiles, and insects. Although their remains occasionally turn up in coyote scat, few animals prey on kit foxes. Unfortunately, humans have been responsible for the decimation of many populations through indiscriminate trapping and shooting, eradication attempts aimed at coyotes and wolves, and the secondary effect of rodent poisoning.

In fall, the vixen begins to search for a den in which to raise her young. She methodically examines and cleans every potential site before selecting the most appealing one. Males join the females in October or November and they breed in December or January. Kit foxes are reported to be monogamous and may mate for life. However, mate switching and even polygyny do occur. There is also evidence from a study of radio-collared individuals that pairs do not travel or hunt together. After a 49-to-56-day gestation, an average of four or five altricial young are born in February or March. Males bring food back to the growing family. Pups emerge from the den after one month, beginning to hunt with their parents at three to four months. In October, the family unit breaks up. Some pups do not strike out on their own, remaining instead in the den with or without the parents.

## GRAY FOX (*Urocyon cinereoargenteus*)

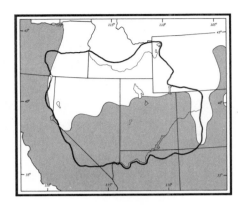

DISTRIBUTION OF GRAY FOX.

Total length: 31 1/2 to 44 1/4 inches; tail length: 8 3/4 to 17 3/8 inches; shoulder height: 14 to 15 inches.

The gray fox is the only North American canid with genuine climbing abilities. So advanced is this skill that it can climb straight up the limbless trunk of a 50-foot tree. It can rotate its forearms at least as much as any other canid, which should aid in climbing. And it is even capable of jumping from limb to limb. Trees are used as foraging and resting places, as well as refuges from predators. Gray foxes are readily distinguished from other canids by their coloration: they are a grizzled "salt and pepper" gray above, cinnamon to buff on the neck and undersurface, white on the chest and throat, and have a black-tipped tail with a stiff, black mane down its middle. In addition, they have distinctive black, white, and red facial markings. These foxes are distributed across the continental United States, except for much of the Northwest, and through Mexico to northern Venezuela and Columbia. They occur in the southern part of the Intermountain West.

More so than any other canid on the continent, gray foxes are inhabitants of deciduous forests. In our region, they occupy rugged, broken terrain with brushy vegetation and old fields. Dens are usually in brushy or wooded areas and thus are not as conspicuous as those of red or kit foxes. In this region, they are typically aboveground in the shade of boulders, cliffs, or trees. The dens are rarely marked with mounds, as are those of the red fox. Throughout the eastern and central United States, rabbits and rodents are their major prey. Yet, in a southwestern

COYOTE

GRAY or TIMBER WOLF

RED FOX

BLACK BEAR

GRAY FOX

Utah study, fruit was most important, followed by mammals, including pocket gophers and mice, as well as numerous invertebrates. They also eat the carrion of animals, such as deer. Insects were most important in summer, with fruit dominating fall and winter diets. Because they eat more berries than do red foxes, their scats are usually darker, especially where wild cherries abound. Humans, interested in marketing their striking pelts, are their major predators. Others are golden eagles, dogs, and perhaps coyotes and bobcats.

The period of breeding varies geographically; in this area, it probably occurs from January through April. Gestation lasts 53 to 63 days, resulting in one to seven, with an average of four, altricial young. At three months of age, the young accompany their mother on hunting trips, learning how to ambush, their primary hunting strategy. Just one month later, they can forage on their own. Females reproduce at 10 months of age and evidence suggests that the majority do so. Like most canids, the gray fox is assumed to be monogamous. A family unit, consisting of the parents and their young, commonly maintains a distinct home range.

## *BEARS—FAMILY URSIDAE*

Bears are the world's largest land-dwelling carnivores. These powerful mammals weigh up to 1,700 pounds and fear no other animal, except perhaps humans. But rarely does a summer pass without a report of a bear attacking a person. Especially dangerous when surprised or with cubs, bears should never be approached. In the lower 48 states, most attacks are by grizzly bears in Yellowstone and Glacier national parks, two of their remaining strongholds. Despite their ferocity, I strongly believe that we must plan and manage ecosystems in national parks, wilderness areas, and other places that include healthy bear populations.

Although regarded by many as the prime example of a hibernating animal, bears are not "true" hibernators. Their blood temperature does not substantially drop below that of the environment, as does that of a hibernating bat or ground squirrel. Finally, a bear's footprint is like that of a human; the entire sole, including the heel, touches the ground when they walk. This is referred to as a plantigrade posture. There are eight bear species in the world. Two occur in the Intermountain West: the black bear and the grizzly bear.

## BLACK BEAR (*Ursus americanus*)

Total length: 4 1/4 to 6 1/4 feet; tail length: 3 to 7 inches; shoulder height: 3 to 3 1/2 feet.

Black bears are the more common species in the region. Compared to grizzlies, they are smaller, usually darker, lack a hump above the shoulders, have much

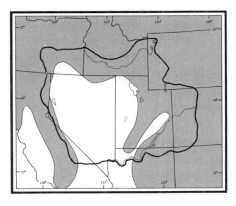

DISTRIBUTION OF BLACK BEAR.

shorter front claws (about one and a half inches versus four inches), and a flat or convex rather than a concave forehead. Not all are black; throughout the West, there are large numbers of brown ones known as "cinnamon bears." Males weigh 250 to 500 pounds, female weights vary from 225 to 450 pounds. Black bears occur throughout most of North America. The largest area from which they are absent is the Desert Southwest, including almost all of Nevada and western Utah. With the exception of this region, they inhabit much of the Intermountain West. The largest populations are found away from areas of human habitation.

In the West, black bears most often occur in forested or brushy mountainous areas and in other wooded locales, such as those along rivers. They are virtually never in open habitats, where grizzlies once reigned. Largely nocturnal and crepuscular, they rely on a keen sense of smell to locate food. Despite a reputation of being vicious carnivores, they are highly omnivorous and will eat almost anything. Recent findings reveal that they are occasionally cannibalistic, attacking others in their dens. Favorite foods include berries and honey, as farmers and beekeepers know all too well. Other typical foods include fish, rodents, birds and their eggs, insects, and nuts. Most meat is obtained from carrion. When the bears are feeding on fruit or berries, their scat is a characteristic flattened "pie." Otherwise, it is cylindrical or coiled. By determining the contents of scat from bears and other species, biologists have learned much about food habits.

During the day, the bears rest in ground depressions lined with leaves and other vegetation. They can be surprisingly fast, running up to 30 miles per hour if need be. From about November until April, they enter a winter dormancy. Although not technically considered hibernation, it is nonetheless a deep sleep from which they are only infrequently and briefly aroused. Winter bedrooms are located in caves, beneath the roots of large trees, or under a pile of large rocks. There, they are kept nourished and warm by a layer of fat several inches thick.

Mating takes place in the early summer. The embryo remains dormant until about November when it implants in the uterus, phenomena known respectively as embryonic diapause and delayed implantation. After a total pregnancy of up to 225 days, the young are born in January or February. Yet, because of the delay in implantation, the actual developmental period of six to eight weeks is short for such a large animal. Two or three extremely altricial cubs are born to a dormant mother. Litter sizes range from one to five. Cubs do not even open their eyes until they are about four to five weeks old, meanwhile nursing in the winter den. Growth is slow; they are but six to eight pounds upon emergence from the den, several weeks after birth. Adult size is not attained until their fourth or fifth year. Still, they remain with their mother for only one year before dispersing. It is at least three years before they enter the ranks of the breeding portion of the population. Females typically bear young every other year. Unusual for a carnivore with altricial young, the father does not participate in parental care. In fact, the female chases all bears away from her cubs. Black bears do not have a well-defined social system, apparently mating promiscuously. A male's home range often overlaps those of several females.

## GRIZZLY BEAR (*Ursus arctos*)

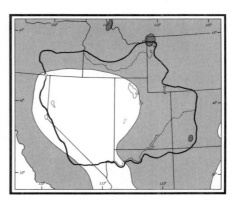

DISTRIBUTION OF GRIZZLY BEAR; HISTORICAL (LIGHT) AND PRESENT RANGE (DARK).

Total length: 6 to 7 feet; tail length: 3 inches; shoulder height: 4 1/2 feet.

My favorite grizzly bear story is about the backpacker who woke up with a start during the night when he felt his tent being pulled around. As he unzipped the door to find out what was going on, he saw a huge grizzly parading about with one of the tent's guylines in its paw. Before the situation worsened, he jumped from the tent and dived into a nearby icy lake, assuming the bear would leave. Naturally, it just walked to the edge of the water and watched the hapless fellow. After a while, it left and the shivering man began wading toward the shore. Just when he was about to exit the lake, the bear reappeared, sending him right back into the deep water. The same sequence of events occurred repeatedly throughout the night until the bear, finally tired of the game, left the area and one numb hiker behind. Such tales usually reveal several attributes about this largest of carnivores: grizzly bears are clever, fearless, powerful, and often ferocious.

One might logically guess that their name reflects grisly or gruesome habits. But "grizzly" refers to their frosted appearance, produced by a yellowish, whitish, or silvery wash over their brown coat, particularly on the shoulders and back. Other distinctive features include a hump on the shoulder region, a slightly "dished" or concave facial profile, and forefeet claws usually about four, but up to six inches long. Weights range from 325 up to a hefty 1,700 pounds in the Alaskan brown bear, which is the same species. Signs include vegetation and earth piled over a carcass on which they have been feeding, ripped-up berry patches, and claw slash marks on trees up to twice the height of an average person. I distinctly recall a queasy feeling upon seeing fresh slashes on the shutters of a cabin I stayed in by Yellowstone Lake's Southeast Arm. The historic range of the grizzly probably included most, if not all, of western North America, with the exception of arid locales. From an estimated population size of some 100,000 in 1800, there are likely less than 1,000 remaining in the lower 48 states. Its present distribution amounts to less than 1 percent of its historic range. By the 1920s, it was virtually eliminated from this region. The one believed to be the last grizzly in Utah, dubbed Old Ephraim, was killed in 1923. Currently, grizzlies occur only in a few spots, from the Yellowstone National Park area northwest to Alaska. There have occasionally been reports of them in the San Juan Mountains of southwestern Colorado.

No one habitat type is preferred by these bears. Today, they are largely in remote forested regions and high mountain country, but this is a result of their elimination from other areas. Once they even prospered on the Great Plains, where they would gorge themselves on bison carcasses. In fact, most of the big game meat they obtain is carrion. They are not the destroyers of big game they are purported to be. Small mammals, such as ground squirrels and marmots, are regularly dug up from dens. Other important foods include fish, pine nuts, berries, fruit, and insects and their larvae. They do not climb trees, as does the black bear. Like their relatives, they sleep through the winter in a large den that is either excavated or modified from a suitable spot. Before dormancy, they can put on up to 400 pounds of fat. They have virtually no natural predators. When both species were plentiful, wolves may have occasionally taken a cub. We are still their principal enemies, only sanctioning their existence in a few restricted settings. Few would argue about the need to control and eliminate grizzlies from areas close to human habitation. The problem for grizzlies, as with most wildlife, is that there simply are too many people and too much habitat destruction. For this animal, which may have a home range of up to 150 square miles, it is easy to see why there are so few places left.

Breeding habits are similar to those of the black bear. Mating occurs in June or July; the embryo does not implant in the uterine wall for several months. Then, following a total gestation of about 185 days, usually two altricial cubs are born between January and March. It is difficult to conceive of a tiny one-and-a-half-pound cub becoming so enormous. The ascent to adulthood is slow; cubs do not eat solid food for about six months, and they den with their mother for the first two winters. Although most females are capable of breeding after four and a half years, they do not become productive members of the population until they are from five to nine years old. The term "promiscuity" best defines grizzly mating habits. Females have cubs only every second or third year. Grizzlies live for about 15 years in the wild; there are records of individuals living for over thirty years.

## RACCOONS AND THEIR RELATIVES — FAMILY PROCYONIDAE

The procyonids are a small group of 18 medium-sized species. All are semi-arboreal and have good climbing skills. Although few in number, they exhibit a wide range of feeding styles. For example, of the two species in our region, raccoons typically forage along streams, whereas ringtails spend more of their time feeding on the ground or in trees and bushes. These two animals and the coati, the other North American procyonid, have long, banded tails. They have blunt, not sharp, cheek teeth, revealing their omnivorous feeding habits. Procyonids are restricted to the New World: North and South America. Some mammalogists previously placed lesser and giant pandas in this family, but each is now regarded as belonging to a separate group.

## RINGTAIL or CACOMISTLE
(*Bassariscus astutus*)

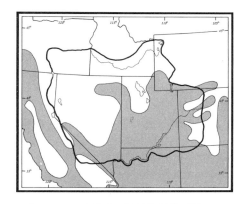

DISTRIBUTION OF RINGTAIL OR CACOMISTLE.

Total length: 24 1/4 to 31 7/8 inches; tail length: 12 1/4 to 17 1/4 inches.

Pity the poor ringtail. It is so often likened to other animals that it must have an identity crisis. It is said to have a catlike body and a foxlike face. In frontier times, it earned the moniker "miner's cat" because it was used around mining camps to dispatch rodents. Another name, cacomistle, is derived from the Aztec Nahuatl term for "half mountain lion." "Cacomistle" is more commonly used for its Central American relative, *Bassariscus sumichrasti*. Ringtails have also been referred to as civet cats, which are African mammals in the mongoose family, Viverridae. This is because the ringtail secretes a smelly fluid from its anal glands when upset. The true civet cat, *Civetticus civetta*, manufactures a musky substance which is used in perfume. Given the above, what does this animal look like? It has a long, slender torso and an equally long, bushy tail with 14 to 16 contrasting blackish brown and white bands. Above, it is pale yellowish gray and whitish buff below. Unlike the raccoon, it lacks a black face mask; instead, a white or pale eye ring surrounds the narrow black circle around the eye. At night, its eyeshine is red to yellowish green. It can partially retract its claws. Ringtails are found in the southwestern United States and Mexico. In the Intermountain West, they occur in southern Nevada, much of Utah, and in adjacent western Colorado and southwestern Wyoming.

Most often, ringtails are found in rough, rocky habitats in dry regions, such as around canyons and boulder-strewn areas,

RINGTAIL or CACOMISTLE

as well as chaparral country. Yet, they usually are not more than
a quarter mile from water. Although less common in wooded
locales, they may occur there if hollow trees are available for
denning. Dens are also made in cliffs, under rocks, in stumps or
logs, and in abandoned buildings. They hunt during the night by
ambushing. After pouncing on their prey, they kill it with a bite
to the neck. They are highly efficient at hunting mice and also
enjoy squirrels, woodrats, and rabbits. Other mammal meat is
obtained from carrion. Their diet includes birds, snakes, lizards,
toads, insects, fruit, berries, and nectar. They have superb
climbing and leaping skills, which are enhanced by their sharp
claws. An incredible adaptation is their ability to rotate the hind
feet at least 180 degrees, affording them superb traction as they
rapidly descend head first down a cliff or a tree. Enemies include
bobcats, great horned owls, and humans.

Their breeding biology is not well understood. In Texas, they
mate in early April, producing a litter of two to four young by
early June. One litter per year is the norm. The newborn are
white and fuzzy. Males assist in rearing the young by bringing
food to the den. After two to four months, they hunt on their

own, leaving their parents in the fall. Ringtails appear to be semicolonial in some areas.

RACCOON (*Procyon lotor*)

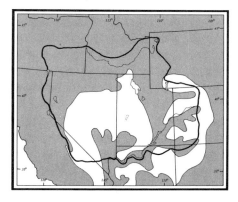

DISTRIBUTION OF RACCOON.

Total length: 23 3/4 to 31 3/8 inches; tail length: 7 1/2 to 16 inches.

If there is an animal with more popular appeal than the masked bandit, I am not aware of it. Raccoons have so many attractive traits that it is hard to begin to describe them. The brownish black mask around the eyes, offset by surrounding white hair, is a good starting point since it alludes to their mischievous ways, like opening up garbage cans. The luxurious fur, dark grayish tinged with red or brown and heavily streaked with black above, and light grayish brown below, has been the object of many a raccoon coat. And what baby-boomer boy went without a Davy Crockett coonskin hat, replete with a bushy ringed tail?

Parts of both the scientific and common names refer to aspects of the raccoon's great manual dexterity. *Procyon* means primitive dog, a reference to canid affinities, and *lotor* means "the washer." The word "raccoon" is derived from the Algonquin Indian term *arakunem* meaning "he who scratches with his hands." It is doubtful that food is washed for hygienic reasons. Raccoons have separate sense receptors in the forefeet, each corresponding with a specific area in the brain. Wriggling food in water may help them to evaluate it because their sense of touch is enhanced when their fingers are wet. Possibly, they wet them simply because it feels good; they massage their hands even when they do not have food. Raccoons range from lower Canada through the United States, Mexico, and much of Central America. The Intermountain West, however, is the one area within this broad distribution from which they are commonly absent. They occur across most of Wyoming, Idaho, and Oregon, into northern Nevada. From southern Nevada, their range extends across southern and eastern Utah into Colorado. They are continually expanding their range in this region; there frequently are reports of new occurrences.

Raccoons are not dependent on any one habitat type. They occur in forests, farmlands, fields, and various other places. Common along streams, marshes, and other wetlands, they feed heavily on the animals in them, such as crayfish, clams, and crabs. Indeed, the relative dearth of water and large aquatic invertebrates in this region has probably precluded their existence in much of it. Additional foods include berries, nuts, seeds, corn, small vertebrates, and young muskrats. They devour the eggs of waterfowl, reptiles, and amphibians. Raccoons are essentially nocturnal. Major predators are humans — who kill millions every year through hunting and trapping, coyotes, feral dogs, and owls. Many places are used as dens, including hollow trees, rock crevices, and ground cavities.

They put on fat through the summer and fall but lose as much as half of their weight over the winter. Those in the north begin this winter weight loss earlier and lose more than those farther south. During the winter in southern locales, raccoons should expend less energy staying warm and have an easier time finding food. Hence, their weight decrease is neither as sudden nor as drastic. Although they den up for long periods at this time, they do not hibernate.

There have been few studies of their reproduction in this region. In the Southeast and Midwest, they breed through much of the early part of the year, with most pregnancies occurring in early spring. Gestation lasts for about 63 days, resulting in litters of two to five altricial young. Litters are larger in northern populations. Weaning takes place between the second and fourth month; the young become independent before winter. In places with cold winters, however, the mother and young may den together. Females can breed as yearlings, but only about half become pregnant. Although juvenile males can breed, most become mature too late in the year for it to matter. They may sire the second litters of some females. Raccoons do not appear to have a tightly knit social organization. Males are promiscuous, seemingly territorial with each other but not toward females. Females, however, probably are not territorial at all.

## WEASELS, SKUNKS, AND THEIR RELATIVES— FAMILY MUSTELIDAE

The Mustelidae is the most numerous carnivore family in the region, containing 11 species. There are approximately 70 species worldwide, making them the second largest family after the Viverridae, the one which includes mongooses and civets. Mustelids vary greatly in appearance and life history, ranging from the thin, elegant ermine to the stout badger. Most, however, are similar in having long slender bodies, short legs, small rounded ears, "pushed in" faces, and especially in being highly efficient killers. Males are usually considerably larger than females.

Their reproduction frequently involves delayed implantation of the egg in the uterine wall. Thus, both mating and birth can occur when food is plentiful. Mustelids are also known and respected for their paired anal scent glands. The scents they produce serve to communicate sexual and other social messages. In skunks, these glands and their secretions have been effectively modified for defensive purposes.

MARTEN (*Martes americana*)

Total length: 19 1/4 to 26 7/8 inches; tail length: 5 1/4 to 9 1/2 inches.

The marten is a close relative of another beautiful furbearer, the renowned Siberian sable (*Martes zibellina*). Both are about the size of a domestic cat. Although

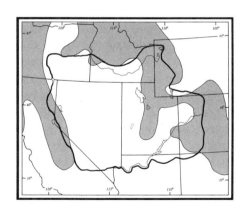

DISTRIBUTION OF MARTEN.

like a weasel with an elongated body, the marten has a bushier tail and the legs are proportionately longer. Both differences are related to its climbing ability; a heavy tail should provide balance, and longer legs enhance mobility while in the trees. Above, the fur is long and silky, but it is dense and soft underneath. It is typically a golden brown, slightly darker below, and blackish brown on the feet and tip of the tail. There is a creamy white to orange patch on the throat that occasionally extends to the chest. The head, including the face, and edges of the ears are all highlighted by buffy hairs. A close relative, the fisher, is distinguished from the marten by its much larger size, darker brown fur, lack of a throat patch, and grizzled appearance on the head and back. Marten occupy the far northern reaches of this continent. In the Intermountain West, their range extends into the Sierra Nevada and Rocky Mountains.

Most common in dense conifer stands of fir, spruce, hemlock, or lodgepole pine, they also occur in mixed conifer-deciduous forests. Prime habitat generally includes fallen logs, stumps, and shrubs which support their prey. In the Intermountain region, they are prevalent at higher altitudes and are frequently spotted on rocky slopes above timberline. I once encountered one upon arriving at the windblown summit of Medicine Bow Peak in Wyoming's Snowy Range. Marten are solitary hunters that basically feed on small- to medium-sized mammals. The larger species they rely on are Douglas' squirrels, flying squirrels, ground squirrels, and snowshoe hares. Red squirrels are concentrated on in some areas; marten also use their seed middens and dens. Meadow and red-backed voles, however, could compose the largest portion of their intake. Berries are a regular addition to their diet in late summer and autumn. In the Sierra Nevadas, they forage at night in winter and by day in summer, apparently coordinating their activity with that of their major prey. Humans are their only significant predator, trapping them for their lustrous, valuable fur. Extensive logging has destroyed their habitat in many areas, drastically reducing populations. They are enjoying a resurgence due to protection, more prudent regulation of trapping, and some reforestation. Other predators may include golden eagles, fishers, coyotes, wolves, and lynx.

Mating takes place in the middle of summer. At this time, communication between the sexes is highlighted by a chuckling "love call." Because the male's home range commonly overlaps those of several females, they may be polygynous. Males are substantially larger than females, about 15 percent longer and up to 65 percent heavier. After only a few divisions, the fertilized egg stops developing; it does not implant in the uterine wall until February or March. The fetus then grows rapidly. After just four weeks, the young are born. Usually three, but from two to five altricial young are produced in this single litter of the year. The female raises the young by herself in a leaf-lined nest located under rocks or within a hollow tree or log. At six to eight weeks, the young accompany the mother on hunts, acquiring the skills necessary for survival. By three months, they are almost adult size and are soon on their own. They do not become part of the breeding population until their second year. Even then, older males do most of the breeding with the recently matured females.

## FISHER (*Martes pennanti*)

Total length: 31 1/8 to 40 3/4 inches; tail length: 11 3/4 to 16 5/8 inches.

Fishers actually do not do much fishing. Instead, the name could be based on their alleged habit of stealing fish from the winter caches that early trappers kept

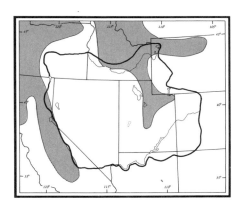

DISTRIBUTION OF FISHER.

for their dogs or from the traps themselves. Others believe that the name is derived from their preying on fish and amphibians in the ponds and lakes of lowland forests. Roger Powell, the leading authority on this mammal, suggests that they are called fishers because early Dutch settlers thought that they resembled the European polecat (*Mustela putorius*). They called a polecat "fitchet" or "fitchew," terms similar to "fisher." These words are derived from *visse*, Dutch for "nasty," a reference to the polecat's odor.

Although similar to marten in many respects, fishers are considerably larger (about the size of a small fox), less slender, and lack the marten's distinctive throat patch. Their long fur is dark brown to blackish above and heavily sprinkled with buff or silver on the face, neck, and shoulders, producing a grizzled look. This appearance is more typical of the males, which are about 15 percent larger than the females. The bushy tail, rump, and legs are black. On the bottom, there can be several white or cream-colored patches which vary in size and number. Historically, fishers occurred across southern Canada and the northern United States. Like the marten, they are found in the Intermountain West, where their range extends south into the Rocky Mountains and Sierra Nevadas.

They prefer dense lowland forests and spruce-fir stands with extensive canopy cover. Canopies are the uppermost, branched, leafy layer of the trees. Major food items are small- to medium-sized mammals, birds, and the carrion of large mammals. In conifer forests, they concentrate on snowshoe hares, attempting to flush them from hiding places. After a quick chase, the hare is killed with a bite to the back of the head or neck and consumed in one sitting. In upland hardwood stands, fishers focus their efforts on porcupines. They often appear to know the precise location of their dens, methodically moving from one to the next. A fisher kills the porcupine by continually biting it on the face, the only unprotected part of its body. The porcupine may circle about, attempting to protect itself. Or it might head up a tree, only to face the quick fisher coming down at it. After the porcupine succumbs, the fisher carefully skins it, eating everything but the feet, large bones, quilled skin, and occasionally the intestines. More so that any other carnivore, fishers are adapted to prey on porcupines due to their overall strength and speed, a height which enables them to attack the porcupine's face, and climbing skills which prevent their victim's escape. Porcupines, however, are not totally helpless. If in a tree den with just one opening, they simply turn away from their foe. Fishers, themselves, are rarely preyed upon, with the important exception of humans.

Mating occurs between March and May. After dividing for about two weeks, the embryo becomes dormant for 10 or 11 months. It develops for about one month after implantation in the uterus. Between February and May, an average of three altricial kits is born. Weaning occurs after two months, but it takes about four months for them to be able to kill on their own. Approximately a month later, the kits disperse. Females reach adult size after half a year; it can take the larger males more than a year to do so. Similarly, although females become reproductively mature at one year, males may not breed until their second year.

Due to overtrapping and habitat destruction caused by logging, fishers were severely reduced or eliminated in much of the continent by 1940. Recently, they seem to be responding well to protection and habitat restoration. They have been reintroduced in some places, including the Rocky Mountains.

## ERMINE or SHORT-TAILED WEASEL (*Mustela erminea*)

Total length: 7 1/2 to 13 1/2 inches; tail length: 1 3/4 to 3 1/2 inches.

Ermine are the smallest carnivores in the region. The least weasel (*Mustela nivalis*) is the tiniest one on the continent but it does not occur here. In our area,

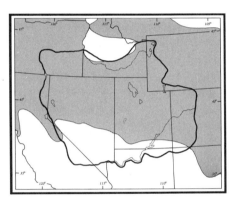

DISTRIBUTION OF ERMINE OR SHORT-TAILED WEASEL.

the only animal with which ermine might be confused is the long-tailed weasel. However, the latter species is usually larger and its longer tail is at least 44 percent of the length of its body. An ermine's tail is normally only a third of the body length. Ermine resemble a typical weasel: their long, thin body is supported by short legs, and they possess a flat triangular head, rounded ears, and a narrow black-tipped tail. In summer, they are dark reddish brown above and whitish below. But in winter, they are completely white, camouflaged against a background of snow. They range throughout the entire northern portion of the continent as well as that of the world. In the United States, ermine extend into the Rocky Mountain and Northwest regions.

Except for some small areas in the southern part, they occupy almost the entire Intermountain West.

They are found over a broad range of environments. The crucial factor determining their presence is an abundance of small rodents, particularly voles, and leporids. They hunt by rapidly moving about, searching holes and crevices for food. Other talents contribute to their hunting success. A fine swimming ability enables them to catch water voles. They are also good climbers, capable of raiding tree nests of birds and squirrels. Surplus food is stored in caches and defended. Apparently, they are not heavily preyed upon. The black coloration on the tip of their tail may have evolved to distract raptors pursuing them in the open.

Typical habitats include brushy areas, forest edges, alpine meadows, marshes, and riparian zones. Ermine are uncommon in deserts. A cryptic winter coloration is not their only adaptation for snowy locales. They can burrow in soft snow and easily run on it when it is compacted or frozen. Females, in particular, hunt for small mammals under the snow. Snow also provides them with insulation in areas with harsh winters. Smaller animals, such as ermine, lose proportionately more heat than larger animals. This is because of the large surface area they have compared to their volume; relatively more heat is lost through this "exposed" surface. Weasels lose more heat than similarly sized animals because their long, slender shape creates an even greater amount of surface area. In places with extremely severe winters, ermine make highly insulated nests, often lined with vole fur.

Of the three closely related weasels on this continent, the least weasel, the ermine, and the long-tailed weasel, only ermine are larger in colder regions. Several hypotheses have been examined to understand this pattern. Thus far, one which has not been ruled out is that they are larger in such places because they feed on larger prey. The skull features associated with feeding are bigger in ermine living in colder areas. Furthermore, the body size of voles is also greater in higher latitudes. The lack of geographical size variation in the ermine's cousins remains unresolved.

Mating occurs in late spring and early summer. As with most other mustelids, ermine exhibit delayed implantation; embryos stop developing after 14 days for 9 to 10 months. They

GRIZZLY BEAR

RACCOON

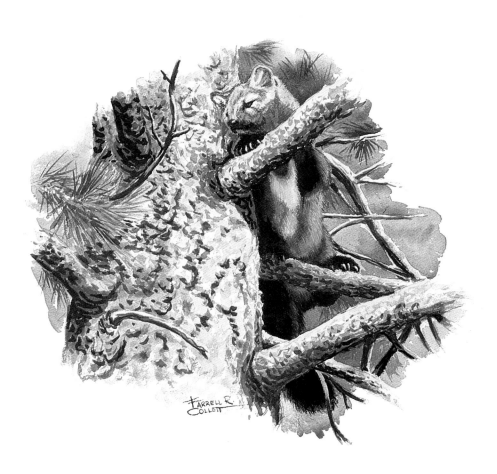

MARTEN

FISHER

ERMINE or SHORT-TAILED WEASEL

MOUNTAIN LION or COUGAR

LYNX

BOBCAT

implant the following spring and birth occurs about four weeks later. Litter sizes are usually between 4 and 8 young; but the range is up to 18. The young normally arrive in April. They are altricial and extremely small, typically weighing less than a tenth of an ounce. Their eyes do not even open until they are at least a month old. At two and a half to three months, they begin to kill small rodents. Males are not opposed to "robbing the cradle"; in temperate areas, females can be fertilized at about five weeks, before they are weaned or even before their eyes open. Alternately, males may not reach maturity until they are a year old.

Ermine exhibit pronounced sexual dimorphism in body size: males are 40 to 80 percent larger than females. In fact, they are the most dimorphic of the three closely related North American weasels. This difference could be related to their reproductive strategies. The female raises the young alone, procuring most of the prey for herself and the litter. Smaller females may be at an advantage because they have both lower absolute energy requirements and better success in hunting abundant small prey. The greater size of the males may be due to the fact that larger ones are apt to attract more mates; ermine are polygynous. The sexes are separate most of the year, but during the breeding season, the home range of one male overlaps those of the several females with which he may mate.

## LONG-TAILED WEASEL (*Mustela frenata*)

Total length: 11 to 21 3/4 inches; tail length: 3 1/8 to 6 3/8 inches.

Unlike other North American weasels, long-tailed weasels do not have a Eurasian counterpart. In many aspects of their ecology and life history, however, they

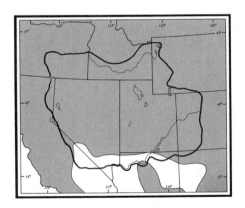

DISTRIBUTION OF LONG-TAILED WEASEL.

are much like their relatives. As the name suggests, their most

LONG-TAILED WEASEL

distinguishing trait is a long, black-tipped tail, which accounts for over 44 percent of the head and body length. In summer, they vary from pale to dark brown above. Paler individuals are found in arid climes. They are white on the chin, upper lips, and occasionally above the eyes, making it appear as if they wear bridles; the name *frenata* is from the Latin *frenum* for "bridle." Below, they are buffy to yellowish. The winter pelage of northern individuals is completely white except for the black tail tip. Those in the south merely become a lighter shade of brown at this time. They are distributed across southern Canada, most of the United States except for the extreme Southwest, and Mexico and Central America. Except for its far southern reaches, they are found throughout the Intermountain West. They are probably the most widely distributed carnivore in Utah and several other states in the region.

Although they occur in a variety of environments, long-tailed weasels are typical of rocky or brushy zones and those close to water. In the West, they also occur at high altitudes, even above timberline. Where they coexist, ermine generally inhabit forests and their borders, whereas long-tailed weasels are more common in open habitats. In this region, pocket gophers seem to be their most common prey. Males may be almost twice the size of females and thus can hunt larger animals, such as cottontails, snowshoe hares, and squirrels. A rabbit is too large to be dispatched immediately, so the weasel first incapacitates it by repeated bites which sever the head-supporting muscles. Then, it finishes the rabbit off by strangulation or by slashing the large blood vessels alongside the neck. Because they lick the blood on their prey's wounds, weasels have been maligned as vampirelike bloodsuckers. Females typically do not engage in such pandemonium, concentrating instead on small rodents and insectivores. In both sexes, the elongated shape enables them to hunt with ease in burrows and hollow logs. Climbing skills are employed to capture tree-nesting species. When prey is abundant, caches of kills are stored under logs or in a burrow. Weasel dens, with their fur- and grass-lined nests, are often the former homes of pocket gophers or ground squirrels, but they may also be found under wood or rock piles. Predators are owls, hawks, foxes, and snakes.

Long-tailed weasels mate in summer and the young are born the following April or May. Embryonic growth is delayed for most of the pregnancy. After a period of cell division that lasts for about a week, embryos cease development until the final four weeks. Most litters have from six to eight altricial young; litter sizes range from four to nine. By the time their eyes open at five weeks, the young are almost weaned. In their second month, they join their mother on hunting trips, but do not disperse until close to four months old. At this time, the females are sexually mature. The males, which are already larger than their mother, do not breed until they are yearlings. There are few studies of their mating system, but some reports indicate that they are briefly monogamous. However, most species in which males are so much larger than females are polygynous, with the male's home range encompassing those of the several females with which he mates.

BLACK-FOOTED
FERRET (*Mustela
nigripes*)

Total length: 19 3/4 to
22 5/8 inches; tail
length: 4 1/2 to 5 1/2
inches.

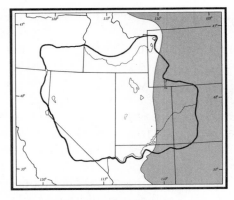

DISTRIBUTION (HISTORICAL) OF
BLACK-FOOTED FERRET.

The black-footed
ferret has the unfortu-
nate distinction of being
the most endangered
mammal in North
America. It once ranged
across a large area in the central part of the continent, but now
there might not be any free-ranging ferrets left. In 1981, a colony was discovered near Meeteetse, Wyoming, some 60 miles
east of Yellowstone National Park. Following a high of about
130 individuals in 1984, the population was decimated by an
outbreak of canine distemper. Late in the summer of 1986, a
team of biologists decided to trap the approximately 15 remaining ferrets and place them in a captive breeding program. In
this program, they hope to replenish the population in an environment free from disease and predators.

Black-footed ferrets are about the size of a mink, buff to
yellowish brown above with whitish areas, especially on the belly
and face. The top of the back is washed with a darker brown.
There is a distinctive dark to black mask around the eyes which
is surrounded by white. The tip of the tail and the feet are also
dark or black. Males are about 10 percent larger than females.
In the Intermountain West, ferrets occurred around eastern
Utah and western Colorado; it is still possible that a few
colonies exist in these remote areas. The word "ferret" comes
from the Old French *fuiret* meaning "thief," a sure reference to
their mask.

Their historic range included the Great Plains, montane
basins, and semiarid grasslands. The boundaries of their distribution nearly coincided with those of the four prairie dog species, which is not a coincidence since the ferret is a "specialist
predator" on prairie dogs. It relied most heavily on colonies of

BLACK-FOOTED FERRET

black-tailed prairie dogs. The ferrets even used their burrows for dens and temporary shelters. Indeed, although they did eat other rodents, it was this dependence on prairie dogs that brought about their demise. Prairie dogs have been the victims of intensive elimination efforts by ranchers who believe that their burrow holes are hazardous for livestock. Due to the success of these efforts and the division of large prairie dog towns by agricultural development, the ferrets lost their food base and never recovered. Additional information is provided in the account of the white-tailed prairie dog.

The ferrets were preyed upon by coyotes, golden eagles and perhaps other raptors, and domestic dogs and cats. Previously, predation may not have been a significant mortality factor in their population dynamics. However, given their present susceptibility to both predation and disease, as well as the potential for inbreeding in small groups, it appears to have been a wise decision to move the remaining members of the Meeteetse colony to a controlled situation.

They mate in March or early April and have a 42-to-45-day gestation. Interestingly, they do not exhibit the long delay in implantation which is so characteristic of other mustelids. The average litter size in one wild population was three and a half; the range was from one to five. The young remain in the burrow for about 45 days. By July, most are close to adult size.

Almost every natural history book makes a statement decrying the fate of species threatened with extinction. It is hard to add to such sentiments in a way that does not seem redundant or trite. But the black-footed ferret, a victim of circumstances if ever there was one, is so captivating that it is easy to make an appeal for it and thus all of the species we have mercilessly driven to the brink of no return. Somehow, for the ferret, the word "extinction" has an especially horrifying ring.

## MINK (*Mustela vison*)

Total length: 19 1/4 to 28 1/4 inches; tail length: 6 1/4 to 7 5/8 inches.

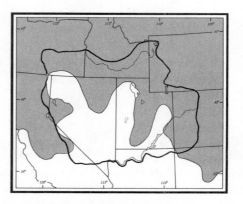

DISTRIBUTION OF MINK.

To most people, the mink is the best-known weasel, even if they do not realize that it is one. This recognition is due, of course, to its beautiful fur. For many, a mink stole or coat is the epitome of "haute couture." Although the value placed on these garments may seem decadent, the fur is certainly deserving of its reputation. The dense, soft grayish brown underfur is covered by the familiar long and lustrous guard hairs. The latter give the animal its color, which ranges from pale chocolate-brown to black; the belly is only slightly lighter. There usually are white markings on the chin and throat. The mink is a large weasel with the characteristic elongated body propelled by short legs. It is distinguished from the others by its slightly bushy tail, which resembles that of the marten but is not nearly as long. Mink also lack the marten's orange throat patch and occur in different habitats. They are differentiated from the other weasels by their lack of white underparts. They have several adaptations

MINK

for their semiaquatic existence, including water-repellent fur and partially webbed feet. Males are about 10 percent larger than females. Mink are more widely distributed than any weasel on the continent north of Mexico. They are found throughout Alaska, in almost all of Canada, and in the United States except for the Desert Southwest, including the more arid portions of the Intermountain West. Here, they occur in the region's northern sections, extending down into the mountains and foothills.

Although mink have a wide distribution, they are almost always found close to water, along the banks of rivers and lakes or in marshes. If a watercourse is strewn with logs or brushy cover, it is especially attractive because it affords them a den and a battery of ambushing stations. The prey with which they are most associated is the muskrat; they appear to be a factor in the muskrat's population cycles in many areas. Yet they are not dependent on muskrats, alternately satisfying their hunger with rabbits, chipmunks, voles, frogs, and crayfish. They also swim well enough to catch fish. Like the other weasels, they cache surplus prey. One den in Illinois contained 13 muskrats, 2 ducks, and a coot. Hence, although largely restricted to watercourses, their opportunistic feeding habits allow them to become established wherever a suitable water supply occurs. Hunting territories are defended and marked with a foul-smelling anal gland secretion. Major predators include other mink, foxes, bobcats, and great horned owls. Pelts from wild mink are still valuable despite the preponderance of the supply from mink farms. Thus, trapping is still an important mortality factor.

Mink usually mate between January and March. Although they exhibit delayed implantation, it is both shorter and more variable than that of other weasels. An average pregnancy lasts for 50 days, but the range is from 40 to 75 days. Embryonic development takes approximately a month of this period. Usually four altricial kits are born, but litter sizes range from three to six. After four weeks, when their eyes are open, the kits are covered with reddish gray fur. Four weeks later, they join their mother on hunting forays, dispersing by early autumn. Both sexes mature by winter, so all individuals can participate in breeding the following year. Some of the younger males, however, may not have the status necessary to attract mates. Males are assumed to mate with several females.

## WOLVERINE (*Gulo gulo*)

Total length: 31 1/2 to 44 1/4 inches; tail length: 6 3/4 to 10 3/4 inches.

The wolverine is a fabled beast of the north, reportedly ferocious enough to scare a bear away from its kill, smart enough to regularly raid traplines, and

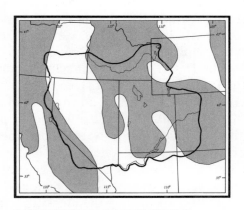

DISTRIBUTION OF WOLVERINE.

capable of roaming great distances to satisfy its gluttonous appetite. But as is the case with most mythical creatures, it is hard to know where the truth begins. Due to the scarcity and secretive ways of wolverines, much of their life history is likely

WOLVERINE

to remain a mystery. Undoubtedly, they are the heaviest, most powerful mustelid in North America. They resemble a large, elongated bear cub on short, heavy limbs. Blackish brown, they have two distinctive, broad yellowish to light brown bands, each extending from the side of the neck to where they meet at the tail. On the top and sides of the head are light gray patches. Irregular pale brown patches dot the throat and chest. This scruffy appearance is accentuated by long, four-inch guard hairs which hang from the hips and sides. Further, the short tail is similarly shaggy, with six-inch hairs swaying from it. Wolverines originally occurred throughout Alaska and Canada and across the northern tier of the United States, extending south into the mountainous regions. A few might still be found in the more remote areas of the Intermountain West.

They inhabit forested areas, particularly those with dense conifer stands. In the far north, they are found on the tundra. Their fur oils are frost resistant, enabling them to remain active in even the roughest of winters. They readily eat carrion and will not hesitate to attack much larger animals. Even moose and elk are fair game, especially when infirm or weary. Other fare includes beavers, porcupines, and ground squirrels, which are dug from their burrows. Yet they are not entirely carnivorous, supplementing their diet with berries and roots. Wolverines cover large areas on their hunting expeditions; a male's home range may be greater than a thousand square miles. Movement is fairly rapid across most terrain. They swim and climb with ease. Dens are located in almost any protected spot. Except for humans, these fierce beasts do not have any enemies.

Mating takes place from April through October. It is suspected that an extended period may be needed for such a solitary, sparsely populated creature to find a partner. Most pairings, however, do occur in midsummer. After some cell division, embryos remain quiescent until January. From one to four altricial young are born in late March or early April after an actual gestation of 30 to 40 days. The mother takes care of the young by herself. Some reports state that the young disperse after six months, whereas others indicate that they remain with the mother for up to two years. In either case, they do not become sexually mature until their second summer. Wolverines could be moderately polygynous since a male's home range usually overlaps those of two or three females. But because it could be difficult to find even a single mate, the potential for polygyny may not be realized.

## BADGER (*Taxidea taxus*)

Total length: 20 1/2 to 34 1/4 inches; tail length: 3 7/8 to 6 1/4 inches.

For an animal that is so widely distributed, surprisingly little is known about the badger. There is scant realization as well that several common items in our culture emanate

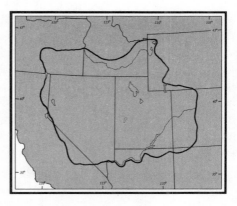

DISTRIBUTION OF BADGER.

BADGER

from them. For example, some of the finest paint and shaving
brushes are made from their stiff hairs. Few know that
"dachshund" means "badger hound." Across the Atlantic, this
dog has long been used to hunt the European badger, *Meles
meles*. Even the use of the term "badger" to indicate harassment
is derived from the cruel European practice of tormenting these
animals. The name refers to their "badges," distinct black and
white cheek patches and a white forehead stripe. The latter
extends to the tail in a southern subspecies, which includes some
found in our region. In most, however, this stripe terminates in
the shoulder region. Badgers are flattish, stout-bodied mustelids
with short legs. Their front paws have long, curved claws, but
the hind-feet claws are shovel-like. The shaggy coat varies from
grizzled grayish to brownish and the legs are black. They have
short, upright ears and a slightly upturned snout. They are
found from the northern Midwest across nearly all of the western United States, including the entire Intermountain West. In
recent years, their range has expanded eastward. They extend far
into Canada and Mexico.

Badgers commonly occur in treeless regions that have soil deep enough for burrowing, particularly open grasslands and deserts. They subsist on a variety of foods, but concentrate on ground squirrels, pocket gophers, rats, and mice. Because of their skill in catching rodents, they are often considered to be beneficial in agricultural areas. Incredibly, they are reported to team up with coyotes, one of their own predators, to hunt rodents. The coyotes, however, simply may watch badgers hunt and then attempt to nab escaping prey. Other items in their diet include lizards, rattlesnakes, insects, carrion, and honeycombs. In addition to coyotes, they are preyed upon by golden eagles. Yet, because badgers are such powerful and ferocious opponents, they are not easily taken. Humans account for a good deal of their mortality. Ranchers, who consider their large, oval burrow entrances to be livestock hazards, trap and shoot them. Many are also caught in traps set for coyotes. Badgers spend much of their time in burrows, using them for dens, escape, and as places to dig out prey. Ground squirrels often use vacant badger burrows as dens. Good swimmers, badgers can even cross rivers and lakes. In hot weather, they often cool off in the water. They are active day or night. In colder regions, they put on fat and become sluggish in winter but do not hibernate.

Except for the breeding season, badgers are basically solitary. Mating occurs primarily from midsummer through early autumn. Implantation of the fertilized egg in the uterus is delayed for varying periods, up until February in colder areas. The blind but somewhat furred altricial young are usually born in early April. Litter sizes range from two to five, with an average of two to three. Nursing lasts through June and the young disperse later in the summer. Both sexes breed as yearlings; some females do so in the year of their birth.

## WESTERN SPOTTED SKUNK (*Spilogale gracilis*)

Total length: 13 to 18 1/8 inches; tail length: 4 to 7 inches.

In North America, there are two types of spotted skunks, each taking its name from the part of the country in which it lives. The eastern United States is home to the eastern spotted skunk (*Spilogale putorius*). Its close relative, the western spotted skunk, is the one found in our region. The latter species is the smallest skunk on the continent. It is jet black with four to six white or yellowish white stripes on its back and sides. Toward the rear and on the sides, these stripes break up into spots. Spotting also occurs on the head and between the eyes. The tip of its bushy tail is white, considerably more so than that of the eastern spot-

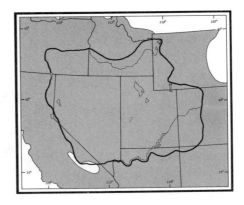

DISTRIBUTION OF WESTERN SPOTTED SKUNK.

ted skunk, which may not have any white at all. The spotted skunk is easily distinguished from the striped skunk, the only other one in the region, by its smaller size and stripe pattern. Western spotted skunks are found throughout the entire Intermountain West.

Largely nocturnal, they occur in rocky or brushy areas, often in foothills and canyons, and along streams and bottomlands. They are reported to be common in several areas, including southern Idaho, Mesa Verde National Park in southwestern Colorado, and the Grand Canyon. They are not found at high altitudes; in Colorado, they rarely occur above 8,000 feet. They make their dens in brush piles, hollow logs, snags, and the burrows of other animals, such as the kit fox. Although opportunistic, they concentrate on rodents and insects. Their diet probably shifts seasonally as does that of the eastern spotted skunk. In one study, the latter species focused on mammal carrion in winter, rodents and insects in spring, insects in summer, with fruit added in the fall. If a farmer could keep his chickens safe, he might find this skunk to be an ally in helping to keep down the area's rodent population. It is a good climber, a skill which sets it apart from the striped skunk.

Only the swiftest or stupidest of predators ventures after a spotted skunk. If it cannot hide, the skunk faces its enemy and begins to stomp its forefeet. Then, it stands up on the forefeet and acrobatically arches its back so that both the head and anal

WESTERN SPOTTED SKUNK

glands are "looking" straight at the foe. If the predator is still around at this point, it gets sprayed with an intensely acrid, temporarily blinding secretion. This well-aimed blast travels for at least 10 feet. Thus, aside from fools, novices to the world of predation, fast-moving birds (such as owls), and humans, spotted skunks encounter relatively little antagonism.

Mating takes place during September and October. A fertilized egg divides a bit at first, but does not implant in the uterine wall for 180 to 200 days. The birth of approximately four immature young usually occurs in May. They are weaned after about two months. A few males and most females breed that fall. Some authorities consider eastern and western spotted skunks to be the same species. However, the eastern form mates in March and its pregnancy lacks the extensive implantation delay. Hence, its total gestation only lasts for about two months. Thus, the two skunks are reproductively isolated, a situation likely to result in their being distinct species.

## STRIPED SKUNK
### (*Mephitis mephitis*)

Total length: 20 1/2 to 31 1/2 inches; tail length: 7 1/4 to 15 1/2 inches.

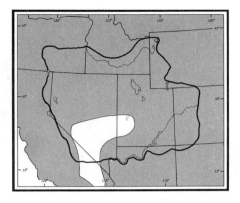

DISTRIBUTION OF STRIPED SKUNK.

The striped skunk is probably the one that most people have in mind when they think of skunks. About the size of a domestic cat, it is deep black, with two wide, white stripes on the back. The stripes usually meet on top of the head to form a white skull cap. Occasionally, they also join at the tail. There is considerable variation in both the length and width of these stripes. A thin white stripe also runs down the middle of the face. The tail is long and bushy, and contains varying amounts of white hair. Striped skunks are differentiated from their spotted relatives by their size and less complex stripe pattern. Naturalists assume that the bold fur patterns of skunks have a warning function; potential predators that associate the skunk's discharge with this coloration might remember to avoid them. Male striped skunks are about 15 percent larger than females. Although found across most of the United States and southern Canada, the largest area from which they are absent includes much of the Intermountain West. They do not occur in most of southern Nevada or adjacent western Utah.

They are found in almost any habitat offering suitable food and shelter. Although generally absent from extremely arid areas, they may spread into them following population increases. Their preferred habitat may be woodland edges; they tend to avoid dense forests. Dens are usually close to water, either in natural cavities or those made by other mammals. They are nocturnal omnivores with a predilection for animals. Major foods include insects, particularly grasshoppers, beetles, and moth larvae; small rodents; birds and their eggs, including poultry; and fruit. Clever animals, they scratch on hives to encour-

STRIPED SKUNK

age the bees to leave, and then kill them. Although their anal discharge is less pungent than the spotted skunk's, it is still effective at deterring predators. Like their cousin, they stomp their front feet before firing, but do not position the anus up above the head. Instead, they twist their body into a "U" and may slightly move their rear while discharging. The golden yellow, slightly phosphorescent musk is released as a spray or stream and is accurate up to 15 feet. Predators include great horned owls, coyotes, badgers, and humans. Except for the last, they usually are not major mortality factors. In fact, most juvenile mortality stems from mothers killing their young.

As an instructor, I once gathered a mammalogy class around to watch a student skin a striped skunk. He had assured me that he was an expert at this, knowing precisely how to cut around the anal glands. Unfortunately, the glands had been smashed when the animal was killed by a motor vehicle. When they became exposed, the odor released into the laboratory was so nauseating that it was disorienting. Indeed, the discharge does temporarily depress the victim's central nervous system. At this time, I had a knife, folded in its case, tucked away in the pocket of a new pair of jeans. Despite such protection, the smell stuck to the blade for several weeks, even after repeated washings with everything from tomato juice to mouthwash. Ironically, the musk is used as a perfume base because of this clinging quality.

Skunks are highly susceptible to rabies and their often great abundance likely facilitates a rapid spread of the virus. In the United States, the incidence of rabies is usually higher in skunks than in any other species. Rabid skunks are atypically diurnal and aggressive; they should be given an even wider berth than uninfected ones.

Striped skunks mate in the late winter and early spring. Gestation lasts for about 63 to 66 days, including a possible brief delay in implantation. Between April and June, a litter of 2 to 11 altricial little stinkers are born. The average litter size is approximately 7. Their eyes open after three weeks and they are weaned by the end of their second month. Striped skunks are usually solitary except during mating, when they are purported to be polygynous. Occasionally, they remain together in winter communal dens, which are composed primarily of females. During the winter in colder places, they become dormant for extended periods. Because they maintain a high body temperature, this is not true hibernation.

## RIVER OTTER (*Lutra canadensis*)

Total length: 35 to 51 5/8 inches; tail length: 11 3/4 to 20 inches.

The river otter is perhaps the most graceful mustelid of all. This is particularly evident when it is swimming, propelling its body through the water with a powerful wavelike

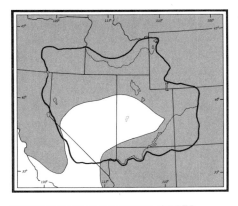

DISTRIBUTION OF RIVER OTTER.

RIVER OTTER

motion. It also uses its webbed hind feet to paddle along. Otters are made all the more attractive by their lustrous, dark brown fur, which appears almost black when wet. On the sides of the head and on the undersurface, they are slightly paler and are often silvery gray on the throat. The underfur is thick enough to be water-repellent. A long, rudderlike tail accounts for about a third of the body length. Finally, the head is broad and flattened. It would be difficult, indeed, to confuse the otter with any other animal in the region, due to its unique appearance and aquatic habits. On this continent, only the sea otter (*Enhydra lutris*) resembles it, but this is a marine mammal of the Pacific coast. River otters occur throughout most of North America. They are absent, however, from a large area of the Intermountain West in the more arid reaches of Nevada and Utah.

These intelligent mammals are found around riparian areas, those surrounding rivers and streams. Active any time of day, they feed almost exclusively in the water, primarily on fish, crayfish, frogs, and turtles. In winter, individuals from the latter three groups are extricated from the mud, where they are lying dormant. Other foods include insects, earthworms, small mammals, and juvenile muskrats and beavers. They are efficient at killing a variety of fish, especially "rough" species, such as carp and suckers, due to an ability to make quick, snapping movements. Game fish, such as trout, are too fast to be relied upon. They can dive to depths of 45 feet and can stay under water for several minutes. Despite their aquatic adaptations and short limbs, otters move well on land and even run. Travel on land is common since they must often leave an area due to food shortages or other unfavorable situations. Dens are dug into banks and usually have both land and water entrances. Abandoned beaver or muskrat lodges are also used. Otters are especially well known for their playful antics, rolling about and sliding down hillsides, seemingly just for the fun of it.

Mating takes place in early to mid-spring following the birth of the litter from the previous breeding. Copulation usually occurs in the water. Blastocysts, the slightly developed fertilized eggs, do not implant in the uterus until winter. From two to five altricial young are born in March or April; the average litter size is two to three. The young open their eyes when about a month old. They do not leave the den until about six weeks old. Otter mothers may have to drag their young into the water when teaching them how to swim. The male is forced away from the young just after birth but, oddly, may return to care for them six months later. When they are eight months old, the young disperse. Females commonly breed in their first year, but males normally wait until their second year. Although they were severely reduced in most of their range by overtrapping and habitat loss, otters have enjoyed a resurgence in many areas. However, the highly variable flow of water in most mountain rivers probably prevents them from attaining high densities in much of this region.

## CATS—FAMILY FELIDAE

Of all the carnivores, the cats stand out as a group of coolly efficient killers. Surely, this is related to their style of predation. After stealthily following their prey, they suddenly rush after it, quickly achieving the kill with a bite to the neck. The shortened, powerful skull is instrumental in producing this devastating bite. But it is the laterally flattened shape of the canine tooth that allows them to quickly slice through the prey's spinal column. It has been suggested that the canine of each felid neatly fits between the neck vertebrae of its most common victim, like a key in a lock. The molars are adapted for shearing; cats are said to slice apart their food before swallowing it. Another predatory adaptation is the retractile nature of the sharp, curved claws, common to all felids except cheetahs (*Acinonyx jubatus*). Usually withdrawn, they extend for grabbing and slashing. Cats rely on superb night vision for their nocturnal hunting forays. In the Intermountain West, there are 3 of the some 37 species of these magnificent mammals.

## MOUNTAIN LION or COUGAR (*Felis concolor*)

Total length: 59 1/8 to 108 inches; tail length: 21 to 36 inches.

Anyone fortunate enough to see a mountain lion in the wild could not mistake it for anything else. But because of its secretive habits, it is rarely seen,

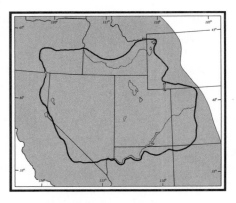

DISTRIBUTION OF MOUNTAIN LION OR COUGAR

even where relatively common. One of the largest carnivores, it is the biggest cat in the region. On this continent, only the jaguar, *Felis onca*, is similar in size, but it is differentiated by its spotted fur. Although the two coexist in the southwestern United States, jaguars are now absent from the Intermountain area. Early in the century, they occurred in north-central Arizona along the Colorado River. All recent sightings, however, are from the southern half of the state.

Mountain lions, or cougars, are yellowish to, occasionally, a dark reddish brown on top. They are slightly paler underneath. The long, cylindrical tail is dark brown to black on its tip. Dark shading occurs behind the short, rounded ears and on the muzzle. Young are covered with black spots until their third or fourth month. At first glance, it appears as if cougars have a thin coat. Yet it is composed of a kinked underfur covered by long guard hairs, which together keep them comfortable even in extreme winters. Due to their size and a serene visage, cougars are portrayed as wilderness symbols. They once roamed from northern British Columbia, across the continental United States, to southern Chile and Argentina. Now, due to habitat destruction and overhunting, they are restricted to remaining large tracts of wild lands. They are found in such places throughout the western United States, including the entire Intermountain West.

Here, cougars chiefly occur in mountainous areas where there is adequate food, stalking cover, and little human disturbance. They prey on a variety of mammals and birds and even eat plants. Their favorite food, however, is mule deer. In winter, deer can account for 75 percent of a cougar's diet. The majority of those killed are older males, the very young of either sex, and the infirm. A cougar stalks a deer until it is fairly close, about 30 feet away, as it can outrun an intended victim only for short distances. After breaking the deer's neck, it feasts until gorged, covering up the remains with nearby vegetation. Hunters have had concerns about cougars decimating big game. In one Idaho study, however, it was demonstrated that deer and elk populations are limited by their own winter food supplies. The cougar's role seemed to be one of preventing rapid increases and decreases of the deer and spreading them over a wide area.

In some locales, particularly the Southwest, cougars prey on cattle and young horses. More cattle may be killed in areas where deer are less available. These problems could also be caused by easy access to the beef. Cougars themselves suffer little predation. But even they have injuries and fatalities, from contact with large prey, falling off of cliffs, and drownings. As is true for so many other species, humans are their principal foe. Some mortality is caused by adult males preying on kittens. Cougars largely hunt at dawn and dusk, but are active at any time of the day or year.

Breeding occurs throughout the year, with most births between April and September. Gestation is variable, lasting from 82 to 96 days. From one to six young are born, with an average litter size being two to three. Covered with densely spotted fur at birth, the kittens are nonetheless altricial. Their eyes and ears stay closed for up to two weeks. After weaning at about six weeks, they begin to eat meat brought by the mother. Soon, they can hunt small prey on their own. Young remain with their mother until close to two years of age. Males do not exhibit any parental care. Females become sexually mature the next year, but are not likely to breed until they establish a territory. A male's home range often overlaps those of at least two females. When this occurs, they are polygynous; a male might mate with the same females for several consecutive years. There are cases of females remaining in breeding condition for at least 12 years.

## LYNX (*Felis lynx*)

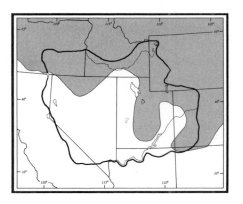

DISTRIBUTION OF LYNX.

Total length: 29 1/8 to 47 1/8 inches; tail length: 2 to 5 3/8 inches.

With its double-pointed beard, long slender ear tufts, and white eyelids, the striking lynx resembles a troll. This appearance is heightened by its beautiful thick coat: buffy to tawny sprinkled with dark brown, black, and white above and cinnamon-brown underneath. Its large feet are well furred, acting as snowshoes in allowing it to move easily across snow. The short tail has a characteristic black tip. Its beard is formed by downward extensions of the large cheek ruffs. The chin, inside of the ears, throat, and belly are all white. Although lynx appear similar to bobcats, they are distinguished by longer, more pronounced ear tufts, larger feet, longer legs, less distinct spotting, and a tail tip which is black both above and below. In this region, lynx are far less widely distributed than bobcats.

They are true denizens of the north, occupying all of Canada and Alaska. Some authorities believe that they are the same species as the Eurasian lynx, a classification followed herein. Others argue that the North American lynx is a distinct species. Largely found in the northern Intermountain West, these cats extend down into the forested mountains of central Utah and Colorado.

Lynx typically occur deep within the forest, in areas with clearings, bogs, thickets, or rocky outcrops. They hunt by night for their most common prey, the snowshoe hare. A lynx population's fate is closely tied to the hare's. From peak to peak, the densities of both species have 9-to-10-year cycles; that of the lynx follows the hare's by a year or two. A scarcity of hares prevents lynx from having enough food to ensure either successful reproduction or survival of their young. In such hard times, they may sustain themselves on ruffed grouse, small mammals, and carrion. They are also capable of taking down young deer. During the day, they rest in any available shelter. Occasionally, they stay in trees, from which they do not hesitate to ambush prey. They have superb hearing and the long ear tufts may function as sensitive antennae. Only humans, who take them for their pelts, kill lynx with any regularity. Other predators include cougars and wolves. However, the greatest cause of mortality seems to be a scarcity of prey, which affects younger lynx the most.

Mating takes place between February and early April, with the time of breeding varying geographically. Young are born after an approximately 63-to-74-day pregnancy. A single litter of one to six, usually three or four, altricial kittens is produced per year. They are able to see within their second week and begin to walk toward the end of their first month. Kittens nurse for over six months, although they take meat after one month. They remain with the mother through their first year. Females become sexually mature as yearlings; males do so in their second year. The proportion of females that breed appears to be determined by prey availability. In a Canadian study, only a third of the adult females conceived when snowshoe hares were scarce, whereas close to three-quarters did in years of hare abundance. Lynx are largely solitary creatures.

BOBCAT (*Felis rufus*)

Total length: 28 to 49 3/8 inches; tail length: 3 3/4 to 6 3/4 inches.

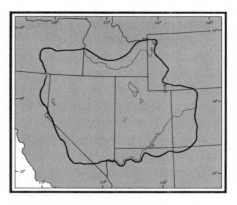

DISTRIBUTION OF BOBCAT.

The bobcat is the wild cat that natural history observers have the best chance of spotting in this area. Generally more common than the other cats, it also is not as restricted to wilderness areas. Even so, the best one may hope for is a fleeting glimpse of this secretive animal. I was once fortunate to see one amble alongside a highway. As this occurred in the Southeast, I had no doubt that it was a bobcat. In the western United States, bobcats could be confused with lynx, so one should be aware of their differences, most of which are reviewed in the previous account. In addition to those mentioned, bobcats are slightly smaller, their grayish to tawny coat is redder, and the underside is pale or white. The stubby "bobbed" tail has two to four blackish bars and is tipped with black only on top. Finally, although they also have broad cheek ruffs, these do not have beardlike extensions like those of the lynx. Conceivably, bobcats could be confused with juvenile cougars, but they have a much shorter tail. They occur across southern Canada, all of the United States, and throughout most of Mexico.

Typical bobcat habitat is rough, scrubby terrain such as that found along rimrock, in canyons, foothills, and chaparral country. These cats also occur in "broken" forested areas and alongside streams. As long as there is adequate stalking cover, they can be found almost anywhere. Although they can climb nearly as well as lynx, they do not use trees as much. Rabbits are their major food, the particular species varying with location. Other common nourishment sources include mice, rats, voles, and ground-nesting birds. They also frequent bat caves, picking off those, mostly young bats, that fall to the ground. Bobcats can take down large animals, such as pronghorn antelope, yet rarely have the opportunity or inclination to do so. Their only consistent predators are humans, who trap them for their fur. In some areas, they are hunted with packs of dogs. Most active at night, they rest by day in any convenient shelter.

Breeding occurs throughout the spring, with pregnancy lasting from 60 to 70 days. Most births take place in May or June. In southern locales, females may have two litters per year, but one is the norm. From one to seven altricial young, with an average of three, are born in a secluded den of dried vegetation. After nine days, they can open their eyes. Weaned at two months, they stay with their mother into the fall and, occasionally, through the winter. Males hardly, if at all, participate in parenting. Although females may breed as yearlings, males do not mature until their second year.

## REFERENCES

Allendorf, F. W., and C. Servheen. 1986. Genetics and the conservation of grizzly bears. *Trends in Ecology and Evolution* 1: 88–89.

Anonymous. 1986. Specialists battling extinction of ferrets. *Salt Lake Tribune*, August 30, 1986.

Bekoff, M. 1977. *Canis latrans*. Mammalian Species no. 79. American Society of Mammalogists.

Brown, D. E. 1983. On the status of the jaguar in the Southwest. *Southwestern Naturalist* 28: 459–479.

Clark, T. W., E. Anderson, C. Douglas, and M. Strickland. 1987. *Martes americana*. Mammalian Species no. 289. American Society of Mammalogists.

Clark, T. W., L. Richardson, S. C. Forrest, D. E. Casey, and T. M. Campbell III. 1986. *Descriptive ethology and activity patterns of black-footed ferrets*. Great Basin Naturalist Memoirs no. 8: 115–134. Provo: Brigham Young University.

Craighead, J. J., M. G. Hornocker, and F. C. Craighead, Jr. 1969. Reproductive biology of young female grizzly bears. *Journal of Reproductive Fertility, Supplement* 6: 447–475.

Currier, M. J. P. 1983. *Felis concolor*. Mammalian Species no. 200. American Society of Mammalogists.

Daneke, D., M. Sunquist, and S. Berwick. 1984. Notes on kit fox biology in Utah. *Southwestern Naturalist* 29: 361–362.

Egoscue, H. J. 1979. *Vulpes velox*. Mammalian Species no. 122. American Society of Mammalogists.

Fritzell, E. K., and K. J. Haroldson. 1982. *Urocyon cinereoargenteus*. Mammalian Species no. 189. American Society of Mammalogists.

Gittleman, J. L. 1986. Carnivore life history patterns: Allometric, phylogenetic, and ecological associations. *American Naturalist* 127: 744–771.

Hall, E. R. 1984. *Geographic variation among brown and grizzly bears (*Ursus arctos*) in North America*. University of Kansas Museum of Natural History Special Publication no. 13. Lawrence.

Hart, E. B. 1982. The raccoon, *Procyon lotor*, in Wyoming. *Great Basin Naturalist* 42: 599–600.

Hillman, C. N., and T. W. Clark. 1980. *Mustela nigripes*. Mammalian Species no. 126. American Society of Mammalogists.

King, C. M. 1983. *Mustela erminea*. Mammalian Species no. 195. American Society of Mammalogists.

Kuban, J. F., and G. G. Schwartz. 1985. Nectar as a diet item of the ringtailed cat. *Southwestern Naturalist* 30: 311–312.

Long, C. A. 1973. *Taxidea taxus*. Mammalian Species no. 26. American Society of Mammalogists.

Lotze, J.-H., and S. Anderson. 1979. *Procyon lotor*. Mammalian Species no. 119. American Society of Mammalogists.

Malcolm, J. R. 1985. Paternal care in canids. *American Zoologist* 25: 853–856.

Martin, S. J. 1983. Additional records of black-footed ferrets in Wyoming. *Southwestern Naturalist* 28: 95.

McGrew, J. C. 1979. *Vulpes macrotis*. Mammalian Species no. 123. American Society of Mammalogists.

Mead, R. A. 1968. Reproduction in western forms of the spotted skunk (genus *Spilogale*). *Journal of Mammalogy* 49: 373–390.

Mech, L. D. 1974. *Canis lupus*. Mammalian Species no. 37. American Society of Mammalogists.

Powell, R. A. 1981. *Martes pennanti*. Mammalian Species no. 156. American Society of Mammalogists.

_____. 1982. Evolution of black-tipped tails in weasels:Predator confusion. *American Naturalist* 119: 126–131.

Ralls, K., and P. H. Harvey. 1985. Geographic variation in size and sexual dimorphism of North American weasels. *Biological Journal of the Linnean Society* 25: 119–167.

Tietje, W. D., B. O. Pelchat, and R. L. Ruff. 1986. Cannibalism of denned black bears. *Journal of Mammalogy* 67: 762–766.

Tumlison, R. 1987. *Felis lynx*. Mammalian Species no. 269. American Society of Mammalogists.

Wade-Smith, J., and B. J. Verts. 1982. *Mephitis mephitis*. Mammalian Species no. 173. American Society of Mammalogists.

White, A. B. 1986. Food habits of a Salt Lake Valley raccoon (*Procyon lotor*) population. Typescript.

Wright, P. L. 1969. The reproductive cycle of the male American badger, *Taxidea taxus. Journal of Reproductive Fertility, Supplement* 6: 435–445.

Zeveloff, S. I., and P. D. Doerr. 1985. Seasonal weight changes in raccoons (*Carnivora: Procyonidae*) of North Carolina. *Brimleyana* 11: 63–67.

Zielinski, W. J., W. D. Spencer, and R. H. Barrett. 1983. Relationship between food habits and activity patterns of pine martens. *Journal of Mammalogy* 64: 387–398.

# The Odd-Toed Hooved Mammals —
# Order Perissodactyla

Today's perissodactyls are the remnants of a group that was considerably more diverse early in mammalian history. Currently, the order consists of only 16 species belonging to three families. Two are familiar: the Equidae, horses and their relatives, and the Rhinocerotidae, the rhinoceroses. The third family is the Tapiridae, the tapirs. These creatures are characterized by stout bodies and an upper lip and nose which are modified into an elongated grasping structure. Tapirs occur on the Malay Peninsula, in Sumatra, and from Mexico through South America.

Perissodactyls differ from other hooved mammals in having an odd number of toes per foot. The equids possess but one toe per foot. In members of the order with more than one toe, the body weight is mostly borne by the middle digit. The different species employ a variety of tactics in dealing with predators. Equids rely on speed to outrun enemies. Tapirs are good swimmers and often head into a nearby river to avoid predation. Once a rhino reaches adulthood it has little concern about predators, given its massive body, thick skin, and horns. Perissodactyls are either browsers or grazers; their elongated faces typically carry many large cheek teeth.

Other than the opossum, horses and burros are the only nonnative mammals for which accounts are included. In much of the Intermountain West, both are important components of the fauna. Following the passage of the Wild and Free-Roaming Horse and Burro Act in 1971, they have been protected by the federal government. In recent years, this has resulted in an explosion of their populations. In 1982, the U.S. Bureau of

Land Management estimated that there were about 45,000 wild horses in the country, the large majority of which are in this region. Because of these numbers, many ranchers are concerned about possible competition between horses and cattle. Many, however, find these graceful animals to be a desirable part of our landscape. Certainly, the image of wild horses against a rugged backdrop evokes a timeless image of the American West. Similar sympathetic views have also been espoused to defend the burro. Thus, due to their ecological impact and the ongoing controversy surrounding their management, I have included these accounts.

## HORSES AND THE BURRO – FAMILY EQUIDAE

Horses, asses, and zebras are seven similar species that compose the family Equidae. All are large grazing mammals that can attain high speeds. This is a useful adaptation for survival in open country, enabling them to travel quickly from one waterhole to the next and to escape from predators. Equids originated and largely evolved in North America, becoming established in Africa more recently. They became extinct in this hemisphere at least 8,000 years ago, for reasons which are likely to remain unknown. Explanations for their demise and that of other large mammals abundant at the time usually address the effects of climatic change, disease, and predation, particularly by humans. Horses were the last common livestock species to be domesticated, between 2,500 to 5,000 years ago. In the fifteenth century they were accidentally reintroduced to this continent, escaping from both Cortes's crew in Mexico and de Soto's along the Mississippi River. All of these, however, are assumed to have perished. Obviously though, there were survivors among those that subsequently came to the New World. The wild equids now in North America are probably descended from animals which escaped from ranchers, miners, and Indians.

HORSE (*Equus caballus*)

Total length: approximately 9 1/2 feet; tail length: approximately 3 feet; shoulder height: 30 to 69 inches.

314

Horses are so well known that it hardly seems necessary to describe them. It is more useful to discuss how to recognize a wild horse in this region. However, this is possible only, if at all, by knowing the areas in which these freedom lovers are found. Almost all wild horses in this region occur in isolated areas

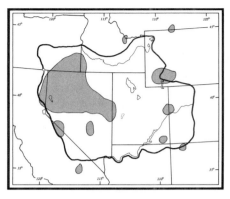

DISTRIBUTION OF WILD HORSE (INTRODUCED).

administered by the Bureau of Land Management. The largest of these includes most of northern Nevada and adjacent southeastern Oregon. Another area is the Red Desert of southwestern Wyoming. Individuals may be any one of a variety of colors. In the beginning of this century, an author named Rufus Steele described a northwestern Nevada herd as consisting of "bays, albinos, chestnuts, red and blue roans, pintos, sorrels, buckskins, and milkwhites." Such an array of hues still characterizes most populations. When one spots individuals or bands in remote areas that appear wild, that is, unkempt and without harnesses or brands, they are likely to be wild horses.

The most comprehensive study of wild horses in this region has been done by Joel Berger of the University of Nevada at Reno. In his book, *Wild Horses of the Great Basin*, he presents his findings from a study of a population in the Granite Range of northwestern Nevada. There, horses are relatively free from disturbances by humans and cattle. Information presented herein is largely based on this population.

Western wild horses feed on a large variety of grasses, such as spike bentgrass, bluebunch wheatgrass, clustered fieldsedge, and Idaho fescue. At home in arid regions, they still depend on the availability of waterholes. From fall through spring, shrublands and grasslands receive the most use. Meadows, however, are used the most, relative to their availability. In summer, when they have migrated to higher altitudes, the horses are virtually restricted to meadows and shrublands. By feeding early in the day on ridgelines or near snow patches, they minimize contact with biting and bloodsucking horseflies.

Like other hooved mammals, horses employ microbial organisms to break down their food by fermentation. But they differ from ruminants like deer and sheep by having a one-chambered stomach. Fermentation occurs in the large intestine and the colon. Horses may improve the habitat for mule deer because their grazing favors the growth of forbs and shrubs. Few predators will tackle a horse. Those most able to, such as grizzly bears and wolves, are usually so rare as to not be important mortality factors. Cougars are probably their most significant predator here, largely striking foals in areas with low deer populations. There is a report of foals dying after being unable to extricate themselves from muddy waterholes. The great majority of deaths are from winter losses due to cold and a lack of nutrition.

Females may first bear young at 2 years and continue to do so until 22 years old. Yet only a third to a half of the two-to-three-year-olds have young; these are usually from the better foraging areas. The most successfully reproducing females are 5 to 17 years old. Gestation lasts for about 11 months. Births occur in any month, but some 85 percent take place between April and June. Foals are typically weaned before the end of their first year. Yearlings attempting to displace a newborn from their mother's teat are treated roughly and are even bitten by the mother. They leave the mother's band at one to four years. Full body weight is not reached until four or five years old.

Bands typically consist of one stallion, two to four mares, and their young. Females regularly switch bands throughout their lives. A nonresident male often fights with the band's stallion in an attempt to take over his females. Biting and kicking are commonly employed during these battles; the stallions rarely rear up on their hind legs during these encounters. A male that takes over a harem can induce abortion in a mare not too far along in her pregnancy. He then reinseminates her. The fetus sired by the previous stallion could be killed by a forced copulation and the stresses associated with it, an event termed "feticide." By such a seemingly brutal act, males avoid rearing unrelated foals and have mares bear their own young. A stallion's fitness is thus enhanced by this process. In other mammals, such as the langur, a primate, males even kill the young in the band they take over. Stallions do not breed until about six years old and vary considerably more than females do in their overall reproductive success. This is typical of polygynous species, those with harem-style mating systems. Indeed, only a few males sire most of the females.

## BURRO (*Equus asinus*)

Total length: 8 to 8 3/4 feet; tail length: 16 3/4 to 19 1/4 inches; shoulder height: 35 1/2 to 59 inches.

Like the horse, the familiar burro needs little description. These reddish brown equids are similar in appearance to the familiar donkey, a member of the same species. They are also called the Somali, Nubian, or Abyssinian wild ass, after their native regions in northeastern Africa. Burros were used as beasts of burden in Egypt and Mesopotamia as far back as 3400 B.C. When the Spanish arrived in North America in the sixteenth century, they brought burros along as pack animals. Because of their endurance and an ability to traverse rugged terrain and subsist in sparsely vegetated areas, prospectors, miners, and sheepherders also took advantage of burros. Those now roaming the West are the descendants of ones purposely or accidentally freed by their early owners. Burros probably did not become widespread until sometime in the nineteenth century, following the first major waves of mineral exploration in the West.

These mammals previously occurred in all western states except for Washington and Montana, principally in California, Arizona, Nevada, and New Mexico. Major concentrations were along the Colorado River from southern Utah to the Mexican border, particularly in the Grand Canyon, and in the desert mountain ranges of southeastern California. Intensive removal efforts have resulted in a scattered and greatly diminished distribution. In 1957, there were estimated to be between 5,500 to 13,000 burros in the United States; few now remain.

It is Grand Canyon National Park where burros have received the most attention. Rangers there, familiar with the animal's impact on flora and fauna, suggested control measures in the early 1920s. From 1924 to 1969, over 2,800 were removed, with the great majority being killed. Toward the end of that period, burro and horse lovers stirred up sentiment for these animals, climaxing in the Wild Horse and Burro Act of 1971. This legislation mandated the cessation of killing them on public lands. Although it does not specifically apply to national parks, opposition to burro-killing made their removal problematic. Nevertheless, their continued habitat destruction and competition with native wildlife necessitated their eviction from the Grand Canyon. By the early 1980s, virtually all of the burros were removed. Some 200 were exterminated. The Fund for Animals, an animal protectionist group, financed the live capture and relocation of another 577. According to Steven Carothers, who has done extensive research on this animal, there are no more than three or four burros left in the park.

Primarily found in rugged locales, burros may occur in several habitats. In basin and range country, they occupy the steep-walled canyons of desert mountain ranges. Occasionally, they are found in the higher mountain reaches above the canyons. Although surefooted, they are not nearly as agile as bighorn sheep or mountain goats and stay out of the more precipitous areas. In winter, they may be found on "flats" surrounding the mountains. There is not, however, a seasonal pattern of habitat use. They exist on a wide variety of plants. Grasses, forbs, and shrubs are their major food items; relative reliance on each group varies with season and place. Drinking water is a necessity, especially in summer. Predators, which include cougars, jaguars, and wolves, do not appear to seriously impact burro populations. Humans are their chief enemy, destroying them for the havoc they wreak on the range and because of their competing with native species for food and water. Burros trample the vegetation surrounding water holes, removing cover for small mammals and birds. As well, they compete for food with mule deer, pronghorn, and especially desert bighorn sheep. There also are concerns that burros interfere with the range's capacity to sustain livestock.

Most mating appears to occur in spring or early summer. This is not set in stone, however, as breeding has been observed throughout the year. Gestation lasts for about a year. Their mating system seems to resemble that of feral horses, with the jacks, or males, gathering a harem of jennies. Fights occur between competing jacks.

WILD HORSE

BURRO (JUVENILE)

# REFERENCES

Berger, J. 1986. *Wild Horses of the Great Basin: Social competition and population size.* Chicago: University of Chicago Press.

Carothers, S. W., M. E. Stitt, and R. R. Johnson. 1976. Feral asses on public lands: An analysis of biotic impact, legal considerations and management alternatives. *Transactions of the North American Wildlife Conference* 41: 396–406.

Jordan, J. W., G. A. Ruffner, S. W. Carothers, and A. M. Phillips III. 1979. "Summer diets of feral burros (*Equus asinus*) in Grand Canyon National Park, Arizona." *In* R. H. Denniston, coord. *Symposium on the ecology and behavior of wild and feral equids*, pp. 15–20. Laramie: University of Wyoming.

McKnight, T. L. 1958. The feral burro in the United States: Distribution and problems. *Journal of Wildlife Management* 22: 163–179.

Potter, R. L., and R. M. Hansen. 1979. Feral burro food habits and habitat relations, Grand Canyon National Park, Arizona. *In* R. H. Denniston, coord. *Symposium on the ecology and behavior of wild and feral equids*, pp. 143–153. Laramie: University of Wyoming.

# The Even-Toed Hooved Mammals — Order Artiodactyla

Artiodactyls are the more successful order of hooved mammals, consisting of some 185 species. They are divided into three suborders: the Suiformes includes the hippopotamus, pigs, and peccaries; the Tylopoda consists of the camels; and the largest one, the Ruminantia, includes deer, sheep, cows, goats, and antelope. All eight artiodactyls in this region belong to the last suborder.

Despite there being such a diversity of forms, several features both unite them and account for much of their success. The first one to consider is limb structure. As revealed by the order's common name, each species has an even number of toes. Except for the Suiformes and the mouse deer, there are two toes per foot. This reduction in digit number and overall fusion of the limb bones considerably lighten limb weight, permitting a more rapid stride. Furthermore, the characteristically long limbs provide for a long stride. A final adaptation for swiftness is the "double-pulley" arrangement of the astralagus, one of the limb bones. It restricts limb movement to just one plane and permits the attached bones to extend forward and backward, resulting in a directed, highly efficient locomotion.

The artiodactyls' great success can also be attributed to their digestive specializations. Like perissodactyls, they break down plant cellulose with microorganisms which are harbored in the digestive tract. In the Ruminantia, this process occurs in large, multichambered stomachs. Food is continually regurgitated and chewed until broken down enough to be passed on to the intestines. Food passes more quickly through the simpler gut of a horse, which therefore must eat more than a comparably sized ruminant to acquire the same nutrition.

## ELK, DEER, AND MOOSE—FAMILY CERVIDAE

The cervids of North America are all large, herbivorous mammals which have long been the objects of our admiration and hunting efforts. Males of the various species bear antlers; in caribou (*Rangifer tarandus*), females also sport such headgear. Antlers are bony outgrowths of the skull which become branched in older individuals. This distinguishes them from horns, which, except for the pronghorn antelope's, are neither branched nor shed. In spring, when they begin to grow, the antlers are encased in "velvet," an epidermal covering of short fur containing blood vessels, which nourish the growing bone and nerves. After they cease to grow, the velvet is shed, leaving the highly prized rack.

To females, antlers provide a basis for judging a male's genetic quality. A large, well-formed rack indicates a superior mate. Males use their antlers in battles that often determine which one will have mating rights to the females. Thus, antler configuration is a result of sexual selection, the process by which behavioral and anatomical traits evolve in relation to sex. After the mating season, the antlers are shed. It is almost incomprehensible that such terrific amounts of material and energy are put into producing items which are discarded every year. But when one realizes that antlers are the objects upon which the crucial processes of mate choice and sexual access hinge, it becomes easier to understand this phenomenon. There are 37 species of cervids in the world. In the Intermountain West, we are fortunate to have four: elk, mule deer, white-tailed deer, and moose.

### ELK or WAPITI (*Cervus elaphus*)

Total length: 6 3/4 to 9 3/4 feet; tail length: 3 1/8 to 8 3/8 inches; shoulder height: 4 1/2 to 5 feet.

The elk is one of a few mammals for which the term "majestic" is commonly used to describe it. Certainly, this is due in part to its size. Elk are the second largest North American cervid; only moose are larger. Males weigh from 600 to over 1,000 pounds and females weigh between 450 to 600 pounds. The sweeping antlers give the bulls a stately bearing. They extend both up and back for up to five feet and, in adults, ordinarily have six sharp points or "tines." Although their size and

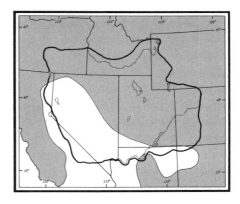

DISTRIBUTION OF ELK OR WAPITI.

antlers are impressive, their powerful body shape is equally important in conveying a regal appearance. The huge, bulky trunk, from which the long, thick neck extends, stands out in contrast to the thin legs, and thus seems especially forceful. Elk are tan or brown above and darker below. After a late-spring molt, they become reddish brown. In late fall, they go through another molt, becoming a darker brown on the head, neck, and legs, with the rest of the body a paler, grayish brown. The small, whitish tail and surrounding yellowish rump area are bordered by darker hairs. A dark shaggy mane which covers the entire neck is pronounced in bulls.

Many biologists suggest that "wapiti," the Shawnee Indian word for "white rump," is a more appropriate name than "elk." This avoids confusion because, in Europe, the name "elk" refers to the moose. However, as "elk" is more commonly used to describe this animal in North America, it is employed here. To further complicate matters, elk and the red deer of Europe are now regarded as the same species. At one time, elk ranged throughout southern Canada and most of the United States, including plains habitats. Due to commercial and subsistence hunting, killings by ranchers concerned about their competing with cattle for food, and wasteful slaughter for such trinkets as their upper canines, elk populations drastically declined at the beginning of this century. They have enjoyed a slight resurgence and are now found in much of the Intermountain region, except for most of Nevada. Transplants were utilized by wildlife managers in the early part of this century to reestablish previously existing herds. Individuals from Yellowstone National Park were released in areas of Utah, including the Oquirrh Mountains, Mount Nebo, and Logan Canyon. Large herds still exist, primarily in mountainous areas, but many are small and isolated.

Elk are creatures of semiopen forests, mountain meadows, foothills, and valleys. Primarily grazers, they largely rely on grasses and forbs, particularly in summer. Woody vegetation can account for much of their intake during winter and where grass is less available. Fire often produces high-quality elk habitat. For example, red-stemmed ceanothus, a shrub which may be an important food, sprouts following a fire. The growth of other deciduous shrubs and herbaceous plants of early plant-succession stages are similarly favored by fires. Suppression of natural fires in much of the West is thus also assumed to be responsible for population declines. Water is consumed through plants, yet elk still drink it and will eat snow to obtain moisture. In the fall, hunters may have difficulty locating one, but in summer and winter elk are one of the most gregarious mammals of all. Winter herds of over 15,000 have been reported on the National Elk Refuge in Jackson, Wyoming. This, however, is not normal; supplemental feeding is used to sustain them now that their native winter range has been altered. Elk are largely nocturnal, but quite active during dawn and dusk. Their choice of daytime locations appears to be influenced by heat avoidance; cool areas, such as snowbanks and ridgetops, are often selected. They exhibit altitudinal migration, traveling to lower reaches in the colder months.

Mountain lions are their major predators; others include grizzly bears and wolves. Other causes of death include harsh winters, starvation, disease, and drownings. One spring day, I found an elk fetus lying at the bottom of Nowlin Creek on the National Elk Refuge. Nonetheless, survival is relatively high, with about 50 to 67 percent of the herd making it from one year to the next. In northwestern Wyoming, calf mortality has been shown to be density-dependent; at higher population levels, calves suffer a decrease in survival.

The sound of an elk "bugling" is a clear reminder that autumn is approaching and that it is time for breeding. A bugle begins as a bellow, changes to a loud whistle, and terminates in a succession of grunts. It is the whistle portion that most people hear. Bugling is a dual-purpose call, serving as a challenge to other bulls and as a domination message for cows. Between August and November, bulls rejoin the herd of cows from which they remained separate all summer. They engage in rutting behavior, which consists of bugling, sparring with antlers, wallowing in water or mud, and urinating on plants that they toss back onto their antlers. This is likely done to exaggerate the headgear, making the bull more fearsome to foes and attractive to potential mates. Bulls successful in this competition may serve as many as 60 cows; 15 to 30 cows constitute a typical harem. After a pregnancy of eight and a half months, the cow gives birth to one precocial, or relatively mature, calf. Although twinning occurs, it is rare. Calves are spotted on the top and sides, but not as much as newborn deer. They can walk within minutes after birth. However, they are totally dependent on their mother's milk for a full month. After beginning to eat grass, they may nurse for an additional eight months. Cows begin to breed at three years of age, bulls usually do so when they are four.

## MULE DEER
*(Odocoileus hemionus)*

Total length: 3 3/4 to 6 1/2 feet; tail length: 4 1/2 to 9 inches; shoulder height: 3 to 3 1/2 feet.

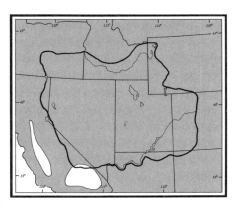

DISTRIBUTION OF MULE DEER.

The mule deer is one of the most exciting animals to watch. With its distinctive stiff-legged bounding movement, which is actually a modified gallop, all legs leave the ground at the same time. This is technically referred to as "stotting." Another unique quality is the size of their ears, from which the "mule" name is derived. Each ear is approximately two-thirds the length of the head; that of a white-tailed deer is only about half of the head's length. The ears seem to be constantly moving about, enhancing their exceptionally sharp hearing ability. Bucks are distinguished from their white-tailed counterparts by antlers which branch equally or "dichotomously." They are divided into two main branches, each of which may again divide, resulting in pairs of points or tines. A white-tail's antler consists of one main branch from which several vertical tines arise. Most mule deer vary from gray to dark brown on the back and sides. In summer, they are a reddish brown. They have a grayish white or yellowish rump patch and one or two white throat patches. The small, thin tail is white and usually terminates in a characteristic black tip. A dark V-shaped mark extends from between the eyes upward and to the sides; it is more evident in bucks. Mule deer are found across western North America. Common throughout the Intermountain West, they are absent only from its far southeastern corner.

They occupy a diversity of habitats including brushy and wooded areas, broken country, and open plains. Correspondingly, they have a varied diet, eating many types of woody vegetation as well as forbs and grasses. The latter items are more commonly eaten in the warmer months. As snow covers up herbaceous matter, they switch to woody plants, especially the terminal shoots of shrubs. The succession of grasses to woody plants, which created an ideal balance of grasses, shrubs, and trees, was likely responsible for their great population irruptions across the Intermountain West in the early 1930s and mid-1960s. This succession of plant communities was largely the result of intensive cattle grazing, which effectively eliminated grasses, and the reduction of fires, which had previously suppressed and even stopped woody plant growth. Ironically, the continued development of woody vegetation here has been detrimental to mule deer because it often leaves little room for the growth of important palatable herbs and shrubs. The deer cannot subsist entirely on woody vegetation. Some wildlife managers suggest that mule deer habitats in the Intermountain region be systematically "disturbed" by activities such as grazing, prescribed fires, and selective tree cutting. This would produce a mosaic of the various plant communities on which the deer depend.

Astir any time of day, mule deer are most active at dawn and dusk and on moonlit nights. In mountainous areas, they migrate to lower elevations in winter months. In the arid Southwest, their migration may follow rainfall rather than snow patterns. They can be very damaging to farms; in one study over 40 percent of their diet consisted of crops. Ranchers occasionally become alarmed by the deer on their property, legally killing large numbers to prevent crop depredation.

They are the principal big game animal in most of the region. Between 1950 and 1975, approximately 1.73 million were killed in U.S. National Forests, with many additional ones taken elsewhere. This is remarkable considering that they were regarded as rare in much of the region when it was first settled. Other than humans, their most common predator probably is the cougar. The young are also preyed on by coyotes and bobcats. Other mortality factors include disease and starvation. Livestock transmit such diseases as "foot-and-mouth" to them, whereas they can infect livestock with anaplasmosis, often a fatal ailment.

No account of mule deer would be complete without the story of the Kaibab Plateau herd in northern Arizona. Until the late nineteenth century, much of the Kaibab was pristine deer habitat; Navajos and Piutes obtained most of their winter meat from its deer. The situation changed in 1885 when 2,000 cattle were introduced. By 1913, the plateau had become home to some 15,000 cattle and 5,000 sheep. Such large numbers of livestock, particularly the sheep, overgrazed much of the area, resulting in deterioration of deer habitat. There was another factor that drastically altered the Kaibab's natural balance. In 1906, the Grand Canyon National Game Preserve was established on what is now the North Kaibab National Forest. To protect big game, a program to remove predators was initiated. Close to 800 cougars, 5,000 coyotes, 550 bobcats, and dozens of wolves were killed within the first 25 years. Initially, the deer increased dramatically, from 3,000 or 4,000 in 1906 to some 100,000 by 1924. But the deteriorated habitat could not support the bloated population and there were too few predators to keep them in check. Eating themselves "out of house and home," thousands starved to death. To forestall die-offs, the government sanctioned the killing of large numbers of deer. By 1940, however, the herd had plummeted to about 10,000 individuals. Several lessons have been learned from the Kaibab. First of all, big game animals cannot be stockpiled. Moreover, predators are natural, if not vital, components of ecosystems, a fact which becomes all too evident when they are removed.

Breeding reaches a peak between late November and mid-December. Gestation normally lasts from 200 to 208 days, but may be several weeks more or less than this. Most births take place from mid-June to mid-July. Fawns are precocial at birth and covered with camouflaging white spots. This pattern and a lack of any noticeable odor for their first few weeks provide them with protection. The majority of older does bear twins, whereas those breeding for the first time have a single young. There have been reports of triplets and even quadruplets in this species. Weaning begins at about five weeks of age. After four and a half months, fawns are sexually mature. Nevertheless, females usually do not mate until they are 2 years old, an age at which they may attain maximum size. Larger males may continue to grow until they are 10 years old.

It threats and posturing are to no avail, bucks will use their antlers to win access to the does. Antlers from two bucks can become entangled, resulting in a slow death by starvation for the headlocked victims. In winter, antlers fall off. They resume growth in spring; the first forks are evident in June. In most populations, the largest buck with the greatest antlers does most of the breeding. Mule deer are polygynous, with the dominant buck tending to the females in his territory which are in heat. Territories may be advertised by scents produced through glandular secretions from the head and legs. Other secretions may function to inform the young about their mothers' whereabouts. During the winter and spring, a "clan" of several females related by maternal descent and their fawns may remain together. Mature bucks usually stay apart. In some areas, herds are formed in the winter months.

## WHITE-TAILED DEER (*Odocoileus virginianus*)

Total length: 4 1/2 to 6 3/4 feet; tail length: 6 to 13 inches; shoulder height: 3 to 3 1/2 feet.

The white-tailed deer is often spoken of in terms bordering on reverential. It has been called the most important and most popular big game animal in North America. Such descriptors are, of course, difficult to quantify to and are based largely on value judgments. In the eastern United States, white-tailed deer are the most numerous big game species. However, the one area they are essentially absent from is the Intermountain West and neighboring California. As a result, they have not received the kind of attention here that they do in the rest of the country.

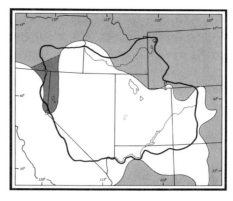

DISTRIBUTION OF WHITE-TAILED DEER.

These graceful mammals are tan to reddish, commonly chestnut brown above in summer, becoming grayer in winter. Much of the body is conspicuously decorated with white: the belly, throat, around the muzzle, the eye ring, and inside the ears. The color pattern of the wide tail is one of their identifying traits. It is brown, fringed with white, and often has a dark stripe down its center. Yet because they are usually seen on the run, "flagging" the tail, all one notices is the bright white rump patch beneath it. Such behavior warns others of danger and may help fawns to stay aware of their mothers' locations. Apparently, it is also the source of the expression "high-tailing it." Bucks, the larger sex, are told apart from their mule deer brethren by the antlers; each has one main beam with several, vertically rising tines. Each of the mule deer's antlers are separated into evenly branching main beams. Found across the continent from southern Canada to Mexico, white-tails occur in this region only around northern Utah, southeastern Idaho, and southwestern Wyoming. They possibly also occur along the northern border between Nevada and California.

They inhabit a wide array of environments, including farms, brushy areas, woodlands, forest edges, riparian zones, and other bottomlands. Open country and dense woods are two habitats which are generally avoided. Although active at any time, they mostly move about in the early morning and throughout the night. Their diet shifts with the seasons. In warm months, they graze on green plants, switching to acorns, nuts, and woody material as green vegetation becomes less available. Where winters are severe, they often seek out spots known as "yards," which offer shelter and food when colder weather arrives. Larger aggregations consist of hundreds of individuals. They can become serious pests around farms and orchards. Indeed, crops such as corn and soybeans may account for over half of their intake in some areas.

Excellent runners, they reach speeds of up to 40 miles per hour to elude their enemies. They are also capable swimmers. Despite such talents, a veritable army of predators feasts upon them. Their most common foes are probably coyotes and feral dogs, but carnivores ranging in size from bobcats to bears readily prey upon them. A deer often makes a loud whistling snort when it senses danger. Other mortality factors include starvation, entanglement in fences, motor vehicles, and various diseases. White-tailed deer originally were a crucial source of clothing and food for Indians and settlers. Although they still account for close to a hundred million pounds of venison a year, hunting is now primarily a recreational activity.

Most breeding takes place in November, although it can occur from October through February. Following a pregnancy averaging 202 days, fawns are usually born in May or June. Single births, twins, and triplets are all common. The newborn are precocial and grow rapidly, quadrupling their birth weight within the first month. Does and bucks alike first participate in breeding when they are a year and a half, although they may be capable sooner. In the spring, bucks start to grow antlers which reach their maximal size by early fall before being shed in winter. Both body size and antler size are affected by an individual's age and nutrition. Sexes remain separate most of the year, except for breeding and associating in the yards. As with the other cervids in this region, white-tailed deer are polygynous. Their harems, however, are often smaller than those of their relatives.

## MOOSE (*Alces alces*)

Total length: 6 3/4 to 9 feet; tail length: 6 3/4 inches; shoulder height: 6 1/2 to 7 1/2 feet.

About the size of a horse, the moose is the largest member of the deer family. In Alaska, some bulls weigh as much as 1,700 pounds. Despite their benign appearance, moose can be extremely dangerous. Rutting bulls and cows with calves, in particular, are unpredictable and never should be approached. Other than

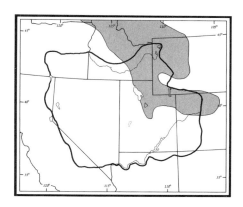

DISTRIBUTION OF MOOSE.

size, there are several features that distinguish them. Adults of both sexes possess a "bell" or "dewlap," a piece of skin which hangs from the throat. Although it has no known function, a male's is usually larger and it thus could have social significance. The dewlap of a mature bull can be as much as fifteen inches across and ten inches long. Another distinctive trait is the top lip, which is large and overhanging. Finally, the antlers warrant discussion because they are unlike those of any other animal. They are "palmate," resembling the palm of a hand with out-stretched fingers. The antler spread is about four or five feet across; the record is close to eight feet. Moose are usually blackish brown, although individuals may be light brown, red-dish, and almost black. With 10-inch guard hairs atop a fine woolly underfur, they have enough insulation to inhabit some of the world's coldest places.

They have a circumpolar distribution, occupying the north-ern portions of North America and Eurasia. Their range extends into the Rocky Mountains, where they are found in the north-eastern corner of the Intermountain West. Not sighted in Utah until 1918, moose numbers rose slowly at first along the north slopes of the Uinta Mountains. An increase in beaver popula-tions and their production of marsh areas in the 1950s is believed to be responsible for the recent growth of the moose population there. From this parent population, others have sprung up in the state. As well, transplants have established moose in suitable areas, such as the north end of Manti Mountain. In 1978, 12 moose from Utah were successfully transplanted to parts of their native range in Colorado. Since then, they have increased to a population of about 100 individuals.

The moose is an inhabitant of the boreal forest. It may be found in various other areas since individuals will meander for great distances. Moose have been recorded as far south as northern Missouri and have even waltzed into residential neighborhoods, such as in Ogden, Utah. Largely browsers, they rely on the stems, bark, and leaves of a multitude of trees and shrubs. A large bull can eat over 50 pounds in one day. Important foods include willow, fir, and quaking aspen. Particularly during the summer, though, they graze on low-growing plants and eat aquatic vegetation as well. Preferred forage is the woody vegetation that appears in the early successional stages of plant communities. As a result, they are common in areas that have been logged, burned, or otherwise altered to induce the growth of "pioneering" plants. Moose travel easily through snow, providing that it is less than about two feet deep. In snow that is deeper, or hard and crusty, it becomes difficult for them to get around. They are excellent swimmers, and run at speeds of over 30 miles per hour.

Major predators are wolves and bears. Although not a factor here, wolves, where they occur in large numbers, can cause declines in moose populations. An interesting situation takes place in eastern and central North America where moose may live in close proximity to white-tailed deer. There, deer are a primary host for the roundworm parasite, *Parelaphostrongylus tenuis*, which they are not harmed by. If a moose ingests it, it can come down with a neurological disorder resulting in a lack of coordination, blindness, and ultimately death. Infestations of this parasite have caused decreases of moose populations in eastern Canada and probably other areas. Moose also fall victim to trains and motor vehicles when they seek travel routes with reduced snow depths. Of course, hunting can be a significant mortality factor. A prized delicacy of the north woods is "moose muffle," the moose's nose. It is reputed to have the flavor of green turtle fat or baked beaver tail.

The height of the breeding season is in late September and early October. Pregnancy lasts for 240 to 246 days in North

America but, oddly, averages 10 days less in Sweden. In late
May or early June, the cow gives birth, usually to a single calf.
Twinning is more common where the quality and availability of
food is high; there are even rare instances of triplets. Newborn
are precocious and usually stand up soon after birth. For the
first two or three months, they are light red to reddish brown. A
yearling is commonly forced away from the mother shortly
before she gives birth. It may be permitted to rejoin her and the
new calf a few weeks later. Although females can breed as yearlings, they reach their greatest potential at 4 to 12 years. Similarly, males reproduce as yearlings, but probably do not become
"effective" until they are several years older. By displaying their
antlers, through direct contact, and simply by staying in the
same area "testing" each other's commitment, bulls compete for
breeding rights to cows. They usually are polygynous, with each
bull mating with several females. However, they tend not to
remain in a group; indeed, moose are the least gregarious of
any North American deer.


## PRONGHORN—FAMILY ANTILOCAPRIDAE

The antilocaprids consist of but a single species, the pronghorn
of North America. Yet, as recently as the Pliocene and
Pleistocene epochs, some 10 million to 10 thousand years ago,
at least 13 different pronghorn genera roamed this continent.
The pronghorn is distinguished by being the only mammal
that annually sheds its horn sheaths. The sheaths are a combination of specialized skin, the protein keratin, and fused hairs,
all covering a bony core. They are shed by early winter, and
new ones replace them by July. The core is bladelike, but the
horny sheath is forked or "pronged" in mature bucks, rarely
so in does. Some authorities contend that pronghorn are too
similar to the bovids, the family of sheep, goats, and African
antelopes, to warrant a separate family designation. This is
because members of both groups have structurally similar horn
sheaths and share some biochemical properties. Nevertheless,
the separate family categorization scheme is still the more
accepted one.

## PRONGHORN
### (*Antilocapra americana*)

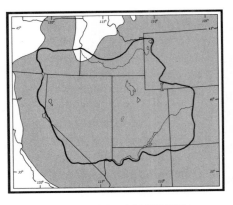

DISTRIBUTION OF PRONGHORN.

Total length: 4 to 4 3/4 feet; tail length: 2 3/8 to 6 3/4 inches; shoulder height: 3 to 3 1/2 feet.

The pronghorn is the fastest animal in the Western Hemisphere and one of the fastest in the world. It can put on a burst of speed up to 70 miles per hour and easily cruise at 30 miles per hour for several miles. Yet, it is one of the smaller hooved mammals on the continent; bucks average only about 125 pounds and a typical doe weighs but 90 pounds. Pronghorn are tan to reddish tan above with a white rump and underparts. On the neck, there is a black mane. Across the throat, two white bands alternate with tan, or occasionally black, markings. Bucks have a broad black band that extends down the length of the snout. They also have a black cheek patch, which they present to the does during courtship. The unique, lyrelike black horns curve back and then inward at the tips. Those of the buck each have a broad, forward pointing prong. Horn length of bucks varies from 12 to 20 inches; many consider one with 15-inch horns to be a trophy animal. The horns of the doe, if present, are usually less than 4 inches long.

Pronghorn are often referred to as "pronghorn antelope" or simply "antelope." But because they are distinct from Old World antelopes, such as gazelles, the name pronghorn is preferred. In Wyoming, I often heard them derisively referred to as "goats," likely because of their appearance and, perhaps, abundance. Yet, although *Antilocapra* is derived from a combination of terms meaning "antelope-goat," they are not close relatives of goats. They occur throughout the western United States, into southern Canada and northern Mexico. Due to insulative features, such as hollow, air-filled outer hairs, they can inhabit extremely cold places. Their range extends over the entire Intermountain West.

These speedsters live in open terrain, primarily grasslands and grassland-brushlands. They are largely browsers, with sage-brush being their major food, especially in winter. Forbs make up much of the remainder of the diet; there is little utilization of grasses. Although active at any time, most feed in the morning or evening. The midday period is normally reserved for resting. Coyotes and bobcats are their principal predators, concentrating on the young. Often, pronghorn are able to make quick escapes; they can detect disturbances up to four miles away. An alarmed individual informs others about potential danger by flashing its white rump patch while taking off. Erecting the hairs on the patch approximately doubles the size of this area, making it visible from afar. But even if the enemy closes in, pronghorn are not without defenses. Groups of them have been known to chase away a predator, even kicking it with their sharp hooves.

Kills by humans, especially illegal ones, are a major source of mortality. Before the arrival of the pioneers, there were an estimated 40 million pronghorn in North America. By 1924, hunting and habitat alteration had reduced their number to less than 20,000. A particularly detrimental event was the fencing of rangelands. Because they cannot leap over fences like deer, they were prevented from migrating to and feeding in critical areas. Deep snow can cause pronghorn to move as much as 100 miles from their summer habitat. Due to complete protection in some areas, stricter hunting regulations, and transplanting of herds, the pronghorn has made a remarkable comeback. Currently, there may be as many as 750,000 pronghorn, making them our second most numerous big game species.

Breeding takes place in early fall. Bucks are territorial, defending areas against other males by ritual displays and battles. They mark taller vegetation in their territories with scent glands located behind the jaw. The largest and most aggressive bucks do most of the breeding. Pronghorn are polygynous, with bucks forming harems of up to 20 does. Following mating, the doe is pregnant for 230 to 250 days, commonly until mid-June. This period includes about a one-month delay for the eggs to implant in the uterus. Usually, twins are born, but some does, particularly those breeding for the first time, produce a single young. As with sheep and goats, the young drops to the ground at birth. The shock of hitting the ground may stimulate breathing; surely, there is a gentler way to go about this. Mothers ingest the odorous urine and feces of the young, likely to prevent predators from detecting them. Newborn are precocial and can outrun a coyote after a few weeks. Does usually become mature at 16 months, but a few breed in their first fall. Although males also can breed as yearlings, older bucks acquire most of the breeding territories. During winter, pronghorn congregate in large herds of 100 or more animals. In summer, they roam about in bands composed of either does with fawns or bachelor herds of yearling and two-year-old males. Older bucks may be territorial from March through October.

## BISON, MOUNTAIN GOATS, AND MOUNTAIN SHEEP—FAMILY BOVIDAE

The Bovidae is the largest and most diverse family of hooved mammals, consisting of some 111 species. Several of our most important livestock species, such as cattle and sheep, are bovids. The group first underwent domestication about 8,000 years ago in southwest Asia. Although bovids occupy a variety of environments, most inhabit grasslands. Adaptations enabling them to effectively exploit these areas include high-crowned cheek teeth for grazing and a four-chambered stomach which harbors microbes that assist in breaking down the cellulose in grasses. Furthermore, their limbs are structured in a way that allows them to attain high speeds; this is often essential in evading predators in the exposed habitats where most live. Bovids have horns consisting of a bony core surrounded by a sheath of keratinized epidermis. Unlike those of the pronghorn, the sheath is neither shed nor branched. In some species, horns continue to grow throughout life. Females occasionally possess horns; they are always present in adult males. Both sexes employ them to defend against predators. Males also use theirs to compete for mates. In the Intermountain West, there are three bovid species: bison, mountain sheep, and mountain goats.

### BISON (*Bison bison*)

Total length: 7 to 12 1/2 feet; tail length: 12 to 18 7/8 inches; shoulder height: 5 to 6 feet.

ELK or WAPITI

MULE DEER

WHITE-TAILED DEER

MOOSE

PRONGHORN

BISON

MOUNTAIN GOAT

MOUNTAIN or BIGHORN SHEEP

No account of the American West would be complete without the sad tale of the bison, popularly known as the buffalo. It is estimated that 60 million roamed the continent in the fifteenth century, although it is impossible to know for sure. By 1890, less than a thousand individuals were left. That bison stand their ground

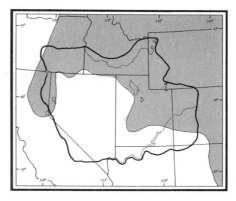

DISTRIBUTION (HISTORICAL) OF BISON.

rather than flee from predators made them all-too-easy a target for our nation's settlers. Railroad crews and army posts often obtained all of their meat from them. Extermination of the bison was part of a United States government policy to suppress the Indian tribes that depended on them for food, clothing, and shelter. At the turn of the century, efforts were finally made to save them from extinction. Since then, populations have been maintained on public and private lands. The two areas where wild individuals were saved are Wood Buffalo National Park in Canada and Yellowstone National Park. In 1983, the total number in all areas was about 75,000.

The bison is the largest terrestrial mammal in North America. Males weigh between 990 to 2,000 pounds, the smaller females vary from 790 to slightly over 1,000 pounds. Their massive appearance is heightened by a broad head atop a short, thick neck, a large shoulder hump, and hindquarters that are not only smaller but lighter in color than the forequarters. The dark brown coat appears unkempt due to the shaggy mane, a beard, and long leg hair. Particularly on older bulls, the long, woolly hair in front often becomes light tan in winter, remaining that way even into summer. Both sexes have short, curved, pointed black horns, but the bull's are proportionately wider. Males also have a considerably larger shoulder hump and longer fur on the forehead, chin, and behind the forelimbs. In both sexes, the tail is tufted at its tip. The recent historic range of the bison encompasses a considerable portion of the Intermountain

West, particularly from southern Idaho to southeastern Utah and eastward into Wyoming and Colorado. The only surviving wild population here is in northwestern Wyoming in Yellowstone National Park. Small, introduced free-ranging herds live in the Henry Mountains of southern Utah, on Antelope Island in the Great Salt Lake, and in Colorado National Monument in the western part of that state.

Bison are grazing animals that largely occur in open habitats. They use forested areas for shade, to escape from insects, and for feeding when snow is too deep in the open areas. They can, however, get to food beneath several feet of snow by digging with their hooves and swinging their head from side to side in it. Grass is preferred, but where it is unavailable they eat sedges and even brushy plants. They are most active in the early morning and late afternoon. During the heat of the day, they ordinarily rest or dust bathe in large depressions that they create called "wallows." In parts of the country, wallows dot the landscape, becoming shallow ponds in some cases. Despite their sluggish appearance, bison can gallop at speeds of over 30 miles per hour. They also are excellent swimmers. Major predators include wolves, grizzly bears, and, of course, humans. Extreme winter weather has occasionally been a significant cause of mortality in the Yellowstone herd.

During much of the year, bulls are either alone or together in small groups. In summer, they join larger herds of cows and their calves. By early September, they have mated. After a 285-day pregnancy, usually one precocial calf is born, although some have twins. Interestingly, mothers not nursing calves from the previous year produce a larger proportion of males than do nursing cows. This finding, from a study on the National Bison Range in western Montana, confirms a prediction of Trivers and Willard that, in species in which there is intense male-male competition, females in comparatively good condition should produce more male offspring than those which are not. This is because females in superior condition are likelier to produce a male of high quality. Such a dominant male would be in a better position to pass on its genes through a greater segment of the herd than would a female. Mothers in superior condition, then, enhance their own fitness by channeling resources into the production of sons.

Just several hours after birth, the reddish tan young follow their mothers about. At five days, they can graze on their own. Males and females alike are capable of breeding by their third year. As in most polygynous mammals, older males sire most of the females and the fathers exhibit no parental care. In the bison, males usually must wait until their sixth birthday to join the ranks of the chosen.

## MOUNTAIN GOAT
### (*Oreamnos americanus*)

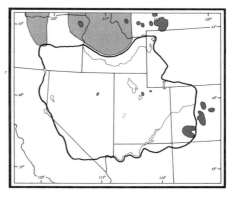

DISTRIBUTION OF MOUNTAIN GOAT; PRESENT RANGE (LIGHT) AND INTRODUCED POPULATIONS (DARK).

Total length: 4 to 5 3/4 feet; tail length: 3 1/4 to 8 inches; shoulder height: 3 to 3 1/2 feet.

With their shaggy, white coats and remarkable climbing ability, mountain goats are true representatives of the high-peak country. Actually, they are not goats, but belong to a group called "rupricaprines," the "goat-antelopes." The chamois (*Rupricapra rupricapra*) of Eurasia is also a member of this bovid tribe. Mountain goats are one of the most striking-looking animals in the region. Although their coat is often tinged with yellow and may have black hairs along the rump and back, its long, snow-white hairs make even the kids appear elderly. In adults, this image is accentuated by a five-inch-long pointed beard. The hooves have sharp outer edges that grip well and large, rubbery soles that provide traction on smooth rock. Both sexes possess sharp, slightly backward-pointing horns that measure up to 12 inches long in males and 9 inches in females. The male's are thicker at the base and taper more. The Dall's sheep (*Ovis dalli*) of extreme northwestern North America is the only close relative that shares the goat's color; it is not found in this region.

It is debatable whether to include the mountain goat in a book on Intermountain mammals. Its native range extends from southeastern Alaska into southern Idaho. However, its southern-most occurrence in Idaho is in the Sawtooth National Forest, just north of the Snake River Plains, along the border of the Intermountain region. It is possible that some animals could enter this region there. Mountain goats have been introduced in several places here, including the San Juan Mountains of south-eastern Colorado, Little Cottonwood Canyon and Mount Timpanogos in Utah's Wasatch Range, and the Ruby Mountains of northeastern Nevada.

They live in seemingly uninhabitable areas: the steep, rocky slopes of high mountains. Characterized by howling winds, extreme cold, and deep snows, these are extremely inhospitable places. The goats are most active at dawn and dusk. In some locations, they forage heavily on grasses, whereas browse is favored elsewhere. Other foods include mosses and lichens. In especially severe weather, even these hardy souls seek shelter in mountain caves and beneath overhanging ledges. By the first heavy snow, they move to more benign wintering areas. Compared with other ungulates, predation on mountain goats is uncommon. Mountain lions, wolves, golden eagles, and humans are their only noteworthy enemies. The lions are capable of fol-lowing and killing them on some mountain stretches. Eagles have been known to knock yearlings off of cliffs and even carry away the kids. The impact of humans on the mountain goat has not been as great as that on most other big game species. How-ever, recent road construction in Idaho and Montana has dis-turbed populations and increased hunting access. Despite their agility, goats can lose their footing and slip off of ice-covered rocks, plummeting to their death.

After being disinterested in each other for most of the year, the sexes begin to interact in October. At this time, males mark females and the surrounding vegetation with a musky oil from their horn glands. These crescent-shaped structures are located just behind the horns in both sexes. They are the continent's only hooved mammal that possesses such glands. Mating occurs relatively late in the year, between November and January. Ges-tation length is variable, lasting from 147 to 178 days. Typically, one precocious kid is born in May or June, high on a mountain ledge. Births of twins and even triplets have been recorded. Sex-ual maturity is reached in the second year. During the rut, males often threaten and swipe at each other with their horns, occasionally resulting in a death. Males do not engage in the head-butting behavior characteristic of bighorn sheep. In comparison with that of the bighorn, a mountain goat's skull is surprisingly fragile.

## MOUNTAIN or BIGHORN SHEEP
(*Ovis canadensis*)

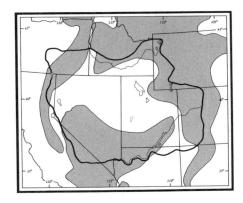

DISTRIBUTION OF MOUNTAIN OR BIGHORN SHEEP.

Total length: 4 1/4 to 6 feet; tail length: 3 1/2 to 5 7/8 inches; shoulder height: 2 1/2 to 3 1/2 feet.

The mountain sheep is another well-recognized member of the alpine world. The familiar head-clanging battles of the rams can be heard for more than a mile, echoing through canyons and valleys. These mammals exhibit considerable geographic variation in color. Individuals from northern mountains are usually dark brown, whereas desert bighorn, a distinct subspecies, are pale tan. In all, the muzzle, rump, back of legs, and belly are generally whitish. Their most notable features are the large brown horns of the adult rams. Each curves up and back, spirals down and then up over the cheeks, creating a "C" shape known as a "curl." A ewe's horns are shorter and but slightly curved. Rams are considerably larger and bulkier than ewes. Like the mountain goat, bighorn are superb climbers. Their hooves have the same hard outer edges and rubbery inner sections that provide for great gripping and traction.

Mountain sheep occur throughout the Intermountain West. As is true for other big game, they were severely reduced by the early part of this century. Populations must have been substantial in much of the region. Osborn Russell, an early trapper, reported seeing a band of about 100 rams in the Wasatch Mountains near Ogden, Utah, in 1840. Some remained until just after World War I. Today, they have rebounded in several areas. They are found in the Rocky Mountains from southern Idaho through western Wyoming, Colorado, and northeastern Utah. Some populations contain individuals introduced to places with suitable habitat, including the Green River area of northeastern Utah, Mount Nebo in the Wasatch Mountains, and Pilot Mountain north of Wendover, Nevada. Desert bighorn occur in the arid rocky country of southern Nevada and Utah and have also been introduced to appropriate locales.

As indicated, they are found in a variety of habitats, from high mountain meadows above timberline to the desert ranges of the Southwest. Before the continent was settled, they were also found in foothills and river valleys. Grasses usually constitute the majority of their diet, with browse assuming more importance in winter. During the latter season, they use their hooves to dig through the snow for food. In spring and summer, they migrate to higher altitudes, likely due to the availability of food in these areas. Most activity takes place during daylight hours. Coyotes, wolves, cougars, bobcats, and golden eagles all prey on bighorn, but often meet resistance from their powerful legs and sharp hooves. Their climbing ability enables them to elude many predation attempts. Some hunters find their large horns irresistible as trophies. Hunting, however, is strictly limited since populations are too low to sustain the type of pressure put on deer and elk herds. In the central Rockies and elsewhere, the lungworm has been a major cause of their mortality. A different threat is faced by the desert bighorn: competition from Barbary sheep (*Ammotragus lervia*), a species introduced to some southwestern states to provide exotic hunting opportunities.

Mountain sheep breed in November and December. Those farther south probably mate earlier; some desert populations may breed throughout the year. The breeding season is generally the only time when rams associate with ewes, likely to reduce competition with them and the young for food and to avoid disturbing them during pregnancy. After a 180-day pregnancy, a single precocial lamb is born in spring or summer; twinning is rare. Mothers and young group together in nursery bands in which the young play with each other. Weaning takes place after about six months. Most can breed by their third year, but rams normally do not reproduce until much older. There is recent evidence of breeding by yearling ewes. The dominant males, which are usually the older ones, do almost all of the breeding. During the late fall rut, dominance is established in contests in which two rams batter each other with their horns and foreheads. The loud crack they make upon contact results from charging at one another at more than 20 miles an hour. A buttressed skull structure and a thick, powerful neck enable them to withstand the terrific force that is generated. Although the dominant ram jealously guards a ewe in heat, other rams may still battle him for temporary access to his ewes. Rams will move their ewes off of traditional tending areas to block the attempts of suitors.

## REFERENCES

Anderson, A. E., and O. C. Wallmo. 1984. *Odocoileus hemionus*. Mammalian Species no. 219. American Society of Mammalogists.

Anonymous. 1987. Uintas new home to Rocky Mountain goats. *Ogden Standard-Examiner*, July 5, 1987.

Bleich, V. C. 1986. Early breeding in free-ranging mountain sheep. *Southwestern Naturalist* 31: 530–531.

Fox, J. L. 1986. Wolf predation on mountain goats in southeastern Alaska. *Journal of Mammalogy* 67: 192–195.

Franzmann, A. W. 1981. *Alces alces*. Mammalian Species no. 154. American Society of Mammalogists.

Geist, V. 1971. *Mountain sheep: A study in behavior and evolution*. Chicago: University of Chicago Press.

Geist, V., and R. G. Petocz. 1977. Bighorn sheep in winter: Do rams maximize reproductive fitness by spatial and habitat segregation from ewes? *Canadian Journal of Zoology* 55: 1802–1810.

Gruell, G. E. 1986. *Post-1900 mule deer irruptions in the Intermountain West*. U.S. Department of Agriculture General Technical Report INT-206. Washington, D.C.: U.S. Government Printing Office.

Hogg, J. T. 1984. Mating in bighorn sheep: Multiple creative male strategies. *Science* 225: 526–530.

Kimball, J. F., Jr., and M. L. Wolfe. 1974. Population analysis of a northern Utah elk herd. *Journal of Wildlife Management* 38: 161–174.

Lennarz, M. S. 1979. Social structure and reproductive strategy in desert bighorn sheep. *Journal of Mammalogy* 60: 671–678.

Madson, J. 1986. The North Woods: A horn of plenty for Old Bucketnose. *Smithsonian* 17(4): 98–111.

Meagher, M. 1986. *Bison bison*. Mammalian Species no. 266. American Society of Mammalogists.

O'Gara, B. 1978. *Antilocapra americana*. Mammalian Species no. 90. American Society of Mammalogists.

Peek, J. M., R. E. LeResche, and D. R. Stevens. 1974. Dynamics of moose aggregations in Alaska, Minnesota, and Montana. *Journal of Mammalogy* 55: 126–137.

Rideout, C. B., and R. S. Hoffmann. 1975. *Oreamnos americanus*. Mammalian Species no. 63. American Society of Mammalogists.

Rutberg, A. T. 1986. Lactation and fetal sex ratios in American bison. *American Naturalist* 127: 89–94.

Sauer, J. R., and M. S. Boyce. 1983. Density dependence and survival of elk in northwestern Wyoming. *Journal of Wildlife Management* 47: 31–37.

Shackleton, D. M. 1985. *Ovis canadensis*. Mammalian Species no. 230. American Society of Mammalogists.

Trivers, R. L., and D. E. Willard. 1973. Natural selection of parental ability to vary the sex ratio of offspring. *Science* 179: 90–92.

Utah Division of Wildlife Resources. 1986. *Utah big game annual report 1986*. Department of Natural Resources; Publication no. 86–3. Salt Lake City.

Wright, J. 1987. Agencies finish bighorn sheep transplant. *Ogden Standard-Examiner*, February 16, 1987.

# General References

Armstrong, D. M. 1972. *Distribution of mammals in Colorado*. University of Kansas Museum of Natural History Monograph no. 3. Lawrence.

Burt, W. H., and R. P. Grossenheider. 1964. *A field guide to the mammals*. 2d ed. Boston: Houghton Mifflin.

Chapman, J. A., and G. A. Feldhammer, eds. 1982. *Wild mammals of North America: Biology, management, and economics*. Baltimore: Johns Hopkins University Press.

Clark, T. W., and M. R. Stromberg. 1987. *Mammals in Wyoming*. University of Kansas Museum of Natural History Public Education Series no. 10. Lawrence.

Dalquest, W. W. 1948. *Mammals of Washington*. University of Kansas Museum of Natural History Publications, vol. 2. Lawrence.

Davis, W. B. 1939. *The recent mammals of Idaho*. Caldwell, Idaho: Caxton Printers, Ltd.

Durrant, S. D. 1952. *Mammals of Utah: Taxonomy and distribution*. University of Kansas Museum of Natural History Publications, vol. 6. Lawrence.

Egoscue, H. J. 1988. Shrew and heteromyid records from the Great Basin of Oregon and Utah. *Great Basin Naturalist* 48. In Press.

Hall, E. R. 1946. *Mammals of Nevada*. Berkeley: University of California Press.

_____. 1981. *The mammals of North America*. 2 vols. 2d ed. New York: John Wiley & Sons.

Hoffmeister, D. F. 1971. *Mammals of Grand Canyon*. Urbana: University of Illinois Press.

Hoffmeister, D. F., and F. E. Durham. 1971. *Mammals of the Arizona Strip including Grand Canyon National Monument*. Museum of Northern Arizona Technical Series 11: 1–44. Flagstaff.

Ingles, L. G. 1965. *Mammals of the Pacific states: California, Oregon, and Washington*. Stanford: Stanford University Press.

Jones, J. K., Jr., D. M. Armstrong, and J. R. Choate. 1985. *Guide to the mammals of the Plains states*. Lincoln: University of Nebraska Press.

Jones, J. K., Jr., D. M. Armstrong, R. S. Hoffmann, and C. Jones. *Mammals of the Northern Great Plains*. Lincoln: University of Nebraska Press.

Jones, J. K., Jr., D. C. Carter, H. H. Genoways, R. S. Hoffmann, D. W. Rice, and C. W. Jones. 1986. *Revised checklist of North American mammals north of Mexico*, 1986. Texas Tech University Museum Occasional Papers no. 107. Lubbock.

Larrison, E. J., and D. R. Johnson. 1981. *Mammals of Idaho*. Moscow: University Press of Idaho.

Lechleitner, R. R. 1969. *Wild mammals of Colorado: Their habits, distribution, and abundance*. Boulder, Colorado: Pruett Publishing Co.

Marti, C. D. 1986. Barn owl diet includes mammal species new to the island fauna of the Great Salt Lake. *Great Basin Naturalist* 46: 307–309.

Murie, O. J. 1975. *A field guide to animal tracks*. 2d ed. Boston: Houghton Mifflin.

Rawley, E. V. 1985. *Early records of wildlife in Utah*. Utah Division of Wildlife Resources, Department of Natural Resources. Publication no. 86–2. Salt Lake City.

U.S. Department of Agriculture Forest Service. 1980. *History of wildlife management in the intermountain region*. Booklet no. 26–31. Washington, D.C.: U.S. Government Printing Office.

Verner, J., and A. S. Boss, technical coordinators. 1980. *California wildlife and their habitats: Western Sierra Nevada*. U.S. Department of Agriculture, Forest Service, Pacific Southwest Forest and Range Experiment Station General

Technical Report PSW-37. Washington, D.C.: U.S. Government Printing Office.

Walker, E. P. 1975. Mammals of the world. 3 vols. 3d ed. (revised by J. L. Paradiso). Baltimore: Johns Hopkins University Press.

Whitaker, J. O., Jr. 1980. *The Audubon Society field guide to North American mammals*. New York: Alfred A. Knopf.

# INDEX

*Page numbers for illustrations in italics.*